Renminbi Rising

Renminbi Rising

A New Global Monetary System Emerges

WILLIAM H. OVERHOLT
GUONAN MA
CHEUNG KWOK LAW

WILEY

This edition first published 2016
© 2016 Fung Global Institute Limited

*The right of **William H. Overholt**, **Guonan Ma** and **Cheung Kwok Law** to be identified as the authors of this work has been asserted in accordance with the Copyright, Designs and Patents Act 1988.*

Registered office
John Wiley & Sons Ltd, The Atrium, Southern Gate, Chichester, West Sussex, PO19 8SQ, United Kingdom

For details of our global editorial offices, for customer services and for information about how to apply for permission to reuse the copyright material in this book please see our website at www.wiley.com.

Wiley publishes in a variety of print and electronic formats and by print-on-demand. Some material included with standard print versions of this book may not be included in e-books or in print-on-demand. If this book refers to media such as a CD or DVD that is not included in the version you purchased, you may download this material at http://booksupport.wiley.com. For more information about Wiley products, visit www.wiley.com.

Designations used by companies to distinguish their products are often claimed as trademarks. All brand names and product names used in this book are trade names, service marks, trademarks or registered trademarks of their respective owners. The publisher is not associated with any product or vendor mentioned in this book.

Limit of Liability/Disclaimer of Warranty: While the publisher and authors have used their best efforts in preparing this book, they make no representations or warranties with respect to the accuracy or completeness of the contents of this book and specifically disclaim any implied warranties of merchantability or fitness for a particular purpose. It is sold on the understanding that the publisher is not engaged in rendering professional services and neither the publisher nor the authors shall be liable for damages arising herefrom. If professional advice or other expert assistance is required, the services of a competent professional should be sought.

Library of Congress Cataloging-in-Publication Data

Names: Overholt, William H., author.
Title: Renminbi rising : a new global monetary system emerges / William H.
   Overholt, Guonan Ma, Cheung Kwok Law.
Description: Chichester, West Sussex, United Kingdom : John Wiley & Sons,
   Inc., 2016. | Includes bibliographical references and index.
Identifiers: LCCN 2015038330 | ISBN 978-1-119-21896-8 (cloth)
Subjects: LCSH: Renminbi. | Finance—China. | China—Foreign economic relations.
Classification: LCC HG1285 .O94 2016 | DDC 332.4/50951—dc23 LC record available at
http://lccn.loc.gov/2015038330

A catalogue record for this book is available from the British Library.

ISBN 978-1-119-21896-8 (hardback) ISBN 978-1-119-21898-2 (ePDF)
ISBN 978-1-119-21897-5 (ePub) ISBN 978-1-119-21899-9 (obk)

Cover design: Wiley
Cover images: Dragon image © ly86/iStockphoto; Gold image © mexrix/Shutterstock

Set in 11/13pt TimesLTStd-Roman by Thomson Digital, Noida, India
Printed in Great Britain by TJ International Ltd, Padstow, Cornwall, UK

To LIU Ming Kang. His reformist integrity inspires us.

CONTENTS

LIST OF FIGURES

LIST OF TABLES

FOREWORD

At a time when effective management of international monetary affairs is fundamental to global economic recovery, the rapid emergence of a new major currency – China's internationalizing renminbi (RMB) – is a transformative event of global significance.

This book analyzes the drivers, progress and likely trajectory of the RMB internationalization. It also looks at what the dawning of the RMB era potentially means for the global financial system, international business and for supporting financial services and products. Overwhelmingly, we see opportunities more than threats.

In tackling this challenging subject Fung Global Institute has, I believe, gone deeper and wider than previous studies on this subject. We have addressed it objectively with a balanced view of different interests and of the welfare of the global financial system as a whole.

True to Fung Global Institute's mission to provide Asian perspectives on global issues, we have taken as our starting point the inner workings and changing needs of China's economy. As China manages its complex transition to a growth model emphasizing domestic consumption and services over investment and export manufacturing, these needs are necessarily expressing themselves through domestic financial reform, with RMB internationalization as an important focal point. We look deeply into these domestic reasons behind the RMB's arrival on the global stage.

A specific example of domestic reform is the Chinese bond markets. We look in detail at how China needs to integrate its bond markets, expand their use and gradually open them to the world, and then how these domestic imperatives support the internationalization of the currency. We also examine China's expanding global network, with Hong Kong as the cornerstone of offshore settlement centers for RMB trade.

We have gone wider by setting the rise of the RMB in a historical context. A century ago, the US dollar overtook sterling in little over a decade to become the leading international currency. While the dollar looks set to remain the principal reserve currency of the world for years to come, its own historical journey is a reminder of how rapidly currencies rise (and fall). In this report, we foresee the RMB possibly challenging in little more than a decade the euro's role as the world's second most important reserve currency. China has already surpassed the euro as a trade-settlement currency.

For some, the speed of this anticipated reordering is surprising, even unsettling. But global businesses have quickly discovered that they can save costs and raise profits by using the internationalized RMB. Provision by the Chinese government of the necessary hard and soft infrastructure has made internationalization of the RMB possible; business profits are making it successful. We have studies of companies in this book illustrating how the RMB's rise is a major opportunity for business to benefit from dealing in RMB.

Having said that, there are inevitable uncertainties as to how fast China can press ahead with domestic economic transformation and RMB internationalization. With these in mind, we offer alternative policy scenarios outlining different outcomes.

Just as the internationalization of the RMB is a moving target, we present this book as a work in progress. Our hope is that it will stimulate debate from economists and professionals in the financial services and industry generally.

Under the project leadership of William Overholt, the authors of this book have taken on one of the hottest topics in international finance with new depth and freshness. I look forward to seeing more such reports from the Asia Global Institute, which, from July 1, 2015, will carry forward the Fung Global Institute's mission to address major global economic issues from Asian perspectives.

Victor K. Fung
Chairman, Fung Global Institute
June 2015

ACKNOWLEDGMENTS

This book is the product of a large collective effort. HSBC provided the funding for much of the research, after which we undertook further research and a colloquium with The Fung Global Institute endowment funds. We are profoundly grateful to HSBC for its support. HSBC gave us complete independence and freedom in conducting the research and publishing this book. The content of this book (including our views) has not been endorsed by HSBC and does not necessarily reflect the views of HSBC. Accordingly, we are solely responsible for the content, any of our views and any possible errors.

William Overholt organized the project, wrote much of several chapters (particularly the first three and the last three) and edited the overall book. Guonan Ma wrote much of several chapters and helped edit and reshape the entire book. Many forecasts in the book derive from Cheung Kwok Law's econometric analysis. In the interest of readability, we have not included regression analyses and extensive methodological commentary in the book.

A broader team made important contributions. Dominic Meagher provided much of the analysis of the history of monetary system transitions. Julia Leung provided the principal input, including decisive case studies, on why business finds RMB-based transactions profitable. Chris Jeffery's verbal comments and consulting paper provided much of our understanding of reserve currency issues. Geng Xiao organized panels at conferences that gave us important insights into Chinese thinking. Mingkang Liu's guidance throughout the project provided indispensable insights and wisdom.

Jodie Hu, Warren Lu, Zhu Yan, Sai Yau and especially Wang Yao provided research support throughout the project.

Andrew Keenan's editing helped make the book more readable for a non-specialist audience.

We held two colloquia on renminbi internationalization to appropriate as many ideas from smart people as possible and to get reactions to drafts of our work. Experts at the first colloquium, on December 1, 2014, in Hong Kong, included Vina Cheung, Victor K. Fung, Montgomery Ho, Haizhou Huang, Chris Jeffery, C.K. Law, Ka Chai Leong, Julia Leung, Mingkang Liu, Guonan Ma, Paul Malpass, Pamela Mar, Dominic Meagher, Kumiko Okazaki, William Overholt, Andrew Sheng, Michael Spence, Angus Tsang, Kai Man Wong and Geng Xiao.

Experts at the second colloquium, on June 7, 2015, in Hong Kong, included Robert Aliber, Suman Bery, John Burns, William Chan, Ka Mun Chang, Richard Cooper, Steven Davis, M. Taylor Fravel, Victor K. Fung, Andy Haldane, Akinari Horii, Fred Hu, Takatoshi Ito, C.K. Law, Julia Leung, Mingkang Liu, Patrick Low, Guonan Ma, Chung-In Moon, Benjamin Mok, William Overholt, T.V. Mohandas Pai, Sebastian Paredes, Dwight Perkins, Michael Spence, Angus Tsang, Mark Tucker, Ezra Vogel, Kai Man Wong, Helen Wong, Chenggang Xu and Jianzhang Zhuang.

We are deeply indebted to these thought leaders. With so many illustrious scholars, regulators and executives on tap, we have no excuse for whatever we have missed and for any mistaken conclusions drawn from among the different and sometimes conflicting perspectives. Errors of fact and analysis are solely our own.

ABOUT THE AUTHORS

William Overholt is President of the Fung Global Institute in Hong Kong and Senior Fellow at Harvard University's Asia Center. Dr Overholt is the author of six books, most notably *Asia, America and the Transformation of Geopolitics* (2008) and *The Rise of China* (1993). Previously he was Director, Center for Asia Pacific Policy at RAND Corporation. For 21 years he headed investment bank research teams, serving as Managing Director and Head of Research at Bankers Trust in Hong Kong, Managing Director of Research for BankBoston's regional headquarters in Singapore and Head of Asia Strategy and Economics for Nomura in Hong Kong. He also spent eight years at Hudson Institute, where he managed research projects for the Department of Defense, National Security Council, NASA and others, and was director of a business consulting subsidiary. He received his B.A. from Harvard and his M.Phil. and Ph.D. from Yale.

Guonan Ma is a Senior Fellow at Fung Global Institute and a non-resident Fellow of Bruegel, the Belgian think tank. He was Senior Economist at the Bank for International Settlements from 2001 to 2014. A veteran investment bank economist, with experience at Merrill Lynch Asia, Salomon Smith Barney, Bankers Trust and Peregrine Securities, he is one of the most widely published financial economists in Asia and also a consultant to major central banks. He holds a B.A. from Peking University and a Ph.D. from the University of Pittsburgh, and has served as a Lecturer of Economics at Peking University and as a Lecturer and Senior Fellow in Economics at the Australian National University.

Cheung Kwok Law is a Senior Researcher at Fung Global Institute and co-author of a forthcoming book analyzing the development of a successful Chinese city, Foshan. He has a distinguished career as an economist, including roles as Senior Economist for the Hong Kong government, Senior Economist for HSBC, Director of Regional Research for Bankers Trust Securities, Research Director at South China Brokerage and Research Director of the Hong Kong Policy Research Institute. He has also had a career in public service, including Member of Hong Kong's Legislative Council 1995–1998 and Member of the Chinese People's Political Consultative Conference for two decades, among many others. He has lectured at Hong Kong Baptist University and the Chinese University of Hong Kong and served as Administrative Director of Graduate Programs at the Chinese University's Faculty of Business. He holds a B.A. from the Chinese University, an M.A. from Thammasat University (Thailand) and a Ph.D. from the University of California, Los Angeles.

CHAPTER 1

INTERNATIONALIZING THE RMB

The rapid internationalization of the renminbi (RMB) is driving – and being driven by – a fundamental and historic transformation of the global financial system. The impact, which is only starting to be felt, will eventually ripple across the entire world, affecting every economy, government, business and household.

The ramifications are clearly profound. While some are predictable, others are poorly understood and much is necessarily plain unknown. However, history warns that no substantial realignment of the global monetary system is without risk. Indeed, as we show in Chapter 2, the results have at times been cataclysmic. While conscious of these caveats and the nascent stage of the current changes, we nonetheless see cause for optimism in both the direction and progress of the RMB's internationalization.

In this chapter, we shall describe our findings with a broad brush, leaving the details and most documentation to subsequent chapters.

Even as recently as five years ago, few could have imagined the rapidity of the RMB's rise. This has been both a cause and a consequence of the "perfect storm" of four key converging trends:

- Increasing international use of the currency, driven by a combination of cost savings for business, Beijing's support – backed by domestic reform and opening – and the growing weight and influence of China's economy.
- US resistance not only to modernizing and expanding the Bretton Woods institutions that have guided global monetary affairs since 1944, but also to accepting new alternatives designed to fill the growing gaps.

■ Deepening skepticism, especially among emerging nations, of the existing system in the wake of the 2008–2009 global financial crisis (GFC). In particular, they are questioning: whether it truly offers the optimal means to achieve stability and prosperity; the continuing relevance of Bretton Woods institutions; and the role of the US Federal Reserve as the de facto world central bank, given that it is required by law to primarily serve US interests.

■ China's promotion – particularly in Central and South Asia, the Middle East and Africa – of the kinds of development that helped OECD (Organisation for Economic Co-operation and Development) countries prosper and integrate, as well as enabling institutions.

The pace and pattern of the RMB's internationalization from here will continue to depend on – and drive – these global and domestic developments.

THE CONDITIONS FOR BECOMING A GLOBAL CURRENCY

Internationalization alone does not guarantee a currency's global importance. The New Zealand dollar, for example, is highly internationalized but of little import beyond its borders. Three connected conditions are required for any currency to become a global heavyweight: a large and growing domestic economy; substantial and open capital markets; and trusted and effective institutions to manage the economy and markets. China faces both improving prowess and serious challenges in each of these areas.

Economic Drivers: Growth and Reform

China certainly appears to meet the first of these three conditions. After little more than three decades of galloping growth, following Deng Xiaoping's "reform and opening," it is now the world's second-largest economy – and the biggest by purchasing power. However, it can no longer continue expanding at the 10% pace of the past 35-odd years. Even to maintain a relatively rapid annual rate of 6–7%, China must overcome four substantial challenges. Combined, they present a formidable hurdle.

First, the most important engines of the economy need to be changed. China has to effect a transition from being driven by investment, exports, catch-up manufacturing and state enterprises and instead look to domestic consumption, services, innovation and small and medium-sized enterprises (SME).

Second, it must manage its way clear of a serious financial squeeze compounded from local-government debt, a housing bubble, unregulated shadow banking and extensive industrial overcapacity.

As if these were not challenge enough, it also faces a rapid decline of its working-age population in proportion to the fast-rising numbers of retirees. To maintain growth and fund social welfare, it needs to use its remaining workforce much more productively.

Finally, it must resolve its current environmental crisis of alarming levels of air, water and soil pollution, with the attendant problems of energy security and food safety.

Beijing's response has been encouraging. Its new leadership has announced plans to pursue a far more market-based economy, has begun judicial and governance reforms, and has begun implementing an ambitious environmental program comprising measures to repair and regulate. To impose politically difficult reforms, it has streamlined its top leadership and wielded an anti-corruption campaign.

Given these aims and China's demonstrated ability to implement major change, we expect it to continue, after overcoming the current financial squeeze, to expand more quickly than most other emerging countries and much faster than the advanced economies. We forecast average annual real GDP growth of 5.0–7.5% over 2016–2020. For the following decade, we expect average growth of about 6.0% if planned reforms are achieved, but only 3.5% otherwise. In Chapter 3, we consider several "surprises" that could push the pace even higher or lower.

The core objective of the economic reforms needed to sustain relatively high growth is more efficient and sustainable allocation of resources by moving to more market-dominated allocation of resources. This is in marked contrast to past practice, whereby bank loans, stock-market listings, land allocations and regulatory permissions have been largely dictated by bureaucrats, with a strong bias toward state-owned enterprises (SOEs). Their preferential access to capital – via both the stock market and bank loans – has been at the expense of smaller, dynamic, private-sector firms, which are now the primary drivers of growth, jobs and innovation. The smaller companies' funding constraints were exacerbated by suppressed interest rates, because, if banks can't charge higher interest rates, they can't cover the risk of lending to SMEs. On top of that, an artificially depressed RMB favored old drivers such as net exports to the detriment of the domestic-market expansion needed to fuel the next phase of growth. Similarly, suppressed exchange rates benefited traditional manufacturing based on cheap labor at the expense of more innovative, high-tech industry and domestic consumers. Meanwhile, controlled capital markets deprived savers of investment opportunities and drove their funds into the unproductive property market.

In a few short years, China has mostly both liberalized interest rates and allowed the RMB to equilibrate to a market level. Consider, for example, that the trade surplus has been running at a small 2% of GDP, capital outflows have been substantial, and the People's Bank of China (PBOC) actually intervened recently to support the currency in the interests of broader stability. As well, the freely convertible offshore and capital-controlled onshore market rates have rapidly converged. In late 2014 and early 2015, senior Chinese officials were indicating privately that the RMB is likely to be basically convertible by 2017 and possibly earlier; whether these optimistic forecasts are realized depends on overcoming the conservative resistance that has been augmented in the wake of the mid-2015 stock-market collapse.

Hence, the fundamental needs of the real economy are driving financial liberalization – and the necessary reforms are proceeding quickly. As it happens, these reforms are also exactly what are required for RMB internationalization.

In turn, RMB liberalization and internationalization are necessary components of further financial liberalization, fueling a virtuous circle of reforms. (They also help drive politically contentious domestic liberalizations.)

More specifically, some key links in this virtuous circle of reforms can be described thus: for the RMB to internationalize, it must be convertible; if it is convertible, capital flows must be open; if they are open, domestic interest rates must be free; if they are free, banks must be sound and soundly regulated so that a rise in interest rates does not risk a banking crisis; if the banking system is to be sound, it must be buttressed against runs by the creation of deposit insurance. We examine these links and the logic behind them in more detail in Chapter 3.

Economists typically describe the links in the preceding paragraph as a set of preconditions. For instance, domestic interest rates must be freed and the banking system fully stabilized before the capital account is opened, because opening capital markets too quickly, for example, can be dangerous. The risk is that money floods in, debt becomes excessive and then the money flees, precipitating a currency crisis. This is what happened in the Asian financial crisis of 1997–1998.

Instead of following a sequence of prerequisites, China seeks to take advantage of the virtuous circle of reforms, and instead takes incremental steps from both ends. This sets in train a virtuous circle, which enables reform to move fairly quickly while also allowing constant checks to ensure the process is safe and stable. Such a virtuous circle plays to China's strength of effecting incremental but rapid reform. When China has, for instance, dismantled rural communes, changed most prices from decreed prices to market prices, put most firms on a market basis and so forth, it has proceeded incrementally (no "shock therapy"), with careful field testing, but in historical perspective quite quickly. That approach has proved brilliantly successful and Beijing is now using it for financial liberalization. We analyze the detailed process in Chapter 3.

The other two conditions for a currency to become globally important, as we noted above, are large capital markets, especially in government bonds, and trustworthy institutions. For huge amounts of money to flow across borders, there must be a sufficiently deep and accessible pool of currency to draw on when things get rough. And they always do get rough eventually. Chapter 4 addresses the creation of a deep and accessible pool of bonds and Chapter 5 looks at other domestic markets.

Institutional Foundations

Conscious of institutional weakness, China initially turned to offshore markets to spur RMB internationalization. As a first incremental step, it allowed simple, individual RMB deposits in Hong Kong, later extending this to a broad range of financial products in a dozen other international financial centers.

More recently, it has established the Shanghai–Hong Kong Stock Connect, which allows restricted cross-border share trading, with plans for a similar scheme involving the Shenzhen exchange. This has required extensive regulatory reforms to ensure compatibility in such areas as taxation and custodian and settlement arrangements.

China is also effecting further reforms by establishing free-trade zones, first in Shanghai and subsequently in three other regions. These zones enable it to incrementally introduce, test and then extend new institutional arrangements for the likes of financial and capital-account liberalization and RMB internationalization.

As well, Beijing has encouraged its commercial and policy banks to follow Chinese firms expanding overseas. Significantly, it has also set about establishing and helping fund alternative institutions such as the Asian Infrastructure Investment Bank (AIIB), the Silk Road Fund and the New Development Bank (NDB, also sometimes called the BRICS Bank). The new alternative institutions appear likely to be soundly governed, sustainable institutions, as the China Development Bank already is.

On top of these measures, within only the past few years, the PBOC has signed bilateral local-currency swap agreements exceeding USD498.5 billion with 29 other central banks in a bid to both provide liquidity for offshore RMB settlement and build trust and confidence.

At home, the most important institution needed to support a globalized RMB is the PBOC, which, happily for this purpose, is the most highly developed institution in China. It has highly professional, reformist management that has demonstrated its ability to control inflation and stabilize the currency – moving toward market interest rates and foreign exchange rates.

More broadly, the central government administration of China has meritocratic personnel development, a technocratic approach to policy analysis and a superior ability (compared with peers like India and Brazil) to confront problems and implement solutions. Its problems include pervasive graft (nearly universal in emerging markets), sometimes weak ability to enforce policies on local governments, and an incongruent balance of budget and responsibilities between the center and local governments. Notwithstanding the weaknesses, it consistently delivers superior results, compared with international peers, in such tasks as building infrastructure, educating the population and maintaining budget discipline.

China's greatest institutional weakness in supporting a global currency is its legal system. A global currency entails huge numbers of transactions, many quite large, and, inevitably, a large number of disputes. International and local participants are anxious to know that any dispute will be settled objectively, by a transparent process based on laws. In the reform period, China's legal system has evolved in very positive directions, and important new reforms were announced in 2014, but a Party commission retains ultimate authority over decisions. Hence, foreign corporations and many Chinese companies prefer to sign contracts under Western-type legal systems, and this will slow the emergence of the RMB as a global currency.

Thus, China's financial-institution building is well under way and, indeed, accelerating, but still far from fully modern. It is sufficient, and becoming more adequate every year, to support an enormous increase in the international use of the RMB, but not yet comparable with the institutions of most OECD countries.

We next consider the final condition: capital markets.

Deepening Capital Markets

An international currency requires deep and accessible capital markets. At the highest level, if other countries are going to use the RMB as a reserve currency, they need to know that they can do huge trades in that currency during periods of crisis without moving the value of the currency disadvantageously. The US Treasury bond market is the ultimate deep and open market; it can accommodate trades of many tens of billions of dollars without excessive price changes, whereas the euro cannot. And other countries know that the US Treasury bond market will not close during a crisis. China's government bond market is growing fast but remains much smaller than its US counterpart, and is fragmented like the euro market although for different reasons. Foreign access is limited by capital controls and potentially subject to curtailment during a crisis.

Bonds

Although China's bond market has expanded massively during the past 20 years, it still amounts to only 40% of GDP, compared with some 200% for the USA and the UK. This is largely because banks dominate China's financial sector.

As well, its onshore bond market is mostly closed to overseas investors. Foreign holdings account for a mere 2.5% of total outstanding onshore RMB bonds. However, the market is quickly opening. More than 200 foreign institutions, sovereign funds and commercial and central banks have gained market access during the past few years.

Corporate and municipal bonds contribute to liquidity, but Chinese government bonds (CGBs) are the core. With about USD4 trillion in capitalization, the CGB market is the world's seventh largest for treasuries, although only about 10% the size of its US counterpart.

However, China's bond market is fragmented, with several different regulators and types of market platforms. As well, most issues are government-related and, thus, subject to moral hazard. Finally, the investor base is narrow, concentrated and almost entirely domestic.

Nonetheless, there is reason to believe that the market might well be largely integrated within a few years. Integrating, or making consistent, the separate bond markets controlled by the PBOC, the Ministry of Finance and the National Development Reform Commission is an important test of China's institution-building process. We think it likely they will pass this test, but readers can monitor it for themselves. The bond market also offers tremendous potential for rapid growth if the following caveats can be overcome. First, the banks' capital requirements reduce their market dominance. Second, local governments restructure their bank debt by issuing bonds. Third, bond issuers and holders become more diverse.

Consolidation is critical if China's bond market is to become one of the top three in size and liquidity by 2020. This would make it structurally more like the deep US treasuries market and far more liquid than the fragmented EUR market, as will be discussed in Chapter 4. It would also significantly bolster the RMB's bid to become a truly global and important currency. However, although China is heading in the right direction in each of these key areas, the extent and pace of change remain unclear.

Stocks

Bond markets provide the principal support for an internationalizing currency, but stock markets are also important. Encouragingly, China's stock markets are rapidly liberalizing domestically and becoming more open internationally, although foreigners still own less than 2% of all A-shares.

The first incremental step in opening the market entailed small quotas for so-called qualified foreign institutional investors (QFIIs). These quotas are rapidly growing. More recently, as noted above, Beijing established the Shanghai–Hong Kong Connect scheme, which since November 2014 has enabled limited but sizable trading between the two cities' exchanges. A Shenzhen–Hong Kong Connect scheme is due to begin soon. Once these are working smoothly, other programs aimed at further opening China's stock markets are likely to be introduced. This will present a substantial opportunity for foreign investors. Shanghai's A-share market, for example, is already the world's second largest and is continuing to expand rapidly.

In the decade after 2004, China's total stock-market capitalization rose from 23% of GDP to 60% of what by then was a much larger GDP. As well, the political imperatives that once drove listing priorities are being replaced by the sort of regulated registration process that applies in most major markets.

Initially, listings were largely confined to SOEs and listings were restricted to create scarcity and thereby maximize their value. The purely political purpose of this approach was to help fund daunting future state liabilities for the likes of pensions and medical insurance. This is contrary to the market's intrinsic role as an efficient allocator of capital, and further denied dynamic private firms access to much-needed funding. (As noted above, their ability to borrow from banks was also severely restricted by preferential policies that ensured the lion's share went to SOEs.) The resulting "immaturity flaws" of the market are detailed in Chapter 5.

These impediments to the efficient working of the markets are now quickly being removed. Two new boards on the Shenzhen exchange, for example, are devoted entirely to small-cap stocks and have experienced spectacular growth.

Such reforms, along with further opening of the market to overseas investors, will help drive substantial RMB-based trading. We expect foreign ownership in China's stock markets to rise from the current low of 1.5% (versus 16% in the USA and 28% in Japan) to about 9% by 2020. Restrictions on foreign ownership and control of brokerages are also likely to be further eased.

As we were writing this book, during late 2014 and the first half of 2015, the Chinese government tolerated and endorsed a huge rise in the stock markets, encouraging people to invest even when valuations were far above what developed markets consider reasonable levels. The bubbles then burst, with markets declining 35% before extraordinary government interventions achieved at least a temporary stabilization. Even after the bursting of the bubble, the markets remained far above where they had been a year earlier, but large numbers of people who joined the latter months of the rise did so with borrowed money and were badly burned.

In the short run, the stock market's volatility means economic growth will be somewhat (but probably not a great deal) lower, heavy government intervention will for some time impede the market's function as an efficient allocator of capital, and the wave of private firms that expected to get needed capital from the stock market will be delayed.

The long-term consequences for the market, for the economic reform program and for renminbi internationalization, remain unclear. The longer-term consequences depend partly on politics. The boom was known as the "reform bull market," and it is unclear whether the ensuing bust will affect sentiment about financial reforms more generally. Although government management of the market was largely responsible for both the boom and the bust, the government's realization that market moves can have such serious and partially uncontrollable consequences may strengthen those who counsel greater caution in liberalizing domestic finances and reducing capital controls. Foreign investors and regulators were taken aback both by the intensity of the government intervention and by a tendency to blame foreigners and alleged "malicious short sellers" for having manipulated the crash. For a time at least, foreigners will be more cautious about treating the Chinese markets as normal "market-driven" phenomena, for instance delaying inclusion of Chinese markets into global MSCI (Morgan Stanley Composite Index) indices. We discuss this in greater detail in Chapter 5.

The sudden and extreme volatility of China's stock market in 2014–2015 is an example of the reason why, throughout this book, rather than providing point forecasts, we speak about ranges of outcomes, alternative scenarios and potential surprises. Both economic and political events can create sharp deviations from the outcomes that simple extrapolation of current trends would lead us to expect.

Banks

Although foreign banks accounted for only 2.7% of total loans in 2013, China's banking sector is the world's largest. It is also more open than that of Japan, for example, where foreign banks had only 1.5% market share in 2013. As well, Beijing is moving more quickly to ease restrictions on foreign firms – such as a recent reduction in their onerous capital requirements. These reforms are helping drive a substantial increase in offshore RMB holdings and an even more rapid rise in onshore holdings by non-residents. Cross-border business of all kinds is also expanding and the use of derivatives, especially for hedging, is surging. As discussed in Chapter 5, China's banking sector may expand at a slower pace than its economy, because of the expected disintermediation process whereby money flows more through the capital markets and less through banks.

BUSINESS AND RMB

RMB internationalization ultimately works only if business finds it profitable. Business seems to be finding it very profitable. As Chinese tourists fan out over the world, accepting RMB becomes increasingly useful; merchants in Hong Kong, Singapore and several other Asian economies now accept RMB cash and, more importantly, electronic RMB-based transactions are readily accepted. Raising money through "dim sum" bonds has become possible and attractive. As the currency is freed from controls and becomes more volatile, more companies want to bet on appreciation or depreciation over varying lengths of time. More companies need to hedge their RMB exposure. More companies find that they can profit from arbitrage between low US interest rates and higher Chinese rates. As Chinese controls are relaxed, foreign companies can transfer RMB between subsidiaries without first converting into USD and then back again; along with many others, Samsung's 130 subsidiaries in China save a great deal this way. Chinese suppliers and purchasers are willing to give discounts to buyers who are willing to deal in RMB and thereby relieve them of exchange risk.

As China punches holes in its capital controls, more foreign funds are allowed to invest in China and more domestic Chinese funds are allowed to invest abroad. The Shanghai–Hong Kong Stock Connect and the forthcoming Shenzhen version allow stock transactions, heavily in RMB. China is beginning to allow some of its citizens to invest abroad. Mutual recognition of fund managers in Hong Kong and in China proper foreshadows broader opening of markets to fund managers.

As these many kinds of transactions proliferate rapidly, banks are rushing to seize the opportunity. And countries are competing to set up RMB settlement centers. This has created a virtuous circle, whereby rising business stimulates the development of institutions that make such business more efficient and reliable.

RMB-PRODUCT MARKETS

Global payments and trade continue to be conducted overwhelmingly in USD. However, the RMB is rising quickly. In the 21 months to October 2013, it soared from 1.9% of global trade to 8.7%, surpassing the EUR as the number 2 currency. About 18% of China's trade is now settled in RMB – equivalent to about USD272 billion in 2013. Even as the value of trade increases significantly, we expect the RMB share to almost double to about 35% by 2020. At current exchange rates, that would amount to more than USD1 trillion.

Most RMB-denominated trade settlement still occurs in Hong Kong, but other major cities – London, Paris, Frankfurt, Toronto, Seoul, Taipei, Singapore and Sydney – are competing to create settlement and business centers. In terms of global payments, according to the Society for Worldwide Interbank Financial Telecommunication (SWIFT), the RMB became one of the top five currencies by the end of 2014, up from number 13 only 24 months earlier.

Foreign-exchange (FX) transactions involving the RMB are also on the rise, increasing by more than 300% from the equivalent of USD35 billion in 2010 to USD120 billion in 2013. We expect this to exceed USD1 trillion by 2020. At that point, the RMB should be one of the top five FX currencies globally, ahead of the highly internationalized GBP and behind the USD, EUR and JPY. In Hong Kong, FX-transaction settlements involving RMB already exceed USD100 billion per day.

This expected rise in the RMB trading in the currency market will be driven primarily by China's growing international trade, its increasingly more open capital account and its more flexible currency. The consequently bigger international balance sheet, larger cross-border capital flows and increased currency volatility will naturally give rise to a growing need for currency hedging, for Chinese and foreign investors alike.

The offshore RMB markets have played a unique role and have also been expanding fast, in terms of size, location and product range. Moving gradually away from the capital controls that were still quite heavy 10 years ago, Beijing's initial strategy is to test out the external use of RMB offshore, first in Hong Kong in 2004 and now offshore. RMB centers have spread from Asia to Europe, the Middle East, Latin America and now North America, knitting a global RMB network, wherein nowadays the currency trades around the clock. Hong Kong remains the premier offshore RMB market, but its dominance has slipped and will continue slipping, indicating that RMB internalization has gained considerable global momentum and will eventually converge with a more open domestic RMB market in Shanghai, together forming a truly global RMB market.

RMB internationalization reduces trading costs and risks, allocates resources more efficiently and reduces dependence on volatile foreign currencies and interest rates. In later chapters, we describe how businesses benefit from RMB-based transactions. Here, we briefly note a likely shift to RMB denomination for some key commodities.

Given its massive and growing manufacturing base, China is the world's largest consumer of several key metal commodities, including iron ore, copper, gold, nickel and platinum. In Q3 2013, it overtook the USA to become the world's largest net importer of petroleum. As well, it is the world's largest producer of steel and gold.

Thus, we would not be surprised if those companies and countries involved in these trades seek efficiencies from quoting the prices of such commodities in the currency of the largest buyer or seller. Hong Kong Exchange and Clearing Limited (HKEx), which bought the London Metals Exchange (LME) in 2012, has already launched commodities contracts quoted in RMB.

Offshore markets for various RMB-denominated financial instruments are well established and growing. The value of bond issues, for example, has risen significantly, albeit from a low base of RMB10 billion in 2007 to RMB140 billion in 2014. As well, there has been massive expansion during the past few years of RMB deposits, certificates of deposits (CDs), loans and FX and rate derivatives. Hong Kong is also seeing growing investor interest in RMB-based funds, including listed, unlisted, exchange-traded (ETF) and those authorized to invest in mainland markets. So far, however, Hopewell Highway Infrastructure is the only Hong Kong-listed company to offer RMB-denominated stock, as part of a dual-currency share offer it launched in October 2012.

To further support RMB internationalization, Beijing is building and strengthening financial networks and ties across the world. In the space of only three years, for example, the number of financial institutions doing business in RMB has risen from 900 to more than 10,000. As well, settlement centers for RMB-based trade now circle the globe. Further, as noted above, the PBOC has established a wide network of swaps with other central banks that helps underpin trade and offers some of the stability normally associated with FX reserves in case of crises. Also, both the China Development Bank (CDB) and the new Silk Road Fund will likely provide more RMB funding for major projects over time.

The extent to which hedging instruments, futures and other derivative RMB markets can expand is constrained by liquidity. Conversely, their development is crucial to further expansion of liquidity. Unless the markets underlying these instruments are deep and liquid, large trades or volatility in related areas can drastically affect their pricing.

The gradual lifting of capital controls creates business opportunities that further extend the use of the RMB. At the simplest level, the ever-growing hordes of increasingly adventurous Chinese tourists are carrying RMB with them to every corner of the globe – and per capita they are the world's biggest spenders after they arrive. At a more sophisticated level, the Stock Connect schemes will create substantial cross-border flows of RMB that may expand rapidly. Growing offshore RMB markets mean the currency will trade around the clock, particularly benefiting banks with global capacity and China expertise.

Allowing foreign companies operating in China to pool their RMB cash from different subsidiaries and branches, thereby achieving cost savings and greater efficiency, is another significant development. This was introduced nationwide late in 2014, after a short and successful trial in the Shanghai Free Trade Zone (SFTZ). The speed with which it occurred was impressive, but it nonetheless followed China's usual strategy of incremental institution-building and liberalization. First, Beijing tests new policies – in this case, using trusted institutions in one of its free-trade zones. The results are monitored closely and adjusted if necessary. Once the process is deemed to work properly, it is introduced more widely.

There are still enormous potential benefits to be realized from further liberalization of capital controls, especially in areas such as insurance and funds management. In Japan, for example, where insurance is largely driven by the private sector, total life premiums amount to about 20% of GDP, compared with less than 2% in China. Also, the Chinese fund management sector has been opening fast in 2015, as the mainland and Hong Kong agreed on a scheme of cross-border fund sales, with an initial quota of RMB300 billion each way. This exceeds 60% of Hong Kong's current annual fund sales.

RESERVE CURRENCY

Popular discussion about the rise of the RMB tends to focus on when it will replace the USD – in other words, how soon before it becomes the principal reserve currency. In fact, this is far away and of little importance. The RMB's rapid adoption for global settlements, FX trading and other key functions, together with the emergence of new Chinese-backed financial institutions, is transforming the world's monetary system.

By contrast, the RMB's use as a reserve currency is much less significant and likely to remain limited – possibly for decades, in the absence of a political or financial cataclysm. The RMB accounts for less than 1% of total global FX reserves, and we forecast that by 2020 it may potentially reach 5%, comparable with the yen's share in 2014.

Although more than 50 central banks hold small amounts as official reserves, the RMB is still not designated as such by the International Monetary Fund (IMF). That may change in October 2015, when the IMF next reviews the composition of its hybrid reserve currency – known as special drawing rights (SDR). This basket currently comprises USD, JPY, EUR and GBP. The criteria for inclusion are that a currency be widely used and freely usable. As we have seen, the RMB certainly meets the first condition. And, by consensus, the second is not strictly defined as "fully convertible." Thus, it will be a matter of judgment – or politics – whether China's remaining restrictions on inflows and outflows mean the RMB is not "freely usable."

As noted above, Chinese officials have said privately that the RMB will be basically convertible by 2016, which would make it freely usable come the next SDR review in 2020. The IMF decision in the fall of 2015 is largely symbolic anyway, given that the hybrid is not widely used, with only SDR210 billion (USD294 billion on June 15, 2015) in existence as of 2014. However, symbolism is important. US opposition to the RMB's inclusion, in the wake of its ill-fated resistance to the establishment of the AIIB, would add to the impression that it is determined to limit China's role in global financial governance. The Chinese government's management of the 2015 stock-market crash (see Chapter 5) will strengthen those who say that the purpose of a reserve currency is to be fully available in a crisis situation and that the stock-market intervention, which included prohibitions on big holders selling their shares, shows that in a crisis the Chinese government might have other priorities than keeping markets open. If financial reform, including capital market opening, continues at its 2014 pace, notwithstanding the stock-market crash, the RMB might be welcomed into the SDR well before 2020.

The RMB is far from becoming a contender to be the primary reserve currency and there is no evidence that it aspires to be. One prerequisite would be that other countries consider it sufficiently liquid to be used during a major financial crisis. In 1997, for example, Thailand went through more than USD30 billion of reserves in a matter of weeks. Had its reserves been in EUR even, this would have sharply moved the EUR exchange rate against the trade, whereas it was easily absorbed in USD. For now, the RMB is considerably less liquid than the EUR.

That more than 50 countries have adopted the RMB as a reserve currency is encouraging for China. However, their holdings are small and serve mainly to hedge trade obligations with China and curry favor with Beijing. Those are reasons enough to expect a growing number of countries to hold RMB reserves, giving the currency wide but thin use. This will undoubtedly deepen as the RMB becomes more liquid. However, to vie for the role of primary reserve currency, the RMB would have to be as liquid as the USD. As well, the PBOC would have to be as trusted as the US Fed. Barring a "black swan" event such as a financial catastrophe or a major war, neither is likely for decades. By 2020, we expect the RMB to be among the top five most-traded currencies globally and foreign holdings of Chinese government and policy bank bonds may well exceed 10% of the 2014 global reserves. Should half of this foreign holding be under reserve asset managers, by 2020 it could reach 5% of the 2014 global reserves (but a smaller proportion of 2020 global reserves).

Although the reserve use of the RMB is small and likely to grow only slowly, swap arrangements will provide some of the stabilizing function normally associated with more significant FX reserves. (This is beyond the trade and other commercial roles the swaps underpin.) As stated above, the PBOC has entered into 28 active swaps worth more than RMB3 trillion (USD498.5 billion). By comparison, due to legislative restrictions, the US Fed has only five standing liquidity swaps – with Canada, the Eurozone, Japan, Switzerland and the UK – worth USD333 billion.

Such large-scale swaps are important for China for three reasons. First, they are increasingly seen as vital crisis-management tools. Second, global confidence in the US Fed has derived in large part from its willingness and ability to offer swaps in a crisis. However, in the aftermath of the 1994 Mexican crisis, the US Congress curtailed the Fed's and the Treasury's power to act. Thus, the USA failed to offer swaps to Thailand or Indonesia in 1997–1998 or to China in 2008. Third, the wisdom of Beijing's decision to offer so many swaps has yet to be tested by a major financial crisis.

THE EMERGING MONETARY ORDER

Reaction to the RMB's rapid rise has ranged from accommodative and supportive, to some anxiety about China's long-term aims. Asian markets, for example, have been quick to create – and profit from – settlement centers. Asian businesses have also jumped at the chance to reduce settlement costs by eliminating the USD "middleman." Further abroad, London was the first city outside Asia to be approved as a settlement and trading center, with the UK even conducting a small RMB bond issue for its FX reserves to support RMB instruments. Frankfurt and Paris have also opened settlement centers in quick succession.

France clearly resents the RMB's potential threat to the EUR's role, but can do little about it. US declaratory policy is to do no more than follow the markets. It will facilitate a settlement center if businesses request it and won't create any regulatory hurdles. However, it will not actively pursue the business.

In contrast to its fairly neutral stance in this area, the USA is more actively opposed to the likely longer-term impact of the RMB's rise on the global monetary system. Senior US government officials, for example, have foreshadowed opposition to the RMB's inclusion in the SDR basket of currencies in October 2015. As well, the US Congress has resisted proposed reforms of the IMF and the World Bank, despite the increasingly obvious need to modernize and expand these institutions. Further, the USA has tried to stymie China's development of alternatives such as the AIIB.

Meanwhile, the USA's use of sanctions against the likes of Russia and Iran, as well as punitive action against colluding foreign banks, is driving significant currency flows away from the USD and US-supported clearing institutions. These include CLS (formerly Continuous Linked Settlement) and the Belgium-based SWIFT.

China's policy has been to eschew transactions that could antagonize the USA. Indeed, Chinese institutions have been among the least problematic for US policy. Nonetheless, its banks are conscious of the risks of USD-based transactions, particularly given the example of French bank BNP Paribas, which was fined USD8.9 billion in mid-2014 for helping clients violate US sanctions.

It is not inconceivable that at some point a critical mass of international institutions will begin to desert USD-based transactions and systems because they either have already fallen foul of US sanctions or fear that they may do so. The logical result would be a wholesale shift to the RMB.

The GFC was a watershed for the world's financial system. Since 1944, it has been based on US leadership, the USD, the Bretton Woods institutions and an open, loosely regulated structure. There was near-universal consensus that this provided the optimal path to prosperity, especially for emerging markets. Now, in the aftermath of that world-shaking crisis, there is deepening skepticism and demand for fundamental change.

This has been exacerbated by growing disenchantment with the US Fed and its inherent conflict of interests. As noted above, the failure of the USA to offer swaps to Thailand or Indonesia in 1997–1998, or to China in 2008, has shaken confidence in the institution. This is especially troubling, given that it is a key pillar of the USD-based system. For Asian countries, in particular, the US Fed's failure to act on these occasions underscores that, although it is de facto the world's central bank, its legal requirement to focus on US employment and financial stability can mean that it ignores potentially severe damage to other economies.

This inherent conflict manifests itself in the US Fed's focus on keeping post-GFC domestic interest rates low to the detriment of emerging economies, which are left to struggle with housing bubbles and staple-commodities inflation caused by the resulting tsunami of money seeking better returns.

Little wonder China's development of alternative institutions has received such strong and widespread support. These include the AIIB, the NDB and the Silk Road Fund, as well as the CDB's international operations and the PBOC's numerous swap arrangements noted above. Collectively, they will have more development clout than the traditional US-led group of institutions that includes the IMF, the World Bank and the Asian Development Bank (ADB).

The USA's failure to win support for its opposition to the AIIB – even from among its key allies, bar Japan – can be seen as a reflection of global disgruntlement with its self-serving approach. On the one hand, it rejects much-needed reforms of the old institutions. On the other hand, it seeks to stymie new ones. Meanwhile, it exploits the prevailing USD-based system to its advantage to the detriment of other economies.

For now, barring financial or geopolitical calamity, the USD position is unassailable. The old system has tremendous inertia and no alternative offers the liquidity of the USD and even the somewhat tarnished credibility of the US Fed. Despite inroads by the RMB, more than 80% of global trade is denominated in USD and it is used for about 75% of settlements.

Nonetheless, US resistance to a growing role for China in global financial governance risks precipitating a schism – unlikely as that may be for many years. In the meantime, a combination of US policies leads to incremental reduction of reliance on the USD and its related institutions: congressional restrictions on reform of the Bretton Woods institutions and on Fed use of swaps to ameliorate foreign emergencies; widespread Asian resentment of US-backed punitive IMF policies after the Asian financial crisis; disillusionment with the existing system after the GFC; proliferation of US financial sanctions; and strong emerging market reactions against the Fed's post-GFC policies.

Having said that, for some time there will be no viable alternative to the USD-based system and even in the long run, schism is hardly inevitable. Some of the US policies that antagonize other countries are based on congressional alignments and could be reversed under a different Congress and stronger executive leadership. Nothing that China has done so far is in any way inconsistent with the orderly expansion of an integrated global financial system.

Meanwhile, aside from the reserve currency role, most aspects of RMB internationalization will continue at a rapid rate – dependent not so much on other countries' approval or otherwise, but the pace of Chinese reform.

CHAPTER 2

THE RISE AND FALL OF CURRENCIES – HISTORICAL LESSONS FOR THE RMB

The rise of the RMB signals a fundamental transition of the global monetary system. Indeed, its internationalization is both a cause and a consequence of this historic change.

The key criterion of an international currency is large-scale international use for such purposes as transaction settlements, FX trading, pricing of commodities and other goods, valuation of financial instruments, value storage and FX reserves. The RMB meets these conditions and is, thus, already an international currency.

However, to be considered truly global, a currency must be among the most important used for these purposes. The RMB is not yet a global currency, though it is well on the way.

Popular discussion about the rise of the RMB typically focuses on the question of if and when it will challenge or displace the USD as the world's primary reserve currency. As noted in the previous chapter, this is an interesting question, but actually not as important as many believe. The rise of the RMB as a trade-settlement currency may seem less "sexy," but it is far more significant for the way the economy actually works – and it is already happening. By contrast, our research indicates that the RMB is unlikely to compete with the USD as a reserve currency for decades, absent a game-changing financial crisis; see Chapter 8 for the detailed analysis. (Of course, as the GFC of 2008–2009 reminds us, such events do occur.)

Meanwhile, we note that the PBOC's bilateral swaps with other central banks are now larger and more numerous than those of the US Fed. This is significant because such arrangements complement and to some extent are even replacing the traditional crisis-management roles of reserve currencies.

Most importantly, the RMB's rise is a key aspect of the global monetary-system transition that is under way. Although the USD remains unquestionably the dominant global currency, there has been a gradual diminution of US monetary leadership since at least the 1990s. Dissatisfaction caused by the growing gaps in global financial governance and, to a lesser extent, risks associated with using the USD have encouraged the development of alternatives, largely led by Beijing.

The pace of the systemic transition from this point is uncertain. Another global crisis could accelerate the process. Equally, it could falter or even fail if China's current round of rapid reform stalls for economic or political reasons. Nonetheless, the trend is clearly toward an important realignment.

Bearing in mind George Santayana's observation a century ago in *The Life of Reason* that "those who cannot remember the past are condemned to repeat it," we review key lessons from previous transitions. Six of the most important are enumerated below. We then go on to examine in more detail their historical underpinnings (with the exception of the fourth, which we deal with in Chapter 3 on economic transition).

Global monetary-system transitions can be highly disruptive and even cataclysmic. This underscores the imperative for prudent management by the major powers of further internationalization of the RMB. However, as the fifth lesson suggests, some disruption may even be necessary.

A relatively insignificant currency can assume a dominant role in the global economy in a breathtakingly short time.

A currency must meet two conditions to be considered truly international:

- significant demand for its use offshore;
- support from the issuing government in the form of enabling global and domestic institutions.

The sequence of supporting reforms is critical. We examine this issue further in Chapter 3. However, China's strategy of gradual reform (trial application, careful assessment, fine-tuning and then widespread adoption) means the cart is unlikely to precede the horse.

Because existing systems tend to be safeguarded by inertia, a disruptive event may be required to precipitate major change. Thus, the GFC helped to launch the RMB's internationalization. However, the USD is likely to remain the dominant currency for decades unless some further shock decisively undermines trust in US-led institutions.

The relationship between international currencies and liquidity is uncertain. Going offshore diminishes control of a currency by its central bank and risks liquidity becoming volatile. It may quickly expand during times of easy money and just as rapidly contract under discipline. The offshore RMB is unique in history and the full ramifications of its internationalization are yet to be felt.

RISKS IN INTERNATIONAL MONETARY SYSTEM TRANSITIONS

History shows all too clearly that global monetary-system transitions can be massively disruptive and enormously challenging to manage. Encouragingly, the internationalization of the RMB appears to be proceeding smoothly, although there is no cause for complacency, given the potential risks.

This section highlights just how earth-shattering those risks can be. It draws on arguments made by economic historians that events as disruptive and even cataclysmic as the Great Depression, World War II, the 1970s stagflation and the GFC were partly caused or exacerbated by mismanaged monetary policy. We do not suggest that these were inevitable or that monetary issues were even the key contributors. Rather, we aim to highlight that the internationalization of a currency has implications beyond business profit and is a matter of global public interest.

The Great Depression

The rapid rise of the USD and its supplanting of the GBP as the dominant global currency was accompanied by significant "teething" troubles. From one view, these contributed to conditions that brought on the Great Depression. That economic crisis, in turn, is widely regarded as one of the factors that led to World War II. Monetarists argue that a fall in money supply caused the Great Depression (Friedman and Schwartz,

1963). Keynesians attribute it to a collapse in aggregate demand. Both explanations have some validity, but only the monetarist view is relevant to RMB internationalization.

In their review of international monetary systems over the past 1,000 years, Eichengreen and Sussman (2000) argue that the international gold standard came about largely as a result of the so-called network effect of Britain's use of the metal. The earliest industrial nation and largest international trader by the late 1800s, Britain regarded investments in countries that did not use the gold standard as relatively risky. As a result, other major economies saw advantage in also adopting gold as the basis of their currencies. Germany was the first, in 1871, followed by the USA in 1879, and eventually Russia and Japan in the 1890s. That system, with global finance and payments centered on London, remained strong until World War I. (China never adopted the gold standard, basing its monetary system on silver instead.) Although the USA was already the world's largest economy before the war, the USD only replaced the GBP as the principal global currency as a result of the associated disruption to the monetary system.

With the rise of the USD, the center of the global-payments system eventually shifted to New York. In turn, regulation of liquidity and banking transitioned to the US Fed, which had been established only in 1913.

Ahead of the US Fed's creation, a National Monetary Commission recommended in 1908 that it use the purchase of "trade acceptances" as a primary tool to smooth interest rates. It did so on the basis that this was the method used by the Bank of England. However, to be effective, it would need a large supply of such acceptances denominated in USD. This was a key reason that the Federal Reserve Act of 1913 authorized US banks to do business offshore. We will return to how the USD became the leading global currency when we discuss the prerequisites for currency internationalization. For now, the important point is that US banks were encouraged to provide trade financing and competed fiercely for it. Later, we will examine how such financing tilted sharply toward China after the GFC.

During World War I, capital flowed from Europe to the USA to pay for machinery and food. Afterwards, the flow reversed as US banks competed to supply reconstruction financing. Lacking international-financing experience, the banks approved many dubious loans. Indeed, in expectation of future loans from the establishment of new trade relations, the banks may have regarded some foreign bonds as loss leaders. However, by the end of the 1920s, refinancing bad debts became impossible and "the majority of the foreign bonds underwritten by American banks lapsed into default" (Eichengreen, 2011). (Mintz, 1951, describes the feeding frenzy that led to this result.) In turn, the credit collapses of these inexperienced banks led to runs.

The naivety of the banks was matched and exacerbated by that of the US Fed. At that time, it was not even two decades old, with an uncertain mandate. In the aftermath of World War I, highly deflationary attempts had been made to return to the gold standard. The following decade was marked by a series of financial shocks. In 1931, Europe's biggest bank, Creditanstalt, collapsed. Across the Channel, the GBP came under attack from speculators and in response Britain withdrew from the gold standard. Other countries followed suit, but the inexperienced US Fed, along with others, decided to abandon its new focus on price stability to defend the standard "at the very time [price stability] mattered most" (Mundell, 2000). Instead of increasing liquidity, this tightened the money supply, dragging the economy into what became the Great Depression. Mundell succinctly tallies the horrendous cumulative cost of this mismanaged transition of the global monetary system:

> *"Had the price of gold been raised in the late 1920s, or, alternatively, had the major central banks pursued policies of price stability instead of adhering to the gold standard, there would have been no Great Depression, no Nazi revolution, and no World War II."*
>
> —(Mundell, 2000)

The Collapse of Bretton Woods and Ensuing Stagflation

The Great Depression and its consequences serve as a stark warning of the risks in monetary-system transitions. Although it is difficult to imagine a more disastrous outcome, the history of such global realignments provides a compendium of cautionary tales highlighting the imperative for thoughtful, prudent management.

After World War II, the international monetary system was defined by the Bretton Woods agreement that again bound exchange rates to the gold standard. By the 1950s, Europe and Japan had largely recovered economically and resumed accumulating USD. However, by 1960 the value of foreign-held USD exceeded the gold holdings of the USA. Eichengreen explains:

"[T]here was an obvious flaw in a system whose operation rested on the commitment of the United States to provide two reserve assets, gold and dollars, both at a fixed price, but where the supply of one was elastic while the other was not."
—(Eichengreen, 2011)

Robert Triffin (1960, 1978) frequently warned of this flaw. He argued that trade would cease if the USA stopped providing USD, but that confidence in the USD would collapse if the supply continued diverging from gold reserves. In his view, this would eventually precipitate a run on US gold stocks and knock the USD off the standard unless the USA moved first to abandon it.

However, the USD remained convertible to gold until August 15, 1971, when President Richard Nixon suspended gold payments as part of his New Economic Program, thereby in effect ending the Bretton Woods system. Since the rest of the world's currencies remained pegged to the USD, Nixon had removed all discipline from the system. In addition, under pressure from Nixon, the US Fed introduced an inflationary policy in 1972 that sparked a run on the USD the next year, leading to the eventual collapse of the fixed exchange-rate system. Monetary systems without discipline are intrinsically inflationary, and the consequence in the 1970s was disastrous stagflation (Barsky and Kilian, 2000). Growth declined, unemployment deepened and interest rates rose to about 20% by the end of the decade.

It took a determined squeeze on the money supply by US Fed Chairman Paul Volcker to bring inflation to heel. This triggered recessions in the rich countries and debt rescheduling in much of the rest of the world. In the aftermath, central banks introduced inflation-targeting commitments (Mehrling, 2014), which ushered in decades of disinflation. Once again, a major transition had been accompanied by significant disruption.

THE ROLE OF EURODOLLARS IN THE 2008 GLOBAL FINANCIAL CRISIS

The somewhat chimeric nature of the eurodollar (a very different animal than the EUR) calls to mind Hughes Mearns's poem *Antigonish*, about the "man who wasn't there" – as many investors discovered to their great cost during the GFC. Indeed, the exacerbating role the eurodollar played in that crisis raises deep questions about the relationship between offshore currencies and international monetary stability. Clearly, this has important implications for RMB internationalization, given the rapidly rising magnitude of RMB balances offshore. To appreciate these implications, we need to discuss certain unique characteristics of euro-dollars. We will then be better able to consider the implications of certain unique characteristics of the offshore RMB.

The most striking anomaly of eurodollars is that they are entirely credit instruments. They are not explicitly guaranteed by any government institution and are issued outside the regulatory authority of the US government. They can be created on the balance sheet of any lender outside the USA without any need for a corresponding entry on the balance sheet of the US Fed. Some 15 years before the onset of the GFC, economist Milton Friedman succinctly and somewhat acerbically noted that both eurodollars and the associated liabilities of US banks derive, in effect, from "a bookkeeper's pen" (Friedman, 1971).

As a result, the eurodollar market as a whole has fewer actual USD reserves than the sum of the reserves of individual eurodollar lenders. This is because many lenders hold other eurodollars as reserves, but these are not at all equivalent to USD accounts at the US Fed. During systemic crises, such reserves provide no security, as demonstrated forcefully during the GFC.

The importance of the eurodollar market should not be understated. It is "the world's funding market" and is governed by different institutions than those that oversee the USD. Most importantly, it is not under the jurisdiction of the US Fed, which is mandated to act only in support of "maximum employment, stable prices, and moderate long-term interest rates" within the USA (Federal Reserve, 2014). Thus, it attends to the domestic money supply and interest rates only. In 2008, when risk tolerance in the banking system was near zero, the eurodollar market had no ultimate source of liquidity. Banks refused to either lend eurodollars or accept those raised in unsecured loans and swaps. Assets that had been assumed to be safe were revealed to be otherwise, and the consequence was a surprisingly protracted and toxic problem.

2008: YEAR ZERO FOR A NEW INTERNATIONAL MONETARY SYSTEM?

As we have noted, a fundamental transformation of the international monetary system is under way. This is being driven largely by a shift in global economic gravity, as China and other developing countries become increasingly more productive and wealthy, while weaknesses in the existing order become ever more glaring.

The end-game remains uncertain. It may be that the system ultimately settles on an equilibrium whereby the USD continues as the leading international currency, with the RMB joining the EUR as a second-tier major international currency. Or the RMB may rise further to join the USD as an equal international currency, with the EUR playing an important regional role. With imagination we can even envisage circumstances under which the RMB would emerge as the sole international currency, supported by a regional USD and EUR. Whatever the outcome, there will be a transition that will tempt many people, particularly in Washington and Beijing, to speak and behave jingoistically.

When economic fundamentals change, tensions arise between prevailing institutional arrangements and pressing economic needs. Institutions need to be stable, but flexibility is the order of the day, especially as monetary management has implications for international affairs.

As we highlighted earlier, previous changes to the global monetary system have been accompanied by economic turmoil and even protracted warfare. So far, the signs provide cause for optimism this time around. US officials claim to be comfortable with the potential for an international RMB, treating it as a market issue (discussed in more detail below), although the US government has resisted the formation of new institutions that would supplement the existing system. Meanwhile, China continues to deploy peaceful rhetoric, while cooperating with other countries to support the establishment of much-needed new institutional infrastructure. Nonetheless, transitions of this order and import are complex and inherently risky. We can only hope that the increasing geopolitical tension between China and the USA does not spread to monetary affairs.

The Pace of Change

Currency systems are characterized by strong network effects that create institutional inertia. In other words, people tend to use particular currencies because others do so. However, recent research shows that, under the right conditions, currency systems can experience drastic change very quickly. The USD, for instance, went from having almost no extra-territorial use to being the lead international currency in just 10 years, by some measures (Eichengreen and Flandreau, 2011). This contradicts the conventional view that the GBP remained the leading international currency until after World War II. In reality, only the GBP and USD have ever been truly global. Although we cannot draw general conclusions from a sample of only two, we can examine their histories for perspective.

The rise of the USD occurred mostly during World War I, between 1913 and 1917. By 1872, the USA had surpassed the UK in terms of output, but still lacked "deep, liquid, dependable and open" financial markets. The New York Clearing House remained "a private bankers' bank," but fulfilled the role of central bank, creating a situation whereby private money was at the top of the monetary hierarchy[1] in the USA (Mehrling, 2014). Not until the Federal Reserve was established in 1913 was public money placed at the top. The significance of this change was that the ultimate source of liquidity became a government guarantee of payment as opposed to a private firm's promise.

Until the Federal Reserve Act of 1913, the USD was scarcely used outside the USA. Nor was it even used to settle a significant portion of US trade. Throughout the 19th century, Canada was the only other country in which the USD was used. (It did not have its own currency until the late 1860s.)

The policy change represented by the Federal Reserve Act was critical for the full development of the US financial system. Subsequently, "large scale wartime lending by the US to Britain and other combatants reversed the 19th Century creditor-debtor relationship and positioned the dollar as a strong currency" (Frankel, 2012). However, the international gold standard left private money at the top of the international money hierarchy (Mehrling, 2014).

The Federal Reserve Act, based in large part on the findings of a National Monetary Commission, had several important implications. First, it helped deepen and internationalize the US banking system. For example, the commission recommended that the new US Fed adopt the Bank of England's (BoE) practice of smoothing interest rates by purchasing trade acceptances. However, such a strategy required USD trade acceptances, which depended on US banks being involved in trade finance in the first place. Thus, the Federal Reserve Act authorized national banks with at least USD1 million in capital to establish branches abroad and purchase acceptances worth up to half their own funds.

Although these two measures created potential for internationalization of US banking, World War I created the demand for US finance.

---

[1]The hierarchy of money is not widely appreciated. We return to this concept in more detail later in this chapter, in the section "Offshore Currencies and International Liquidity."

As the USA switched from being a debtor to a creditor nation and became a major net exporter, USD trade financing became increasingly important, just as trade finance in Europe was being disrupted by the war (Eichengreen, 2011).

The instability of the GBP during the war was a third factor supporting internationalization of the USD. Traders from South America and Asia became increasingly willing to accept USD trade finance because the USD was pegged to gold, which was flowing into the USA in exchange for exports.

A fourth factor was the rapid establishment of US bank branches abroad, with 181 in operation by 1920. They encouraged local traders to accept USD loans instead of drawing on accounts in London (Eichengreen, 2011).

As the market for USD banking acceptances expanded and became more liquid, the interest charged fell. By the late 1920s, traders could receive finance in New York a full percentage point lower than in London. The city's growing status as a center of global finance was further boosted as the USA became the preferred source of reconstruction financing after the war. (The League of Nations was the main alternative.)

Thus, as Eichengreen (2011) has observed: "From a standing start in 1914, the dollar had already overtaken sterling by 1925."

Fast-forwarding to the present, we can consider the ongoing internationalization of the RMB by comparison with the early-20th-century experience of the USD. China's economy is already the world's largest in terms of purchasing power parity (PPP) and is expected to be the largest in nominal terms within a decade. Beijing is actively promoting the RMB's internationalization and has established many of the necessary enabling institutions. Given that the transition from the GBP to the USD arguably took only a decade, it is imperative that we explore how quickly the RMB could become a rival of the USD.

CONDITIONS FOR CURRENCY INTERNATIONALIZATION: MARKET DEMAND AND INSTITUTIONAL SUPPLY

The foundations of market demand[2] for internationalization are among the most widely studied aspects of currency internationalization. There is

---

[2]In this chapter, demand for a currency does not mean that people want to "hold" it. Rather, it refers to people's desire to "use" the currency. There is no clear relationship between this type of demand and the price of the currency.

broad – though imprecise – agreement about what influences use of a particular currency. Most analysis implicitly assumes that, if market demand exists, a currency will be made available. History shows this is probably not the case.

Two key conditions must be met for a currency to become international. Neither is sufficient on its own. They are as follows:

1. Market demand must exist for use of the currency beyond its borders – the economic condition.
2. The issuing country's government must actively support international use of the currency by creating or supporting international and domestic supporting institutions – the political condition (see Campanella, 2014).

Frankel observes that, historically, governments have not made a deliberate attempt to internationalize their currencies:

"[T]o promote internationalization as national policy would depart from the historical precedents. In all three twentieth-century cases of internationalization, popular interest in the supposed prestige of having the country's currency appear in the international listings was scant, and businessmen feared that the currency would strengthen and damage their export competitiveness. Probably China, likewise, is not yet fully ready to open its domestic financial markets and let the currency appreciate, so the renminbi will not be challenging the dollar for a long time."

—(Frankel, 2012)

While Frankel's observation of scant government support for currency internationalization is mostly correct, the two exceptions (the USA and the UK) are also the only two countries to have successfully created international currencies. The US Fed worked proactively as market maker to promote use of the USD outside the USA, while the British Empire was the major factor in the earlier internationalization of the GBP (Eichengreen and Flandreau, 2011).

In stark contrast, Germany and Japan most clearly demonstrate that market demand alone is not sufficient for the regular and reliable international use of a currency. The deutschmark never became an international currency, for one principal reason: German government policy. The Bundesbank was so scarred by memories of hyperinflation in the 1920s that it preferred capital controls to any hint of capital inflow. After World War II, Germany maintained relatively high interest rates, making it attractive for capital. However, capital-account controls made the deutschmark too frustrating for investment.

During the late 1970s, the deutschmark was considered the main rival to the USD, but Germany's economy remained small relative to that of the USA, and the government's balanced budget meant it issued few bonds that were attractive to foreign central banks and risk-averse institutional investors. Moreover, approval was required to sell fixed-income securities to foreigners, and foreign-owned banks were subject to high reserve requirements. Germany was hawkish on inflation and actively discouraged other countries from trying to bring in large volumes of savings. (Among the countries warned off the deutschmark was Iran, which made overtures in that direction during tense bilateral relations with the USA.) Consequently, less than 15% of FX reserves was denominated in deutschmarks for most of the 1980s (Eichengreen, 2011).

The experience of the JPY also reveals the importance of government support for currency internationalization. The idea of the JPY as an international currency arose in the wake of the Bretton Woods collapse and the adoption of a floating exchange-rate system in 1973 (Ministry of Finance, Japan, n.d.). Faith in existing structures was lost. In particular, trust that the USA could support the global economy was weak, whereas both Japan and Germany appeared to be in the ascendant.

Tokyo traditionally had been concerned that convenient use of the JPY abroad would be detrimental to domestic financial and capital markets. Not until May 1998, after the Asian financial crisis and final decisions about the creation of the European Monetary Union, did then-Foreign Minister Hikaru Matsunaga declare an intention to deliberately "boost the international role of the yen" by implementing the Foreign Exchange Law (1998) and liberalizing the capital account. Aside from this change in the official tone, the concept of deliberately internationalizing a currency was novel. Murase (2000) claims that, "a public pronouncement made by a finance minister of a sovereign nation's plan to internationalize its currency . . . has been virtually unheard of."

However, by the time the Japanese government had embraced the notion of an internationalized JPY, the lure of Japan's economy had faded. The bursting of the stock and property bubbles in 1989 was the beginning of a long period during which Japan struggled to inspire economically. Market interest in the JPY as an international currency faded before the government had the opportunity to make any serious moves to facilitate it.

JPY faded, but the main lesson for the RMB does not depend on those details. The critical point is that market demand and government institutional support for internationalization must both be present. As we shall discuss later, China has been rapidly building the institutions, such as settlement centers, needed to support an internationalized currency. Business has eagerly responded because dealing in RMB can often save money. Thus, the fact that both conditions have been met suggests that the RMB will not follow the path of the JPY – or, if it does, not for the same reasons, at least.

One other implication of the need for both market demand and proactive supply of institutional capacity with respect to RMB internationalization is that other countries would be misguided in viewing China's proactive approach as necessarily nationalistic or competitive. Awareness that internationalization requires at least some of these efforts should put into context some of China's policy initiatives vis-à-vis the RMB.

Factors Creating Market Demand for Currency Internationalization

The growing importance of the RMB has led to an increasing body of research examining the determinants of currency internationalization. Scholars focus on a variety of factors, typically economic gravity, ease of transaction and risk.

For instance, Cecchetti and Schoenholtz (2014) focus on "a reliable legal system, backed by a stable political system with an independent judiciary that efficiently enforces property rights" (all risk factors), while "an economy's size alone does not make its currency an international leader" and "the rise of a new international currency requires effective financial markets and institutions, in addition to a supportive external environment."

Ultimately, whether a currency is truly international depends on the extent to which people around the world trust that it will continue being accepted as final settlement of accounts. This begs the question: What builds such deep and wide trust?

Aliber (2011, ch. 7) describes currencies as "brand names." He points to the "economic and financial events associated with the First

World War" (p. 117) as having tarnished the value of the GBP's brand. By contrast, the USD brand became more attractive because it retained value (relative to gold) and a broader range of securities was offered in US financial markets than elsewhere. Aliber identifies three factors that strengthened the USD brand over the second half of the 20th century. First, the size of the US economy. Second, the relative stability of US financial markets and relatively low rate of inflation. Third, the USA was considered "militarily and politically secure." The first of these is based on economic geography, while the other two are based on risk.

These factors consistently appear in explanations of why people trust particular currencies – or, using Aliber's analogy, what builds a strong currency brand. Such considerations will be just as significant as purely economic calculations in deciding how the USD and RMB evolve over the coming decades. The GFC shook global confidence in the US-based system of economic and financial management. However, although some countries have since changed the way they manage their financial affairs at the margin, the core remains as incontestable as ever. The established system is basically intact and confidence in it remains higher than in any visible alternative. That said, if a plausible alternative were to emerge, the aftermath of any subsequent crisis could be significantly different.

People must be confident that their use of a currency will not be impeded. This requires deep and liquid markets linking different-quality financial assets. There are three important prices in such a system: the exchange rate; par (the price of deposits in terms of currency, normally kept at one-to-one by law); and the interest rate.

When considering RMB internationalization, there is a temptation to focus on people's acceptance of RMB for settlement of accounts in the current context of high Chinese economic growth and low European and US growth. But for the RMB to be truly international, global confidence that it will be accepted to settle accounts must continue through a financial downturn. The Chinese government's policies in the stock-market crash of 2015 are significant here, because it forbade large investors from selling stock; the analogue in foreign currency markets would be to (re)impose strong capital controls, thereby limiting currency trades.

There are a number of potential benefits to RMB internationalization that create demand for the process and for the RMB outside China, which is driven primarily by trade settlement. Currently, all currency risk on trade and investment between Chinese and foreign firms is held by

Chinese parties, despite the potential that the partner may have better risk-management techniques, lower expected costs of risk or lower risk-aversion (Ballantyn, Garner and Wright, 2013). A survey of Australian firms trading with China clarified the thinking behind private-sector demand for settling trade in RMB, identifying three perceived advantages:

- improved terms with trading partners due to reduced currency risk;
- a marketing advantage for foreign firms that can better satisfy Chinese demand if RMB settlement services are available; and
- improved currency-hedging capacity among existing exporters (Ballantyn, Garner and Wright, 2013).

The structure of trade may also be important for generating market demand for international use of a currency. For instance, in the 1980s Japan exported highly differentiable goods that had few substitutes and imported a high proportion of commodities (especially food and raw materials), trading in a single global market. Taguchi (1992) argues that these factors gave Japanese exporters a competitive edge by allowing them to pass currency costs on to their customers, whereas Japanese importers had no such competitive power, resulting in relatively poor take-up of JPY denomination for Japanese imports.

Similar analysis of the Chinese trade structure yields further insights. China's position in the middle of many global value chains may strengthen its bargaining power over which currency to use. However, such a statement remains in the realm of hypothesis, pending further research.

INSTITUTIONAL INERTIA AND DISRUPTIVE EVENTS

The international currency system is sustained by inertia, meaning that a disruptive event may be required before the system responds to shifts in economic fundamentals. Although 2008 may be "year zero" for RMB internationalization, and although the Chinese economy now has similar size to the US economy (smaller in nominal terms, larger in purchasing power terms), and although Chinese institutions may improve from their current immature state, the USD is likely to remain the leading currency, with RMB use not exceeding that of the USA for decades unless some additional shock reduces trust in US institutions.

History suggests that major changes to the global monetary system are often precipitated by a crisis. Indeed, it may not be possible to dislodge a dominant currency unless trust in the prevailing system is significantly damaged.

The USA had been the world's largest economy for at least 45 years before the USD began to be used abroad. It had even become the largest exporter a year before the Federal Reserve Act of 1913 allowed national banks to engage in international trade financing. How likely is the USD to be displaced today? Eichengreen strongly cautions against complacency:

> *"To be sure, it took an exceptional shock, World War I, and the market-making efforts of the Fed to effect this changing of the guard. Still, it is not impossible to imagine something analogous today. For the wartime shock to sterling, substitute chronic US budget deficits. And for the efforts of the Fed to establish a market in trade acceptances in New York, substitute the efforts of Chinese officials to establish Shanghai as an international financial center. The renminbi replacing the dollar may not be anyone's baseline scenario, but it is worth recalling the history of the 1920s before dismissing the possibility."*
> —(Eichengreen, 2011)

However, it is equally worth recalling that it took an exceptional shock for the USD to overtake the GBP. The GFC may spur the internationalization of the RMB. It has certainly damaged confidence in the existing system. Japanese lack confidence in their currency. Europeans lack confidence in their currency. So do Americans. Everywhere people express a lack of confidence in the overall system. Nonetheless, the aftermath of the GFC has not reduced use of the USD. Absent an additional crisis occurring after a viable alternative currency has been established, it is unlikely that the USD will be displaced any time soon.

OFFSHORE CURRENCIES AND INTERNATIONAL LIQUIDITY

Aliber explains offshore currencies ("external currency markets") as those by which "a banking office in a particular city produces a deposit denominated in a currency other than that of the country in which the office is located" (Aliber, 2011, p. 102). Eurodollars are simply short-hand for any external-currency deposit, regardless of whether they are in Europe or denominated in USD.

The relationship between global currencies and the stability of the international monetary system is uncertain. Eurodollars diminish central-bank control; they quickly expand during good times and just as quickly contract under stress. Although eurodollars raise interesting and important considerations for RMB internationalization, the offshore RMB (CNH) is a unique creation different from any currency in history. Thus, the impact of the CNH on international-liquidity stability is uncertain.

A critical difference between eurodollars and the CNH is that China has created an officially sanctioned offshore currency and tethered it in certain ways to the domestic RMB (CNY). The CNH is separated from China's onshore currency yet linked through a series of offshore clearing houses, each of which receives liquidity through RQFII quotas and a series of central-bank swap arrangements. Hong Kong is positioned as the main point of entry by virtue of its having the largest RQFII quotas, the largest swap arrangement and the Shanghai–Hong Kong Stock Connect, which went live on November 17, 2014. Previously, Hong Kong residents could exchange HKD for CNY up to a daily limit of RMB20,000. Since the establishment of the Shanghai–Hong Kong Stock Connect, that cap has been removed.

An important lesson from the eurodollar is that it dilutes the monetary-policy mechanism. Whereas eurodollars were originally balance-sheet creations of financial-services institutions outside the USA (or the respective currency's issuing country), many banks inside the USA borrow USD from institutions whose USD assets are simply balance-sheet creations. Often, these transactions occur between different divisions of a single multinational company.

Because eurodollars exist in a jurisdiction outside the currency's issuing country, but are denominated in a currency foreign to the jurisdiction in which they are deposited, they are subject to minimal regulation. For instance, a USD-denominated deposit in a London bank is outside US jurisdiction just as a JPY deposit in a Hong Kong bank is outside Japanese jurisdiction. In these cases, neither the UK nor Hong Kong would have much interest in regulating them because they are foreign currencies (Aliber, 2011, ch. 6). Thus, eurodollars largely escape regulations such as reserve requirements.

The existence of a currency over which central banks can exert only minor influence has important implications for the stability of global liquidity and the smooth functioning of payments systems. In essence, eurodollars form a credit market denominated in a currency that appears to be similar to domestic currencies (such as the USD, for example) but is ultimately unsecured. Consequently, it is more elastic than any domestic currency. Liquidity is determined purely by market forces without the counter-cyclical efforts of a central bank. This makes the eurodollar market a volatile and unstable source of liquidity. Do multiple unsecured currencies support or undermine the stability of global payments and liquidity compared with a situation where only one major unsecured currency exists? We don't know.

Answers are necessarily speculative. It is possible that a world with two or more offshore currencies would be more resilient to the business cycle or financial problems in just one of the primary countries concerned, but less resilient to problems that simultaneously disrupted both or all home markets. We hope we never have to find out the answer to this question with any certainty, but institutions with large exposure to, or responsibility for, the smooth functioning of international liquidity and payments must consider these risks. It is by no means clear whether the type of "once-in-a-century" events witnessed in the 1930s and again in 2007–2008 are likely to become more or less frequent in a world with multiple offshore currencies. Nor is it clear whether responding to such events is likely to be made more or less difficult. China, Russia and others have reacted strongly against the instability of the GFC by urging transition to a different system, less dependent on the USD. Their reactions are understandable but their assumption that an alternative system based on multiple currencies or more widespread use of SDRs remains untested and largely unsupported by strong arguments, as does the contrary view that the current system is optimal.

One of the most fundamental insights to understanding money is that "always and everywhere, monetary systems are hierarchical" (Mehrling, 2012). This statement is most easily understood by realizing that payment systems are almost always credit systems, and that most money is in reality a form of credit backed in part by reserves of actual money. When a national currency becomes international, there is a change in the hierarchy of money. It is not clear where the CNH may fit into an international hierarchy of money, although we present relevant data in subsequent chapters. Much will depend on how integration of the CNH and CNY progresses.

Addressing this question involves a return to fundamentals. What is meant by an international currency is both simple and profound. Money is commonly defined as a means of exchange, a measure of account and a store of value. An international currency, then, is simply one that performs these three functions internationally (including in situations not directly involving the currency's issuing country in any way) and for both private and public sectors.

However, Allyn Young argues for a more basic understanding of money:

"The one really essential characteristic of money is that the holder should be able to get rid of it without undue loss. Other commodities have their ultimate consumers; money never finds an ultimate destination or resting-place: it is tossed about from person to person until finally, worn out, lost, or melted down, it passes out of use."

—(Young, 1924)

According to Young, convertibility is the ultimate definition of money, implying that global convertibility is the ultimate definition of an international currency. This makes one implication of RMB internationalization apparent immediately: we are talking about the integration of China's financial system with that of the rest of the world. The changes brought about by China's accession to the World Trade Organization (WTO) and integration of its trading system with the global economy provide some guide to the potential significance of finishing the job.

Aside from the implications of integrating one of the largest financial markets and pools of savings in the world with the rest of the global economy, there are implications for the creation of global liquidity. Fluctuations in liquidity are a monetary way of saying "the cycle of booms and busts." Changing the way liquidity is created at the global level is directly related to the frequency and severity of crises and recessions.

Mehrling distinguishes different qualities of money by their ultimate liquidity. He is not, however, referring to different currencies – rather, to the difference between an IOU, a bank loan, a cash deposit, a reserve deposit and a reserve-backed hard currency. He demonstrates the fact of this distinction with the gold standard, under which gold was the ultimate money and all other forms of settling accounts merely derivatives of a promise to pay gold. A fiat system is fundamentally the same, but gold is replaced by currency. A global currency, then, is one that is accepted for settling accounts at all levels of the global economic system. After all, no one considers settlement in an international currency to be merely a promise of future payment – it is the actual payment.

The apex of the monetary system is the fundamental source of liquidity. Ultimate money is no one's liability. Under the gold standard, the supply of gold was the ultimate source of liquidity: only gold could be reliably used to settle international accounts. Under the USD standard, the US Fed is the ultimate source of liquidity, since only Fed-backed USD can reliably be used to settle international accounts.

Mehrling explains monetary-system dynamics as a balance between liquidity and discipline – the scarcity of ultimate money and the elasticity of derivative credit:

> *"[S]carcity comes from the fact that agents at any particular level in the hierarchy cannot by their own actions increase the quantity of the forms of money at a higher level than their own. Just so, central banks cannot increase the quantity of gold, and ordinary banks cannot increase the quantity of central bank currency. At every level of the system, the availability of money from the level above serves as a disciplinary constraint that prevents expansion; credit is payable in money, but money is scarce."*
>
> —(Mehrling, 2012)

Liquidity can be created by increasing the supply of ultimate money or by increasing credit at various levels of the monetary system: central banks, private banks, shadow banks, the private sector and households. Discipline is created either by decreasing the supplies of ultimate money or decreasing the supply of credit. In a fiat system, the supply of ultimate money is a policy decision, but the supply of credit is a market outcome.

Thinking about the difference between ultimate and derivative money (or money versus credit) makes clear how important the source of ultimate money is for global financial stability and liquidity:

> *"At every time scale, we see expansion and contraction of the hierarchy. As it expands, the hierarchy flattens and the qualitative difference between credit and money becomes attenuated, but then the system contracts and the hierarchy reasserts itself."*
>
> —(Mehrling, 2012)

There are two sources of fluctuation: the expanding and contracting quantity of credit (the total leverage in the system, or the money multiplier) and fluctuations in the degree of "moneyness" of credit. It is the "moneyness" of the CNH that has not yet been tested under stress. Who would act as lender of last resort for CNH deposits? Which jurisdictions have standing to regulate the market? Such critical questions were not raised during the development of the eurodollar market. They should be raised and answered at an early stage of the creation of the CNH market.

A multi-currency global monetary system, in which people around the world accept a variety of different currencies in settlement of accounts, has multiple independently governed sources of liquidity. Global liquidity would be determined by distributed authorities. While there have been periods of multiple international currencies in the past, there has not previously been a period in which a major international currency was not freely convertible with its own onshore version, nor a time when the quality of key economic institutions in the issuing country was uncertain. In subsequent chapters we address China's development toward increasing convertibility and the pace of development of its major financial institutions.

CURRENT INTERNATIONAL REACTIONS TO THE RMB'S RISE

Reactions to the rapidly increasing global importance of the RMB vary widely in emotional tone and in the details of regulatory responses – although none of these would inhibit progress and many will actually prove helpful. The global business community mainly sees opportunities to make money, reduce costs and cultivate China relations. In the absence of a comprehensive survey, it is hard to find evidence of any significant negative reactions within this community. Regulatory and political actions (as distinct from the wider range of expressed sentiments) have been generally either supportive or passive.

European countries have responded far more quickly than the USA to the market opportunities they see in RMB internationalization. London, Paris and Frankfurt have all established settlement centers. London even floated a small RMB-bond issue for its FX reserves in order to have backing for RMB-based instruments. By contrast, whereas Paris has responded positively to the market opportunity, French politicians clearly resent the emergence of a competitor to the EUR – all the more so because there is so little they can do about it. The non-US financial centers all face the problem that there are not yet sufficient RMB deposits and transactions to support the infrastructure they are creating. In the short run, US complacency looks efficient and UK enthusiasm looks expensive. However, barring a crisis or stagnation in China's economy, the UK investment may well pay off.

In Japan, the business community mainly sees a plethora of opportunities. There is no sense that the internationalization of the RMB creates major problems or dilemmas. Among politicians, there is an intense sense of geopolitical competition with China, but it is not particularly focused on currency. Japanese officials – and citizens who are conscious of currency issues at all – are quite aware that the failure of the JPY to internationalize is entirely a consequence of domestic decisions and problems, rather than foreign competition. Some parts of the political community have a vague sense of unease about the emergence of an additional dimension of China's rise. Indeed, Japan expressed this by refusing to join the Chinese-sponsored AIIB, which adds a Chinese-led institution alongside the Japanese-led ADB.

For now, only Hong Kong has the critical mass to support an RMB settlement center financially. The other centers are subsidized in hopes of future profits.

The US Perspective

US officials say they have no objections to gradual internationalization of the RMB per se, but they have grave concerns about the emergence of Chinese institutions and roles that could challenge US dominance of the global financial system. They have indicated that there are no significant regulatory hurdles preventing the establishment of a US-based settlement center for RMB transactions when demand develops. Both US business and regulators appear to be less conscious of the emergence of the RMB than their global counterparts. US regulators say that the Treasury is in charge of currency-related issues, although businesses are unclear about this and more often than not approach the US Fed for guidance.

More generally, US regulators indicate that they are comfortable with the RMB's internationalization. They officially see it as a market phenomenon, not a political competition. They believe that the shifts of balance can be accomplished smoothly and that there is no particular reason for the USA or other nations to fear them. In discussions, they are very clear that markets, rather than politicians or regulators, will decide. General Electric, for example, decides in which currency to settle trades based only on profit considerations. Similarly, the Chicago Mercantile Exchange decides whether to denominate derivatives in RMB based on market demand and profit potential. US regulators see offshore and onshore RMB exchange rates converging and welcome this as a sign of a maturing market. Whereas London opened its settlement center in response to private-sector demand, the US Treasury and Fed note that they have been approached on the issue by only one big firm – and a foreign one, at that. With Toronto having established a settlement center, US authorities appear content that the needs of the time zone have been met for now. (However, to ensure liquidity, a US swap agreement will eventually be necessary.)

Despite this seemingly sanguine view, the USA increasingly shows reluctance to accept rising Chinese influence in the global financial system. It does not oppose internationalization of the RMB, but conversely it does not support China's attempts to become more involved in global governance. As we detail below, this has perversely enhanced Beijing's influence at Washington's expense.

Looking further ahead toward the possibility that the RMB may one day challenge the USD to be the world's dominant currency, US politicians' competitive juices start to flow.

Since 2009, the US Congress has been unwilling to support expansion of the capital bases of the IMF and World Bank (the "Bretton Woods institutions") and has rejected proposed reforms of their governance to reflect the changing structure of the world economy. By contrast, the US Executive Branch is clearly conscious that such a stance risks eventually condemning those institutions to irrelevance. However, it nonetheless is resisting Chinese efforts to create new institutions (such as the AIIB, the NDB and the Silk Road Fund) that bypass the Bretton Woods institutions. Taken together, this stance positions the USA as a "King Canute," trying to halt the incoming tide. By trying too hard to defend the status quo, these policies almost certainly will hasten its demise. Already, for example, the CDB dwarfs the World Bank.

Other US policies are inadvertently hastening the emergence of a system that will be less dominated by the USD. The US Fed's and Treasury's unique willingness and ability to provide liquidity in a crisis has been a foundation of the USD-based system, along with the unique liquidity of US capital markets. However, in the aftermath of the successful and costless intervention (using the Treasury's Exchange

Stabilization Fund) to limit the Mexican crisis of 1994, Congress restricted the executive branch's ability to undertake such action. Hence, it could not legally help Thailand or Indonesia during the 1997–1998 crisis. Those countries' resulting disillusionment with the US was deepened by disastrous IMF austerity policies and opposition to the establishment of a Japanese fund that would have supplemented the IMF. Southeast Asian trust in the existing US-dominated system significantly declined.

Extensive use of financial sanctions (regardless of their justification) has provided a powerful incentive for foreign banks to try to avoid USD transactions and established clearing institutions to preclude any potential punitive legal action. This has been the case for banks not only from Russia and Iran but also France and other European countries, as well as across Asia. With the global financial system still primarily USD-based, this has created a remarkable burst of activity in the HKD, which is a proxy for the USD but does not have to clear through any US institutions. So far, this reaction does not even approach the critical mass of a system-changing development. However, we can imagine a scenario under which US-driven sanctions and its refusal to adapt to the changing world economy could combine to foster the emergence of a significant non-USD-based subsystem. The trajectory of this trend will depend on whether the current flurry of major financial sanctions broadens and becomes more frequent in response to the urgings of the US Congress or contracts as the current wave of anti-bank sentiment subsides, as seems likely.

Most importantly, the GFC shattered the beliefs of many countries that the Bretton Woods and USD-based system represented the best means of achieving global prosperity and stability. The crisis inflicted extraordinary external shocks on their systems that put their own growth and stability at terrible risk. This was exacerbated by Western monetary-policy responses that sent tsunamis of money rushing into emerging markets – and likely rushing back out later, with potentially destabilizing consequences.

RMB INTERNATIONALIZATION

The initial impetus to internationalize the RMB came from the Chinese leadership's shocked reaction to the GFC in 2009 – five sleepy years after authorizing a tiny retail offshore RMB market in Hong Kong. The collapse of trade finance hit China hard. It was made worse by the subsequent sharp contraction of US and European demand for its exports. This forced the leadership to consider how to mitigate such risks in the future. We see three possible considerations in this context.

The first reaction was that an exclusively USD-centric international monetary system posed too high a risk. Thus, in their view, the RMB should join the system as an international currency in itself – possibly by becoming one of the constituents of the IMF's SDR basket. To accomplish this would require the RMB to become widely used abroad.

Second, internationalization effectively involves some partial opening of China's capital account and, thus, could serve as an external pressure to accelerate domestic financial liberalization in a similar way to China's WTO accession. The argument here is that a more open capital account forces faster domestic financial reforms. This consideration is controversial, even inside China. Many economists and officials argue that it contradicts a key supposed lesson of the Asian financial crisis: that capital markets should be opened only after domestic interest rates are liberated and the banking system is fully stabilized. However, the political reality is that, so long as the capital-account opening does not get too far ahead of domestic reforms, it can be used to push forward domestic reforms. In any case, RMB internationalization itself partly liberalizes the capital account and stimulates further opening.

Third, China has a huge net foreign-currency exposure because of both a net creditor position vis-à-vis the rest of the world and its skewed international balance sheet. Most of its international assets are denominated in foreign currencies, whereas most of its international liabilities are in RMB. This net foreign currency exposure could be as large as 50% of GDP. Such mismatch risk needs to be mitigated by denominating more assets in RMB, which requires wider international use – hence, Beijing's efforts to promote RMB internationalization (Cheung, Ma and McCauley, 2011).

Many Chinese officials also express a desire for the prestige that they see accompanying a rise of their currency to a stature more proportionate to China's role in the global economy.

These motives complement and reinforce each other to incentivize greater external use of the RMB. This is quite distinct from any alleged ambition to dominate in the global financial system. Far from it, China appears keen to share the risk and be a stakeholder.

Nonetheless, if China's economic success continues, albeit at a slower rate, the internationalization of the RMB will integrate more closely with – and even eventually change – the global monetary system. What we have seen so far may well prove to be only the first small steps of a "Long March" toward internationalizing the RMB in the coming decade.

Although the GFC provided the motivation for RMB internationalization and the initial impetus for achieving this quickly was policy-driven, its success so far has been largely because it delivers cost savings and increased profits to business. One of our tasks in later chapters is to understand the extensive advantages and opportunities that global business obtains from RMB internationalization.

CONCLUSION

From the mid-1800s, global finance was centered on London and money was ultimately a promise to pay gold. World War I saw the center shift to New York, but the transition was poorly managed and the Great Depression followed. In 1971, the USA unilaterally broke the gold standard. The existing hierarchical monetary system quickly became one of floating national currencies. Again, the transition was poorly handled. All monetary discipline was removed and an extended period of stagflation ensued, lasting until the mid-1980s, when key central banks adopted inflation-targeting.

The GFC of 2007–2008 hastened the next major monetary system transition. The shock encouraged Chinese policymakers to become proactive in building the enabling institutions to underpin international use of the RMB – thus making it unlikely to follow the path of the JPY. However, history shows that any such transitions are risky. Wisdom and prudent management will be needed to avoid disruptions and keep adjustment costs low. Such an approach is more likely to come from careful and early consideration of the fundamental economic and political nature of the emerging system.

The epicenter of disruption to the existing system is China. Thus, ascertaining how the monetary system needs to adjust requires understanding what is happening there, specifically with respect to the process of internationalization of the RMB. Jeffrey Frankel (2012) argues that the "fundamental determinants of international currency status are economic size, confidence in the currency, and depths of financial markets." China's economic size is forcing change. Its government is creating the institutional capacity to administer an international currency. How other countries respond to Chinese policy initiatives will also be important. Early signs are positive, but work may be needed by China to ensure they remain onside.

The internationalization of a currency entails a change in equilibrium – a shift in the demand for the currency's international use and in the supply of the currency beyond its borders. The demand shift is primarily a market outcome: firms choosing to settle trade in RMB instead of another currency; investors choosing to denominate financial assets in RMB; businesses choosing to quote prices in RMB. The supply shift is principally a regulatory outcome: lifting restrictions on China's capital account; granting permission to foreign firms to invest in Chinese equities and other financial products; allowing people to convert money from one currency to another without prior approval; establishing easily accessible and reliable real-time payment systems. History is replete with examples of poorly managed transitions. The advantage this time is that the transition can be a conscious, systematic one, managed with awareness of the risks – if officials in the USA, China and Europe are willing and able to do so.

REFERENCES

Aliber, R. (2011) *The New International Money Game*. Palgrave Macmillan: Basingstoke.

Ballantyn, A., Garner, M. and Wright, M. (2013) Developments in renminbi internationalization. RBA Bulletin, June.

Barsky, R. and Kilian, L. (2000) A monetary explanation of the great stagflation of the 1970s. NBER Working Paper, No. 7547.

Campanella, M. (2014) The internationalization of the renminbi and the rise of a multipolar currency system. ECIPE Working Paper, No. 01/2014.

Cecchetti, S. and Schoenholtz, K. (2014) To RMB or not to RMB? Lessons from currency history. *Money and Banking*, August 18.

Cheung, Y.-W., Ma, G. and McCauley, R.N. (2011) Renminbising China's foreign assets. *Pacific Economic Review* 16(1), 1–17.

Eichengreen, B. (2011) *Exorbitant Privilege: The rise and fall of the dollar and the future of the international monetary system*. Oxford University Press: Oxford.

Eichengreen, B. and Flandreau, M. (2011) The Federal Reserve, the Bank of England, and the rise of the dollar as an international currency, 1914–1939. *Open Economies Review* 23(1), 57–87.

Eichengreen, B. and Sussman, N. (2000) The international monetary system in the (very) long run. IMF Working Paper, No. WP/00/43.

Federal Reserve (2014) What are the Federal Reserve's objectives in conducting monetary policy? Available at: www.federalreserve.gov/faqs/money_12848 .htm.

Frankel, J. (2012) Internationalization of the RMB and historical precedents. *Journal of Economic Integration* 27(3), 329–365.

Friedman, M. (1971) The Euro-dollar market: Some first principles. University of Chicago, Graduate School of Business, Selected Papers, 34.

Friedman, M. and Schwartz, A. (1963) *A Monetary History of the United States, 1867–1960*. Princeton University Press: Princeton, NJ.

Mehrling, P. (2012) The inherent hierarchy of money. Duncan Foley festschrift volume and conference, April 20–21.

Mehrling, P. (2014) Chartalism, metallism, and key currencies. *Economics of Money and Banking*. Coursera Lecture Notes.

Ministry of Finance, Japan (n.d.) Chronology of the internationalization of the Yen. Available at: www.mof.go.jp/english/about_mof/councils/customs_ foreign_exchange/e1b064c1.htm.

Mintz, I. (1951) *Deterioration in the Quality of Foreign Bonds Issued in the United States, 1920–1930*. NBER: Cambridge, MA.

Mundell, R. (2000) A reconsideration of the twentieth century. *The American Economic Review* 90(3), 327–340.

Taguchi, H. (1992) On the internationalization of the Japanese Yen. In Ito, T. and Drueger, A. (eds), *Macroeconomic Linkage: Savings, exchange rates, and capital flows*. NBER-EASE: Chicago.

Triffin, R. (1960) *Gold and the Dollar Crisis*. Yale University Press: New Haven, CT.

Triffin, R. (1978) Gold and the dollar crisis: Yesterday and tomorrow. Essays in International Finance No. 132, Princeton University, Princeton, NJ.

Young, A. (1924) The mystery of money: How modern methods of making payments economize the use of money. The role of checks and bank-notes. The enormous edifice of credit. In *The Book of Popular Science*. The Grolier Society: New York.

CHAPTER 3

ECONOMIC AND INSTITUTIONAL FOUNDATIONS FOR THE RISE OF THE RMB

The success and scale of RMB internationalization depend on both the importance of China's economy and the institutions that facilitate the currency's use internationally. China needs to transition to a new growth model if it is to achieve a robust and open domestic economy. This requires faster economic reform and financial liberalization. Greater opening of capital markets, in turn, complements RMB internationalization. We expect China's contribution to global GDP to rise from 13% in 2014 to around 18% in 2020.

Institutional quality is also important for a global currency in the long run. This chapter discusses core elements of institution-building generally and particularly explores one of the key conditions required to support the RMB as an international currency: the central bank's (PBOC's) ability to manage inflation, exchange rates, financial stability and reform.

ECONOMIC FOUNDATION

China's recent economic slowdown has raised questions about the prospects of RMB internationalization. While many challenges exist, the country's continued growth is likely to create a solid foundation for full convertibility, provided the economy can move to a new growth model. A large, sustainable and open domestic economy is essential for RMB internationalization. The possibility of disruptive "black swan" events should not be ignored; some analysts believe the stock-market collapse of mid-2015 risks being a "black swan" for the larger economy.

A New Era of the Chinese Economy

In the early decades of reform, China focused almost exclusively on economic growth. This is understandable, given the imperative of trying to quickly catch up with the developed world from a low base. Given an obsessive focus, it was able quickly to acquire the necessary technology and management skills. It also had a model it could emulate in the form of the earlier "Asian Miracle" economies, with their strategy of building infrastructure, gradually marketizing and opening the economy, and relying heavily on exports. Its young and growing labor force, boosted by rising education levels, delivered rapid productivity gains. On top of this, China was able to ride a favorable globalization wave.

The result was stunning growth, averaging 10% a year for three decades from 1978. Along the way, hundreds of millions were lifted out of poverty. As we shall see, however, the figures for the final decade would prove to be somewhat deceptive. And the social and environmental costs were enormous.

Among the first signs of stress were cracks in the "iron rice bowl" – a term used to describe the old Communist guarantee of lifetime employment. Under pressure to improve efficiency, state-owned enterprises (SOEs) began massive layoffs from the mid-1990s. This was the first of a "double whammy" of blows that would preoccupy the authorities and even retard China's growth. Between 1994 and 2003, some 50 million SOE employees lost their jobs, including 25 million in manufacturing. Yet a more efficient Chinese economy joined the World Trade Organization (WTO).

Following this painful restructuring under Zhu Rongji, and faced with deep popular reform fatigue, market and political reforms stalled under the weight of vested interests for the next decade. Although rapid growth continued, China was largely coasting on the easy gains of its previous tough reforms. Beijing did not move fast enough to implement or even devise a new, sustainable growth strategy to meet the new challenge. SOEs continued to receive preferential access to capital via the capital markets and bank loans, to the detriment of private-sector SMEs. Despite these smaller firms increasingly being key drivers of jobs and growth, they were largely left to fend for themselves.

The second blow came in 2008, in the form of the GFC. Beijing's response to the crisis was a RMB4 trillion stimulus package that was initially applauded for its role in stabilizing a plunging global economy. However, its critics argue that it also worsened misallocation of resources, misdirected funds to less productive sectors and SOEs, encouraged a rapid build-up of debt, led to increases in both party and state bureaucracies, bolstered anti-reformist interests and deepened what was already widespread corruption. Meanwhile, both environmental degradation and economic inequalities were growing worse.

Under Xi Jinping's leadership, armed with a next-generation "fast enough" economic growth strategy, Beijing has begun tackling these and other issues. Nonetheless, China's growth potential, while still high by international standards, has begun to decline. As a base case, we expect an average annual pace of 6.5% over 2015–2020. This is due to a combination of factors, on top of some of those mentioned above. They include now-unfavorable demographics, fewer low-hanging fruits from economic liberalization, increased debt – particularly by local authorities – plus a more saturated housing market, weaker global growth and serious environmental issues (Ma, McCauley and Lam, 2012). Given that most of these are structural, trend growth is likely to slow.

A reduced workforce and an aging population, due to decades of the one-child policy, will soon adversely affect labor costs and reduce returns on capital. China's dependency ratio (non-workers to workers) is projected by both the World Bank and the United Nations to rise from the current low of 35% to 65% by 2050 (see Figure 3.1). The days of abundant cheap labor are over. The growing numbers of elderly, many of whom have inadequate savings for their retirement, will put an increasing strain on social-security resources.

On top of this, past efficiency gains derived from labor migration – both from farms to factories and from SOEs to SMEs – have dwindled (see Figure 3.2). At the same time, productivity gains from massive restructuring following the WTO accession have also been gradually diminishing, as vested interests have become more entrenched. These include state monopolies, central- and local-government bureaucracies and the military. By stalling further market opening and liberalization, they also contributed to the slowdown of productivity growth.

In the wake of the GFC, an increased debt burden on both local governments and firms suggests that growth from 2008 to 2010 was in part borrowed from the future. A more stretched balance sheet may

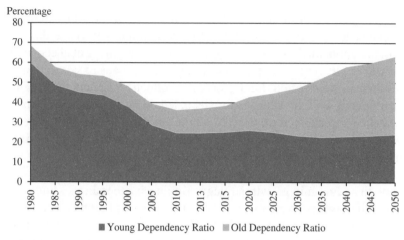

Percentage

■ Young Dependency Ratio　■ Old Dependency Ratio

FIGURE 3.1　China's age dependency ratios: young and old
Note: The young (old) dependency ratio is defined as the population
aged 0–14 (65 and above) over the working population aged 15–64.
Data Sources: CEIC, State Administration of Foreign Exchange

eventually slow growth. To make things worse, the increased debt
burden may coincide with weaker corporate cash flows.

Moreover, after 20 years of a booming housing market, China's
property sector appears to have peaked, relinquishing its role as an
economic driver. This, in turn, is likely to drag on a wide range of

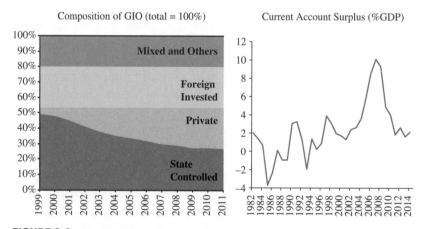

Composition of GIO (total = 100%)　　　Current Account Surplus (%GDP)

FIGURE 3.2　Composition of gross industry output and current account surplus
Data Source: CEIC

upstream and downstream industries, from cement and steel to white goods and furniture. It may even pose a threat to the banking system if not handled carefully, in part because many investment projects have been financed by property.

China's debt problem is serious. Standard & Poor's recently warned that about half of China's provinces would fall into the junk-bond category. Shadow banking is a potential exacerbating problem. It has built up huge positions that have bypassed the over-regulated, repressed banking sector. Much of the lending of the shadow banks is good for the economy, but much must be judged as risky because these institutions are poorly regulated and often lack transparency. To make matters worse, many commercial banks have funded shadow operations and are, therefore, exposed to the potential problems (Sheng and Ng, 2015). As well, many SOEs are heavily in debt. As a group, they are earning less than their cost of capital (Lardy, 2014). The industrial debt burden is exacerbated by serious overcapacity in many industries.

We estimate that total debt of all types – including households, enterprises and central and local governments – is probably equivalent to about 250% of GDP. Other estimates range from 230% to 282%. Even the most conservative of these is high enough to raise concern. Worryingly, the debt level appears to have risen at a faster rate than banks can manage properly. It included extraordinary levels of margin lending for stock purchases, inflating a stock bubble whose rapid deflation caused serious damage.

Although China's aggregate debt numbers are worse than those for other major emerging markets such as India and Brazil, we see cause for greater optimism as well. First, the central government's financial position is exceptionally strong, with CGBs equivalent to less than 15% of GDP (see Chapter 4 on the bond market). Second, although growth is now slower, it should still be fast enough to help alleviate some of the financial problems. Third, domestic saving is high, so servicing the debt does not require foreign or inflationary borrowing. Fourth, China's debt therefore is mostly in its own currency, whereas many other emerging countries have borrowed heavily in foreign currencies, incurring additional risk from FX volatility.

As well, China's economy is heading in a more favorable direction, from being driven by inefficient investment to a greater dependence on consumption. By contrast, other emerging nations face the even more difficult reverse transition from excessive consumption to a need for increased investment. Most encouragingly, Beijing appears determined to face up to and overcome its problems. It has announced a sweeping reform program that squarely confronts the entrenched interests, and it has reorganized its political leadership for decisiveness in confronting those interests (Overholt, 2013, 2015). China's debt overhang will unquestionably slow economic growth. However, there is no reason to believe it will stall, as has occurred in Brazil, or collapse into financial crisis.

The IMF expects China's growth to slow to 5.5–6.3% in 2020, while the OECD forecasts a more robust 6.8–7.1% in 2020, depending on the success of reforms. The World Bank, optimistically in our view, expects an average of 7.0% growth between 2016 and 2020. Our own 6.5% baseline assumption for 2015–2020 could prove optimistic, especially if the political consequence of the stock-market crash is to slow market reforms.

The consensus is that "fast enough" growth will continue if the reform program is effectively implemented. Nonetheless, for the first time in recent history, the pace of China's GDP expansion looks likely to lag that of India – and will remain suppressed by its debt and transition problems for some years to come. That aside, it should be sufficient to support both domestic stability and a further increase in China's weight in the global economy.

Four Economic Transitions

Despite its problems, the Chinese economy has undergone four healthy transitions in recent years: slower but more sustainable growth; lower, more stable inflation; a less investment-intensive pattern; and a smaller current-account surplus. All should help strengthen the economic foundation for a more internationalized RMB.

First, China is now the second-largest economy in the world, thanks to spectacular growth averaging 10% each year for the three decades to 2008. It then slowed to 8% over 2009–2014 and according to market consensus, will ease to 7% in 2015. Yet China's per-capita income, at USD7,500 in 2014, is only one-sixth that of the USA, with ample room to catch up in the decade ahead.

Second, its economy has transitioned from an era of high and volatile inflation over 1984–2000 to one of more stable prices. Given an improved and stronger monetary policy framework and slower economic growth, to be discussed later in this chapter, inflation should remain low relative to both the past and most other emerging markets.

Third, as consumption's share of GDP stabilizes and even gains, both savings and investment rates appear to have peaked at about 50% during the past two years, after having risen steadily for 15 years from about 30% (Ma and Wang, 2011). But 2011–2014 already witnessed a greater contribution from consumption to GDP growth than investment. From here to 2020, we expect the economy to become less investment-driven as an expanding middle class augurs a more consumer-oriented society.

Fourth, the current account oscillated between deficit and surplus throughout the 1980s and 1990s, before eventually bursting into a massive surplus of 10% of GDP in 2007. This has since contracted to about 2%. Following 2005, the RMB has appreciated more than 50% against a broad basket of trading partners' currencies (after adjusting for inflation differentials). The Chinese economy is now far less export-oriented, and from here the RMB may be influenced more by capital flows than current-account balances.

Notwithstanding the previous decade of hesitant reform and the coming era of slower growth, these transitions are remarkable and positive. Also, given the scale of China's economy, they have important implications for RMB internationalization. An end to overinvestment indicates that a transition to a new economic strategy is under way and that "fast enough" growth will be sustainable. Successful management of inflation and the current-account balance underpin a stable currency. If these favorable conditions continue, investors and traders will be able to settle accounts and trade in RMB with a degree of trust. However, if the debt problem and its many associated risks are not addressed, both capital-account liberalization and full RMB internationalization will be impeded.

China's economic prospects will influence the degree to which the RMB is used offshore. Given the intrinsic uncertainties, we consider three scenarios as a broad backdrop to our discussion of internationalization. Table 3.1 summarizes these scenarios over 2015–2020 and 2021–2030. Our base case is for real GDP growth to average 6.5% per annum over 2015–2020 and trend toward 5.0% over 2021–2030. We expect nominal GDP growth (which includes inflation) to average 10% over 2015–2020 and 6.5% over 2021–2030.

We also envisage the RMB appreciating 1.5% vis-à-vis the USD each year to 2020 and then averaging flat from there. China's labor-cost advantage has disappeared and with it the era of ever-growing current-account surpluses. Outward investment should roughly balance inward

TABLE 3.1 Three GDP-growth scenarios (2015–2020 and 2021–2030)

Scenarios (probability)	Real GDP (CAGR, percentage)		Nominal GDP (CAGR, percentage)	
	2015–2020	2021–2030	2015–2020	2021–2030
High growth (10%)	7.5	6.0	11.0	8.0
Base case (60%)	6.5	5.0	10.0	6.5
Slow growth (30%)	5.0	3.5	7.5	5.0

Source: FGI analysis.

foreign investment. Potentially net private capital outflows on fuller capital-account opening can be partly offset by a drawdown of the huge official reserves (Hooley, 2013; Ma and McCauley, 2014).

The baseline scenario projects much slower growth than in the recent past, because China needs to deleverage from the high debt of its state enterprises and local governments and manage its property bubble. This requires the government to manage deftly a balance between market deleveraging in some areas and stimulus in others. It has done so before, but the balance now is more delicate and the consequences greater. China must work off tremendous overcapacity in some sectors. It must also address serious environmental problems. And it must navigate a complex transition from growth based on exports, investment, SOEs and low-level manufacturing to a greater reliance on consumption, domestic demand, SMEs, higher value-added manufacturing and services. In the face of these challenges, our baseline scenario assumes a reasonable reform pace, deft macroeconomic management, stable domestic politics, stable commodity prices and an accommodating external environment.

Lower growth could result if all of these highly demanding conditions are not met. For instance, state and party bureaucrats could collude with SOEs and local-government officials to stall reforms. Efforts to level the economic playing field and channel funding to smaller and more innovative enterprises may take effect more slowly than we hope. A Middle Eastern crisis may see a surge in oil prices, while a European crisis could reduce demand for exports. Equally, the big banks' non-performing loans may turn out to be substantially worse than we believe, and the housing bubble could prove to be more serious than we assume. The stock-market collapse could empower opponents of rapid reform. The government's management of the delicate balance between deleveraging and stimulus may misjudge the risks. Anti-monopoly and cyber-security campaigns could lead to a serious decline in foreign investment, and the anti-corruption campaign, combined with market opening, could trigger a large acceleration of capital flight.

If some but not all of these conditions occur, we envisage a scenario of sharper economic slowdown to an average 5.0% of real GDP growth over 2015–2020 and 3.5% over 2021–2030. We judge such a scenario to be less likely than the baseline scenario, but far more likely than a high-growth scenario. *China's risks today are weighted to the downside.*

A high-growth scenario, albeit still low compared with the first three decades of reform, is possible if financial liberalization proceeds relatively smoothly. A more market-based economy would move labor and capital more quickly out of sectors with too much capacity and excessive leverage. (Such rapid shifts are why the US economy recovers relatively quickly whereas Europe's is much slower.) This would shift funding relatively quickly to SMEs and private enterprises and reduce wasteful over-allocations of funds to bloated SOEs. A nimble macroeconomic policy complements the tough supply-side restructuring (Ma, 2015). The anti-corruption campaign could reduce transaction costs across the board. Export customers in the USA and Europe would recover gradually but steadily while commodity prices, especially energy, would not rebound to previous hey-day levels. The anti-monopoly campaign would reduce predatory behavior by both Chinese and foreign enterprises, freeing investment for businesses and allowing consumer discretionary spending. Such a positive scenario could sustain real GDP growth at the 2014 pace of 7.5% over 2015–2020 and 6.0% over 2021–2030.

Higher potential growth tends to provide greater headroom for tough reforms and restructuring, facilitating financial liberalization. Decent nominal income growth also assists with the tricky but necessary deleveraging. Strong and sustainable economic expansion naturally gives rise to a weightier Chinese economy globally, providing a solid anchor for a global RMB.

In the long run, economic and trade weights are important. The World Bank estimates that in 2011 PPP terms, China's aggregate GDP in 2014 was already neck-to-neck with that of the USA, if not larger. Many forecasts see the Chinese economy overtaking that of the USA (at the 2014 market-exchange rate) by about 2025. As a baseline case, China's contribution to global GDP reached 13% in 2014 and is likely to rise above 18% by 2020. In short, as the largest trader, second-biggest economy and a top-three net-creditor nation, China has achieved the global weight required as a foundation for a global RMB.

SURPRISES

Evaluation of alternative scenarios helps illuminate less-likely but none-theless possible paths. It enables consideration of a broader range of uncertainties and should result in more accurate – or, at least, considered – economic and political forecasting. In our view, the above three scenarios and resulting RMB outcomes span the most probable paths. However, history shows all too clearly that unexpected events occur – and they can be momentous. The traditional literature calls these outliers "surprises" or low-probability but high-impact events. More recently, the term "black swans" has become popular for bad surprises. The GFC was one such gigantic bird. The drastic decline in oil prices that has coincided with the writing of this chapter is another surprise. The stock-market collapse is a third. Clearly, our scenarios could fall foul of such fowls.

Surprises could occur on both the upside and the downside. One positive surprise would be more rapid consolidation of reforms and orderly deleveraging than we project, even under our fast-growth scenario. None of the following outcomes, for example, is beyond the realms of possibility, albeit highly unlikely on present indications: rapid consolida-tion of power by the reformist leadership in the face of resistance from self-interest groups and the bureaucracy; quick culmination of the anti-corruption campaign; speedy consolidation of the fragmented bond market; faster fiscal reforms that lift most local governments clear of excessive debt; firm and unambiguous regulation of shadow banking; and early stabilization of the property market. In other words, there is a small probability (on the back of a great deal of good luck) that we will see a highly accelerated version of our fast-growth scenario. In that event, the RMB could be floated and the capital account largely opened very quickly. All global uses of the RMB would then surge and its use in FX reserves would be far greater than we forecast. Such a "super-fast" outcome would be a surprise because it would entail a virtual suspension of political and bureaucratic conflicts. However, the new Chinese administration's deter-mination to enact its reforms quickly suggests that this is a possibility we should at least consider.

Equally, there could be downside surprises. These include victory by interests opposed to further financial liberalization and SOE and fiscal reform. Beijing has shown great resolve in pursuing its agenda – particularly its anti-corruption campaign. However, reform damages the interests of powerful groups such as the SOEs, big banks, central bureaucracies, local governments and the military, any or all of which could strenuously resist. These vested interests will seek leverage from the stock-market collapse, arguing that the government must maintain control of markets (and ignoring that it was government institutions' encouragement of unsophisticated market participants and pumping up of extraordinary margin credit that caused the bubble).

If they were able to stall reform, growth would remain deceptively high for a year or two, but then stagnate. As a result, China would lose its prestige and the currency its attractiveness. Japan suffered just such a fate. Moreover, income stagnation could foment political unrest, triggering a vicious circle that would feed back into the economy and derail RMB internationalization.

A severe financial crisis would be an even more immediate downside surprise. This could stem from some combination of the following: bursting of the property bubble; defaults in the unregulated shadow-banking market; more and more rapid collapses than expected in industries with severe overcapacity; and a local-government debt debacle. A variety of studies has shown that any one of these should be manageable and that China has sufficient assets to offset its financial liabilities (Sheng and Ng, 2015). However, they are so interrelated that they could combine to create a sudden collapse. Shadow banking, for example, depends on property collateral and lends heavily to local governments; they, in turn, also rely on property income. Meanwhile, the big banks' assets are tied to all three. Such a crisis would cost China a couple of years of growth, at the least, and delay significant global uses of the RMB.

Similarly, a major geopolitical clash could seriously exacerbate China's financial problems. Any of the following, for example, especially if it were to occur during the next few years, could catch China at a time of financial vulnerability: a severe military clash over the East China Sea or South China Sea islands also claimed by Japan and Southeast Asian countries; prolonged and severe cyber-warfare; or a substantial loss of access to US or European markets.

We suggest that a final surprise involving the RMB, rather than the wider economy, is separate from both our upsides and downsides, and would upset our forecast that the USD is likely to remain the world's lead currency for decades. If China continues to open its markets, the RMB could become very important soon after about 2025. If the USA were to overuse sanctions, a critical mass of banks could start to avoid USD-based transactions. If another US-based global financial crisis were then to occur, the RMB could quickly challenge the USD as the dominant international currency.

Any of these surprises is possible; none, in our view, is likely. Then again, nobody thought the GFC was likely.

NEW GROWTH ENGINES

China's economic prospects, and thus our expectations about RMB internationalization, depend heavily on the country's ability to transition to new growth engines. The economy requires formidable transformation. China's past three decades of growth derived largely from exports produced with cheap labor. However, it has now gone from labor surplus to shortage – and its labor is no longer cheap. Growth based on infrastructure investment was hugely productive when that meant building a high-speed rail from Beijing to Shanghai. Now, it too often means building an outsized government-administration center in a small city. SOEs were often highly profitable in building such infrastructures. Now, however, these large enterprises are earning less than their cost of capital.

The new era of growth must come from technological improvements, more highly skilled and productive activities, accumulation of a more highly trained workforce, greater innovation and a stronger services sector on the supply side, as well as greater consumption on the demand side. It means less reliance on major construction projects such as expressways and airports. Even Chinese exports have to climb the value chain. The job at hand amounts to a far-reaching overhaul of the growth model.

Among possible future growth engines, we highlight two principal categories that are associated with the market-oriented reforms needed to support RMB internationalization. The first is increased investment in education, research and development, and technology. This is needed to counter diminished lower-end competitiveness, slower labor-force growth and the effects of an aging population. It also relies on increased international scientific cooperation, better property-rights institutions and greater openness to the global economy. All of these are important for RMB internationalization. High per-capita income makes such investment possible.

Internationalizing the RMB will also be made easier by a second growth-oriented reform: the reduction of regulatory and structural impediments to reduce the monopoly power and inefficiency of SOEs. Market and financial liberalization, in particular, will be important in ensuring resources are used more efficiently. To this end, China's latest Five-Year Plan (2016–2020) emphasizes the following three areas:

- further transition of economic development from investment to consumption and services, by improving investment efficiency;
- raising living standards for the poor, environmental protection and innovation and upgrading information technology;
- deeper marketization of a wider range of factors and products, in particular financial liberalization.

Since the core of China's economic problems is capital misallocation, greater efficiency in this area is key to successful transformation. For decades, bureaucratic/political allocation of capital through state banks favored SOEs. Party decisions served China adequately when the economy's needs were simple – creating growth by building roads, ports, telecommunications and basic heavy industries, as well as adopting policies that encouraged exports. However, the economy is now far more complex, and the giant industries and bureaucracies have evolved into interest groups serving themselves and each other rather than allocating capital where the economy needs it most. That is why the Third Plenum in 2013 announced one of the most far-reaching and radical policy changes in the nation's history: henceforth, the market will dominate the allocation of resources.

Putting the market in charge entails thorough and wide-ranging banking and industrial-sector reform. This explains the emphasis on financial liberalization in the 13th Five-Year Plan. The financial-reform program features these five core elements: interest-rate deregulation; a flexible exchange rate; lower barriers to market entry; strengthened regulatory framework and infrastructure; and capital-account liberalization. RMB internationalization is an integral part of this tricky process.

Accompanying financial-market reforms are some vital changes for SOEs, competition policy and fiscal management. With SOEs highly in debt and earning below their cost of capital, the health of both the real economy and the banks that finance them depends on reform. To increase economic efficiency, the government is promoting greater competition by opening new sectors to competition. It is also introducing a "negative list" system, whereby investment is allowed so long as the particular sector is not on a (shrinking) prohibited list; eliminating some monopolies; and cracking down on a number of anti-competitive practices.

The reforms needed to stimulate China's new growth engines will also tend to make RMB internationalization more viable. Since China's leaders have every intention of pushing growth-oriented reforms, we believe conditions are likely to be favorable.

CAPITAL-ACCOUNT LIBERALIZATION

Sustained economic growth alone is insufficient to expand the international use of the RMB. China's economy must also be more fully integrated globally. On the back of already high trade integration, substantial opening of its capital account is the key economic reform in this regard, so that the RMB can be more actively used in global commerce and finance.

China's capital account previously was heavily managed, but it has incrementally become more open. Two-way cross-border capital flows used to be extensively regulated in terms of foreign-exchange controls, external borrowing and overseas investment by Chinese residents, and access to domestic financial markets by non-residents. Capital controls were substantially tightened during the Asian financial crisis, as Beijing vigorously defended the pledged USD peg amid a sharp competitive devaluation of many neighboring Asian currencies. Offshore uses of the RMB were banned until 2004, when deposits were permitted in Hong Kong for the first time in the People's Republic of China's (PRC) history.

Therefore, a strictly regulated capital account was a major institutional reality that shaped the initial approach to promoting external uses of the RMB: trading of the currency in offshore markets before the capital account becomes highly open (see Chapter 7).

A major international currency is, by definition, one that is freely used by non-residents in all international commercial and financial transactions. It should also offer deep domestic and international liquidity, so it can widely trade in the currency markets and move in and out of its home financial market. Hence, a deep domestic capital market, expanding offshore markets and an open capital account linking these are all vital for RMB liquidity.

Over recent years, China's capital account has become more porous, but the economy remains less open financially than India's (Ma and McCauley, 2013, 2014). Increased RMB cross-border flows since 2009 have also effectively opened the capital account further.

However, opening too quickly can be perilous. The Asian crisis of 1997–1998 resulted in part from some countries in the region opening their capital accounts prematurely to flows of international funds (BIS, 2003). Local debt, stock, bond and property markets became engorged with borrowed foreign funds, and then collapsed when conditions shifted and funds flowed out. Likewise, poor risk-management at Australian banks in the late 1980s (when foreign capital was accessible and credit unrationed) was exacerbated by inadequate regulation and intense interbank competition, resulting in a property-price boom and bust (Lowe, 2014).

The Japanese experience is particularly relevant to China's current situation. In 1983, Tokyo began to encourage the development of an offshore euroyen market (analogous to today's offshore RMB, or CNH, market) that became very large. In 1986, an offshore market was also established in the capital. This was the first round of internationalization of the Japanese currency (JPY). The combination of this offshore market and tardy progress in liberalizing domestic interest rates proved catastrophic. With rates strictly regulated, the authorities had to depend heavily on "window guidance" of bank lending to control credit growth and inflation. (China uses similar techniques, whereby regulators direct lending into certain sectors, while restricting total loans through high reserve requirements.) However, banks were able to fund euroyen in the offshore market, send them to their Hong Kong branches, and then bring the funds home in massive quantities, fueling inflation and inflating bubbles. Had interest rates been fully liberalized, the Bank of Japan (BoJ) could have managed the money supply through open-market operations. Interest-rate liberalization was too slow, though, and the authorities could not control the money supply, with the result that inflation and bubbles got out of control. Eventually, the bubble economy collapsed.

In its strongest form, the form that now pervades the economic policy literature, the lesson is that domestic interest rates must be freed before the capital account is opened. More broadly, the sequence of financial reforms is critical. In more careful phrasing, the capital-account opening must not get too far ahead of domestic interest-rate liberalization.

China is choosing to take the lesson in its weaker form; its strategy is to make incremental, parallel relaxations of both capital and rate controls, in addition to a less managed RMB. It punches holes in the capital controls (Table 3.2), monitors the results, then moves forward. This plays to China's strength of achieving gradual reform through trial

TABLE 3.2 Selected capital market openings

Year	
1994	Removal of most restrictions on inbound FDI
2003	QFII – qualified foreign institutions get quotas to buy Chinese securities
2004	Hong Kong individuals can have RMB accounts, converting RMB 20,000 per day
2006	QDII – domestic institutional investors may buy foreign securities
2007	First "dim sum" bond
2008	First currency swap
2009	Trade settlement in RMB
2012	RQFII – qualified foreign institutions may use offshore RMB to buy Chinese securities
2013	Qianhai Equity Trading Center raises RMB finance in Hong Kong for Qianhai enterprises
2014	Shanghai–Hong Kong Stock Connect RQDII – domestic investors may buy offshore RMB products
2015	China–Hong Kong reciprocal recognition of funds QDII2 – high-net-worth Chinese may invest overseas Shenzhen–Hong Kong Connect (expected)

and observation. Systematic, orderly, well-timed and interactive measures can create liquid markets. As an example, after the bust of the 1980s, Australia gradually liberalized by first developing hedging markets, which facilitated both currency flexibility and market stability. It then proceeded to a phased capital opening (Lowe, 2014).

The Chinese authorities so far have adopted an approach of pushing for financial liberalization with many half-steps on many fronts at the same time. Most local interest rates have been liberalized, and even bank-deposit rates have been largely deregulated. The daily trading band for the RMB has been widened, with much less foreign-exchange market intervention. As well, more private banks have been licensed and approved. A deposit-insurance scheme is now in place. It will not only protect small depositors, but signals clearly that depositors cannot expect to be bailed out in full on an unlimited basis; this should lead depositors to be more careful where they put their funds, rather than just seeking the highest interest rate. Simultaneously, the government has started allowing some bond defaults, including by SOEs, thereby putting bonds and shadow banking on more of a market basis.

This progress is substantial but, given the complexity of the overall financial-liberalization task, the pace of capital opening must be managed with care. In particular, we can start from the lesson that capital-account opening must not get too far ahead of interest-rate deregulation.

Domestic interest rates have mostly been liberalized, but the benefits may be diluted if a majority of local governments and SOEs fails to respond properly to market rates. Instead, new distortions and risks could arise in such an environment. For instance, if liberalization leads interest rates to rise (as they almost certainly will initially), companies and local governments that have to roll over maturing loans may be unable to pay the higher rates. That problem caused a serious crisis in the USA in the early 1980s, when rates were liberalized and many homeowners were unable to pay. As a consequence, large numbers of banks collapsed. Beijing plans fiscal reforms that should strengthen SOE and local-government financial accountability, but these will take time.

Similar issues arise for increased currency flexibility and a deeper hedging market. Without a sufficiently high degree of exchange-rate flexibility and an active foreign-exchange derivative market, increased and volatile cross-border capital flows could result in either excessive government intervention or currency volatility (Lowe, 2014). Both could seriously damage China's financial system if the capital account is opened too quickly.

Other key issues must also be resolved prior to – or in the process of – capital-account liberalization to avoid excess volatility in cross-border capital flows. For instance, imperfect delineation of property rights creates an incentive for officials and business managers to "strip" assets, particularly when they can easily move inappropriate acquisitions overseas. With a highly open capital account, the ongoing anti-corruption campaign could potentially make China vulnerable to capital flight because officials and business executives who enriched themselves may fear losing their assets and, therefore, hastily move them overseas. Some of this is happening. A sharp weakening of the RMB in this case could create stress in China's corporate sector and financial system.

Conversely, surging net capital inflows could give rise to marked RMB appreciation, fueling domestic asset bubbles and damaging the manufacturing sector. Either way, it is risky to completely open the capital account in a rush.

The problems that must be addressed in pursuing capital-account liberalization are difficult and time-consuming. Solutions will be found over a period of several years. Even under the most optimistic assumptions, the issues are unlikely to be fully resolved much before the end of this decade. While some aspects of capital opening, such as elements of RMB internationalization, can proceed quickly, our projections must take full account of the constraints policymakers face. Our base case assumes that it may take China's authorities until the end of the decade (2020) to implement a very high level of liberalization, comparable with that of major OECD economies.

The past few years have witnessed steady but cautious and incremental but accelerating capital opening in China, mostly via various expanding management schemes of portfolio investment,[1] and together with the four free-trade zones in Shanghai, Guangdong, Tianjin and Fujian, as well as the Shanghai–Hong Kong Stock Connect, with the launch of a similar Shenzhen scheme imminent as this chapter was being written. Moreover, Chinese citizens currently can send USD50,000 abroad per person per annum, no questions asked, and may soon be able to freely invest half of their net worth offshore in bonds, stocks, properties or paintings of choice if their personal net worth exceeds RMB1 million (USD160,000) under the forthcoming pilot QDII2 scheme.

Many RMB-internationalization measures themselves are effectively punching holes in the Chinese capital account by stealth. Of special importance are the cross-border RMB settlements in trade; cross-border RMB cash-sweeping schemes; and wider access for foreign investors to the onshore interbank bond market. The overall picture is one of numerous small liberalizing steps on many fronts, translating into a gradual but significant capital opening.

We anticipate that the strong momentum of incremental capital-account liberalization will continue and probably accelerate over the next few years. This scenario could prove optimistic if the 2015 stock-market crash empowers opponents of liberalization. We believe that

---

[1] These schemes of managed-portfolio investment include the Qualified Foreign Institutional Investor (QFII), Qualified Direct Institutional Investor (QDII), Renminbi Qualified Institutional Investor (RQFII) and Renminbi Qualified Direct Institutional Investor (RQDII) programs. Under these schemes, permission to invest in onshore or offshore markets depends on specific qualifications, investment quotas and regulations regarding exits.

China's capital account will become "basically convertible" by 2020 and propose a summary indicator reflecting possible changes in its financial openness between 2015 and 2020. If, for instance, China's capital-account convertibility is only half of Hong Kong's (our real-world benchmark for "perfect" capital mobility), our baseline scenario is for China's financial openness to reach a high of 80% of Hong Kong's by 2020. This is also consistent with the notion of "managed capital-account convertibility" coined by PBOC Governor Zhou Xiaochaun. This projection is based on analysis of China's relative financial openness using India as a benchmark (Ma and McCauley, 2013, 2014) and, inter alia, assumes a fairly aggressive but sensible pace of capital opening over 2015–2020.

RMB internationalization, domestic financial liberalization and capital-account opening move forward in incremental steps, like participants in a three-legged race. (In such a contest, teams of two are tied together by one leg and then try to run.) RMB internationalization eventually requires foreign access to domestic financial markets (that is, capital-account opening), which is dangerous without fuller domestic liberalization. Another complication is that it is impossible for the authorities to achieve the so-called "Impossible Trinity"[2] of policy goals simultaneously: an open capital account, a fixed exchange rate and an independent national monetary policy. Hence, a highly flexible currency is warranted before a highly open capital account, especially for a large economy such as China's (see Chapter 6 for more details).

In sum, there are three ways a country can manage these interconnections. One is to liberalize everything at once. That approach risks the sort of catastrophic economic damage that "shock therapy" caused in Eastern Europe. A second is to think in terms of prerequisites. For instance, a currency can only become convertible under an open capital account when the domestic financial sector is mostly liberalized and the exchange rate is floating. But completing one process and then undertaking another in sequence may entail a prolonged, bumpy road. China has chosen a third way, consistent with its overall process of reform. It

---

[2]An important economic theorem holds that no economy can simultaneously maintain an open capital account, an independent monetary policy and a pegged currency. For instance, Hong Kong has open capital flows and a currency pegged to the USD. If US interest rates decline, enormous amounts of capital flow to Hong Kong, drastically increasing its money supply. Hong Kong could only control supply by breaking the currency peg.

takes a series of incremental, linked, carefully tested steps in each of these three areas simultaneously.

Chinese incrementalism means gradual and field-tested, but it does not mean slow. In fact, the multi-legged process of liberalization is proceeding quite swiftly. RMB internationalization is an integral part of China's financial liberalization process, with benefits and risks that are closely tied to capital-account opening.

INSTITUTIONAL QUALITY

Institutional quality is crucial for a global currency in the long run. Its core pillars range from rule of law to reliability and transparency of domestic legal and political systems, corporate governance, effective policymaking, crisis-management capacity and a stakeholder record of an evolving international monetary system.

While an encompassing discussion of institutional quality is beyond the scope of our book, the most pertinent component is the record of, and trust in, the currency's central bank. The standard demanded by the central bank of an international currency is far higher than that of a small, local currency.

The US Fed enjoys a proven record, despite having lost some global trust as a result of its inability to assist Thailand and Indonesia during the Asian financial crisis and the consequences of its low-interest policies creating a tsunami of money into emerging markets after the GFC. The European Central Bank (ECB) faces internal challenges that limit its decisiveness and global trust during crises. The PBOC is a new institution on the international stage. It has an improved record of controlling domestic inflation and stabilizing the currency value, but still lacks experience and needs to improve its monetary-policy framework.

The PBOC's institutional quality is crucial to RMB internationalization. A second key institution is a well-functioning bond market. To back a global currency, the domestic bond market must be large, liquid, consistent, market-driven and stable. As discussed in Chapter 4, China's bond market is moderate in size, though growing fast, but still working on other qualities. Different parts of the market are driven by different government regulators – including the PBOC, the Ministry of Finance, the National Development and Reform Commission, the China Securities Regulatory Commission (CSRC) and the China Banking Regulatory Commission – adversely affecting market efficiency.

Corporate issuance to a large extent is by regulatory decision, not market criteria, and local government-bond issuance is just beginning. In the corporate bond market, most big state enterprises receive very high identical ratings – akin to the children in the American novel *Lake Wobegon*, who are all above average. These are standard developmental issues, not character flaws, and Chinese capital markets are maturing much faster, from a later start, than most of their emerging-market counterparts. In analyzing the implications for RMB internationalization, it is crucial to maintain perspective from multiple angles: the major remaining developmental issues; the speed with which Chinese reforms occur; the considerable time that full modernization will require; and the political will needed to meld the multiple contradictory regulatory systems into a consistent market.

Likewise, the stock market is a case of rapid late development from a low base. China's formal markets in Shanghai and Shenzhen began only in the early 1990s. For many years, the market has been mostly closed to foreigners and largely (but not exclusively) confined to large state-dominated enterprises selected by the CSRC on a non-market basis. As discussed in Chapter 5, the goal of the regulator was to list those companies most valuable to the state and to limit listings to keep prices high. The leadership was concerned about how the loss-making SOEs were to be kept afloat. Because the Chinese government realized that it faced formidable future costs for social welfare, inflating the price of state assets and giving preferential market access to SOEs were two important government policies governing the development of a stock market in the earlier years.

Gradually, foreigners have been allowed to invest in local stocks and the Chinese to invest in foreign securities. With the creation of an open pipeline between Shanghai and Hong Kong and more to come soon, that opening is now accelerating. Even more gradually, the market has opened to private companies. The Chinese authorities have forecast a shift from a certification system (by which the regulator carefully selects companies) to a registration system (where companies need only fulfill basic market criteria). Managed perpetual overvaluation seemed by 2014 to have mostly vanished. However, for much of 2014 and early 2015, the authorities condoned an extraordinary ballooning of margin finance and talked the market up to levels that were clearly unsustainable. When they started to put limited prudential controls on margin finance, the market crashed. The authorities then mounted an extraordinary intervention to stabilize the market (see Chapter 5).

The stock market, as in many emerging economies, has been dominated by individual investors and intrusive institutions. The fundamentals of growth and profits have not been the primary drivers. But now there are numerous competent analysts. Pension, insurance and mutual funds, guided by those analysts, will increasingly tether market prices to underlying business realities. This is the way all stock markets develop. China started far later than Indonesia or the Philippines, but has developed much faster – though not fast enough to avoid the crash of 2015. (It is worth noting that when the Hong Kong stock market, now one of the world's best regulated, was at a similar stage of development it crashed by 50% more than once and in one case by 90% – far more than the 35% crash experienced by the Chinese market.) Alongside the PBOC and the government bond market, the most important institution for the emergence of a global currency is the legal system. A global currency experiences trillions of dollars of transactions, of which many are quite large. Numerous disputes are inevitable. When disputes occur, investors want to be sure that the resolution will be based on clear laws, a transparent process and objective – i.e., non-political – judgments. This is the internationalizing RMB's greatest weakness and the one that is most difficult to remedy.

China's legal system has come a long way from the pre-reform period, when a judge, often a retired army officer with no legal training, made judgments based on personal moral judgment and political correctness. China has made a great effort to codify a formal legal structure, to improve legal training, to raise standards for judges and to introduce certain rights, like the right to a lawyer. Following the 2014 Fourth Plenum, it is initiating a new wave of legal reform in which the key reform is central appointment of judges. Until this reform, the local Party Secretary was in charge of the local state enterprises and also in charge of appointing local judges. If a company from another city or another country had a dispute with one of the local SOEs, the judge was not likely to risk his job by ruling against the local company. Thus this reform is crucial.

The functioning of the system in Shanghai for resolving major disputes meets the needs of Fortune 500 companies with big operations there. The biggest companies say that the system works well because Shanghai mayors are very interested in maintaining their city's reputation for fairness, so that it can become a major international hub. In interviews conducted by one of the writers of this book (Overholt) in 2003, they consistently expressed a preference for the Shanghai system, where the mayor makes quick and generally fair decisions, over Hong Kong, which is famous for its British legal system but, as is typical of Western legal systems, is quite expensive and ponderous.

Having acknowledged the system's reforms and virtues, they remain vastly insufficient to bolster a major global currency. The inevitable number of disputes means that most will have to go through regular courts, not the mayor's office. (Even today, smaller companies strongly prefer to domicile in Hong Kong, because the Shanghai mayor generally would not have time for them.) Property rights in China are not yet defined with sufficient clarity. Above all, the ultimate decision in any court case rests with a Communist Party commission, not with an independent judiciary.

Solving these problems does not necessarily require abandonment of the overall structure of China's judicial system. Property rights are gradually being defined. In principle, a separate court could be established to hear major financial and business cases, or China could delegate a wide range of cases to the Hong Kong judicial system. But such changes are not even under discussion today. Therefore, the legal system will be inadequate to support a major global currency like the USD for many years.

The accounting system is another key institution. China's accountants have long met a very high emerging-market standard: they could create three or four sets of books, each internally consistent, for any company, and in many cases back those accounts up with receipts for vast fictional transactions among different companies. As in other areas, China has moved faster from this base than its counterparts.

From the earliest days, companies that wanted to list abroad were required to meet international accounting standards and use top-tier international accounting firms as auditors. Far older markets, like Indonesia's, lagged. All too frequently, the initial high-quality audits were followed by rapid deterioration of both accounting standards and corporate results. Some firms, like Sino Forest and China Metal Recycling, managed to evade the tests of business reality. Until recently, even when Chinese companies used international auditors, their auditors were not allowed to release the documents outside China, so foreign investors and regulators could not pursue normal investigations.

Gradually, the markets have matured, much too slowly for current frustrated investors but much more rapidly than emerging-market peers. As with the bond markets, these are developmental growing pains, not cultural infirmities. Nonetheless, it will be a long time before China's markets attract the level of trust achieved by London, New York or Hong Kong. (As investors in Enron can testify, the growing pains never completely cease. And after the GFC, Western markets as a group have powerful justifications for humility.)

China's markets are now entering a period of accelerated development. Tougher rules, more transparency, the rapid emergence of institutional investors, registration-based listings, a corruption crackdown and far greater opening to foreigners are combining to transform the way China's markets work. By 2020, they should be almost unrecognizably improved – not fully mature, but much more so than today.

As China internationalizes its currency, such institutional development underlies the whole process. To understand the prospects of any currency, the most important institution is the central bank. Here, China has already reached a level of considerable maturity.

Central Bank Trust: International Perspectives

An important aspect of liquidity for a major currency is trust in the willingness and ability of the central bank to both safeguard and intervene in markets when necessary and help its foreign counterparts to deal with exceptional liquidity turbulence. From the perspective of its principal counterparts, the US Fed and Treasury have established a superb reputation for quickly stepping in and providing liquidity in a crisis. This reputation is unexcelled, but not completely unblemished. After the Mexican crisis of 1994, when timely, effective US intervention – using the Treasury's Exchange Stabilization Fund – had prevented a financial catastrophe, the US Congress prohibited further such action. This prevented the USA from offering monetary support to Thailand or Indonesia during the Asian financial crisis of 1997–1998. That inability to intervene has led to some skepticism, especially in Asia, about relying on the USD-based system. This was exacerbated by the Fed's failure to offer China a swap line during the GFC. (Although China had huge official reserves, USD trade financing nearly dried up and the offshore market was vulnerable to hedge-fund attacks, so a swap line would have helped.)

Also, controversy continues over the implications of the US Fed's conduct of quantitative easing (QE) and eventual exit, since its legal mandate confines its monetary-policy considerations to domestic concerns. In the eyes of many international observers, USD dominance endows the Fed with some responsibility as steward of the global financial system. The argument that the Fed's low-interest policies are essential to ensuring US economic growth, which in turn is essential to prevent global relapse into recession, is a powerful one. But when other countries judge Fed policies, they wonder whether there aren't larger problems with the US government/USD-dominated system. If Washington politics was different, couldn't fiscal stimulus have been used to eliminate some of the need for extreme monetary policies?

The degree of trust that international markets have in the Fed will be seriously tested and affected by the results of its eventual exit from QE. The Fed and its Japanese and Eurozone counterparts have flooded the world with cheap money, stimulating asset prices or even bubbles in some cases, along with excessive leverage and possibly inflation of staple-food prices. If its exit from QE is gradual and uneventful for emerging markets, global trust will remain high. If, on the contrary, widespread emerging-market turmoil ensues, the clamor for a new international monetary system will greatly increase. In either case, there is at present no effective rival for the high degree of trust that the Fed enjoys, nor is there any prospective rival for many years.

The ECB has not had time to establish such a reputation. Its counterparts believe that the complexity of its decision-making process means it would be less able to respond quickly and decisively in a major foreign crisis. (Its response to the internal crisis of the EUR has been relatively effective so far, notwithstanding a very high level of politicization and tortuous decision-making.) Competing sovereign interests definitely muddy the waters for the ECB. More importantly, when monetary and fiscal policies mingle, such as the large-scale central bank purchase of government and private debt, the conflict between a unified monetary system and independent treasuries comes to the fore (see Chapter 4). Since the European sovereign debt crisis in 2008, the ECB has struggled with internal tensions within the euro area and may not take on bigger international roles for some time to come.

The PBOC is currently even further behind in establishing trust on the international stage. Over a period of decades, it may be able to earn the confidence of global markets. As the central bank of one sovereign nation, it does not have the decision-making complexity that inevitably slows the ECB. Therefore, unless there is a drastic change in the European political structure, China could enjoy a decisive advantage over the longer term. However, the process of establishing this has yet to begin. As will be explored in detail below, while the PBOC has done a good job of stabilizing inflation and the RMB, many investors still think it lacks the independence, legal foundation and sophistication that are essential to trust in major Western central banks.

Record of the PBOC

There is little doubt that the PBOC has been a champion of RMB internationalization, making the issue of trust even more relevant. What is its institutional quality as the central bank behind a potentially global RMB? The PBOC formally acquired its legal status and mandates only in 2003. Arguably, it has an even shorter history of playing a significant role on the international finance stage. In our view, however, it has built a solid and credible base.

It is commonly believed that the PBOC still lacks a high degree of independence, because some of the important monetary policy decisions often have to be agreed and approved by the State Council, China's cabinet. Accordingly, the PBOC enjoys only limited discretion in that area, relative to its international peers. It employs the gamut of policy tools to manage multiple and sometimes conflicting goals, and often operates under specific political constraints (Ma, Yan and Liu, 2013), which can somewhat dent its credibility in the eyes of the markets.

While the market consensus is that lack of independence reduces the PBOC's credibility, PBOC Governor Zhou argues that by being part of the government, the PBOC can more effectively participate in the broader policy debate and decision-making. It can thus play a more influential role than it could if it were merely another "independent" government agency. More generally, the issue of central-bank independence may come under intense scrutiny in the wake of the GFC, when many major central banks have pursued unconventional monetary policy that may have potentially serious redistributive consequences. Finally, the relative merits of central-bank independence and effective cooperation across policymaking agencies are far from being settled.

A simple benchmarking of the SDR-member central banks may also be useful in discussing central-bank independence in the context of the RMB's internationalization. As former Fed Chairman Ben Bernanke reminded his successor Janet Yellen during his handover, the Fed is required to heed the US Congress. Moreover, the independence of the ECB is mostly defined and often constrained by competing needs of sovereign members of the monetary union. In other words, even in the West, central-bank independence is relative and incomplete.

Furthermore, the 1997 Bank of Japan Law requires the central bank to cooperate with the government. The BoJ fought hard and vigorously to gain greater independence by establishing its inflation-fighting credentials at a time when the biggest challenge to Japan was persistent deflation. Current Prime Minister Shinzo Abe ran on a platform of changing BoJ monetary policy and imposed leadership there that made the changes he wanted. Finally, even the Bank of England (BoE) gained its high degree of independence only in 1997 to pursue an explicit inflation target set by the UK Treasury.

In any case, one good way to view the trust and institutional quality of the PBOC naturally centers on its performance in terms of maintaining the internal and external values of the RMB. In other words, its record on domestic inflation and exchange-rate management. The best summary indicator for checking the record of the PBOC, therefore, is the real effective exchange rate (REER) of the RMB – the trade-weighted exchange rate of a basket of bilateral exchange rates against China's trading partners' currencies, adjusted for their corresponding consumer price index (CPI) inflation differentials. We first start with separate discussions of the PBOC's inflation record and currency performance.

The left panel of Figure 3.3 indicates a possible distinct regime change in China's inflation dynamics around 2000 (Amstad, Huan and Ma, 2014; Girardin, Lunven and Ma, 2014). Before 2001, the Chinese inflation rate was much higher and more volatile, fluctuating between

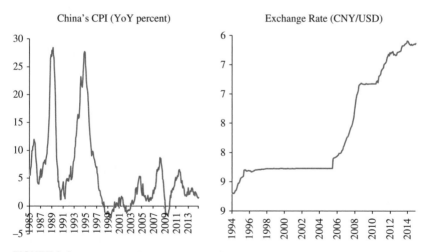

FIGURE 3.3   China's inflation and exchange rate record
Data Source: CEIC

peaks of above 20% and troughs of outright deflation. The mean and standard deviation of monthly year-on-year inflation between 1987 and 2000 reached 8.8% and 8.7%, respectively. From 2001 to 2014, however, they dropped markedly, to 2.5% and 2.4%, respectively. In sum, the PBOC has maintained a much improved and impressive record of low and stable inflation over the past 15 years, even though it is not an official inflation targeter.

China's exchange rate has mostly appreciated against the USD over the past two decades (Figure 3.3). More importantly, the RMB was steady against the USD during both the Asian and global financial crises, when most emerging-market currencies plunged. The pledge of "no devaluation" by Beijing subjected its economy to brutal deflationary shocks in 1998 and stiffened its capital controls, winning itself widespread international praise, but making the RMB a more rigid currency. The PBOC has built a solid record of resisting competitive devaluation in times of financial stress. It even signed a bilateral currency-swap agreement with the Bank of Korea during the GFC, enhancing its credibility and trust among many emerging-market central banks.

The price for such a hard-earned reputation is an undesirable "PBOC put" instilled into market expectations about the RMB exchange rate. Trust is based on performance, at least over the long term. One useful way to examine the performance of, and trust in, the PBOC is to look at the RMB's REER and benchmark it against those of other major emerging-market currencies. A rise indicates real and broad-based currency appreciation, whereas a fall indicates depreciation. Figure 3.4 shows a very strong RMB, vis-à-vis not only major emerging-market currencies but also the G4 currencies that make up the hybrid SDR basket.

Table 3.3 reveals three further messages (Ma, 2015). First, over the past two decades, the RMB has strengthened by more than 60% in real effective terms. This is the best performance among major emerging-market currencies. Second, three-quarters of this 60%-plus REER appreciation has come from nominal effective exchange rate (NEER) appreciation over the past 20 years. Third, relative inflation has played a reinforcing but secondary and minor role in the REER appreciation of the RMB. For China, the contribution of relative inflation to the REER appreciation is one of the smallest among the listed major emerging-market currencies. In other words, China's inflation has averaged modestly higher than that of its advanced trading partners but substantially below that of its major emerging-market peers.

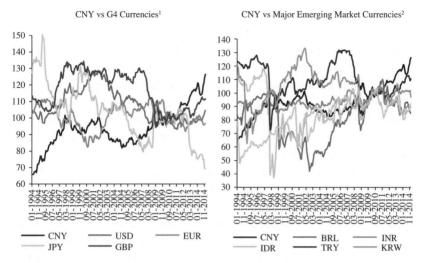

FIGURE 3.4 Real effective exchange rates, 2010 = 100
Notes: Currencies[1] refer to CNY = Chinese RMB, USD = US dollar, EUR = euro, JPY = Japanese yen, GBP = sterling. Currencies[2] refer to BRL = Brazil real, INR = Indian rupee, IDR = Indonesian rupiah, KRW = Korean won, MXN = Mexican peso, TRY = Turkish lira.
Data Source: BIS

TABLE 3.3 Contributions to changes in REER from NEER and CPI by percentage

	China	Brazil	India	Indonesia	Korea	Mexico	Turkey
January 1994 and December 2014							
REER	65.6	2.0	−3.7	−19.9	−11.0	−20.9	13.0
NEER	50.2	−264.8	−59.4	−175.8	−23.1	−150.5	−493.6
CPI	15.3	266.8	55.6	155.9	12.0	129.6	506.6
March 2005 and December 2014							
REER	42.6	33.7	−2.8	13.5	−10.1	−9.7	2.9
NEER	36.9	16.3	−35.9	−31.4	−11.0	−27.1	−49.8
CPI	5.7	17.4	33.0	44.9	0.9	17.3	52.7

Note: Natural logs of REER and NEER. A positive (negative) number indicates appreciation (depreciation). Contribution from CPI is computed as the natural log of REER less that of NEER.
Data Sources: BIS and author's estimation

These three observations combine to highlight one central contrast between China and the six big emerging markets. In the RMB's case, both its NEER and trade-weighted CPI differential have complemented each other to share the sizable adjustment burden of real effective appreciation. In contrast, for most major emerging-market currencies, typically much higher local inflation has precipitated currency depreciation, resulting in either noticeable real depreciation or insignificant real appreciation. Hence, on the performance of both inflation and currency, the PBOC's record is quite strong.

Another way to assess the quality of the PBOC is to examine its capacity to prevent, or respond to, financial crises. For instance, it was instrumental in cleaning up Chinese banks' non-performing loans, recapitalizing the commercial banks and assisting the public listing of most major state banks in the equity market since the mid-2000s (Ma, 2007; Okazaki, 2007). It has also been at the forefront of China's financial liberalization and regulatory reform and creative in developing the onshore interbank money, bond and FX markets. The PBOC has fought hard to contain excess leverage by local governments in more recent years. It is also at the forefront of building institutions that may support RMB internationalization, such as the Silk Road Fund (see Chapter 7). So the PBOC enjoys a decent record in liberalization and financial stability. The principal failure of the PBOC in preventing potential financial crises is the way senior PBOC officials encouraged the excessive stock-market rise in 2014–2015 and failed to take proactive measures to control the extraordinary build-up of margin financing that inflated the bubble. On balance, unless the stock-market crash undermines ongoing financial reforms, the PBOC's overall record is relatively solid; OECD countries have not avoided stock-market crashes, and China's performance compared with emerging market peers is outstanding.

Finally, the PBOC has behaved responsibly in the international financial sphere. It has resisted competitive depreciation and supported international and regional financial arrangements such as the IMF, the Bank for International Settlements and the Chiang Mai Initiative. Its efforts to promote offshore use of the RMB complement China's financial-liberalization agenda. Importantly, a good number of the many swap agreements China has entered into with other countries are intended not just to underpin commercial transactions but also to enhance currency and financial stability in the event of market turbulence. These new swap arrangements in some sense are offshoots of the

Chiang Mai Initiative, a system of mutual support that many Asian economies agreed on after 1997–1998. They still lack sufficient scale to cope with a major crisis, but they may well provide a budding mechanism for China to offer a meaningful buffer and assistance to its neighbors in times of stress and thereby build trust in the PBOC for a much greater global role.

In short, a strong record of currency stability, sustained low inflation, financial stability and a constructive and stabilizing role during recent international crises have earned the PBOC a solid reputation, as a start.

Nevertheless, to be an issuing central bank of a global currency, the PBOC still needs a more robust policy mandate, more time to climb the learning curve and more work to gain the trust of its peers and international investors. This is so, even though the PBOC acted in a highly responsible manner in the wake of the GFC. Beijing should allow the PBOC a higher degree of independence in both monetary policy-making and implementation.

The PBOC has a long way to go before it is able to stand shoulder-to-shoulder with other major central banks such as the US Fed, the ECB, the BoJ and the BoE. It cannot afford to aim lower.

We see three missions potentially adding to the trust and credibility of the PBOC as an issuing central bank of a global RMB.

First, it needs to move toward a new monetary-policy framework comparable with those of the top OECD economies and consistent with a more liberalized financial environment. Such a regime would feature low and stable inflation as a core mandate and some policy interest rate as the principal operating target. The transmission of monetary policy to the real economy then should be through the financial market and the banking system, not through bureaucratic allocation of credit.

Yet China's monetary-policy regime remains a hybrid based on both quantity and price, deploying multiple instruments such as central bank bills, bank reserve requirement ratios (RRR), indicative loan quotas and window guidance (Ma *et al.*, 2013). This is so even though the new policy tools recently introduced by the PBOC are more price-oriented and market-based. China's previous monetary-policy regime is appropriate for a small but growing economy where the export market takes a high proportion of final consumption. It is not appropriate for a large economy issuing a global currency. The emerging regime will take time to be road-tested and for both domestic and international investors to become acquainted with it.

Second, the PBOC needs to send clearer messages that convey its monetary-policy stance to both domestic and international investors. As an issuing central bank of a global currency, it would have to be more forthcoming in its stance and intentions. Neither the global market nor international investors will welcome a major central bank that is elusive in that regard.

Although the PBOC has come a long way in terms of expressing its views via its *Quarterly Monetary Policy Implementation Report* (PBOC, 2014), much remains to be done. Barclays' latest survey (2014) suggests that, of the 14 central banks reviewed, the PBOC's communication with the financial market and public ranks third-last, barely ahead of Turkey and Russia.

Third, the PBOC must make a more concerted effort to provide a wider range of monetary, banking and financial market statistics to facilitate market functioning and price discovery, rather than being reluctant to contribute to international financial-monitoring initiatives. Financial markets function more efficiently when information is amply and reliably available. The selective release of market data can damage both investor confidence and a central bank's credibility, especially in times of stress.

The PBOC has just officially subscribed to the IMF Special Data Dissemination Standard (SDDS), taking another big step in complying with international practice. It ought to contribute to the BIS's international and cross-border statistics, as do more than 40 other central banks from advanced and emerging-market economies. This is a basic and essential obligation of a central bank aspiring to issue a global currency.

CONCLUSION

A major international currency requires both strong economic fundamentals and quality institutions that facilitate its international use in commerce and finance. With full acknowledgment that China's economy faces important risks and a complex transition, its economic fundamentals in terms of growth momentum, reform and liberalization nonetheless provide a favorable foundation for RMB internationalization. A high degree of capital-account convertibility naturally encourages wider international uses of the RMB. While institutions such as its capital markets are still in an upper-middle level of development, the country is also building its key institutions, both international and domestic, in a solid and systematic way. Significantly, its most important monetary institution, the PBOC, has already achieved a relatively high level of maturity.

REFERENCES

Amstad, M., Huan, Y. and Ma, G. (2014) Developing an underlying inflation gauge for China. BIS Working Paper, No. 465.

BIS (2003) China's capital account liberalization: International perspective. BIS Papers, No. 15.

Barclays (2014) 2014 Survey of Central Bank Communication: The gap narrows but the Fed still sets the standard.

Girardin, E., Lunven, S. and Ma, G. (2014) Understanding the monetary policy rule in China: What is the role of inflation? In *Globalisation, Inflation and Monetary Policy in Asia and the Pacific*, BIS Papers, No. 77, pp. 159–170.

Hooley, J. (2013) Bringing down the Great Wall? Global implications of capital account liberalization in China. *Bank of England Quarterly Bulletin* 53(4), 304–316.

Lardy, N. (2014) Markets over Mao: The rise of private business in China. Peterson Institute for International Economics.

Lowe, P. (2014) Some implications of the internationalization of the renminbi. Conference on the Internationalization of the Renminbi, Centre for International Finance and Regulation, Sydney.

Ma, G. (2007) Who pays China's bank restructuring bill? *Asian Economic Papers* 6(1), 46–71.

Ma, G. (2015) A compelling case for Chinese monetary easing. In Song, L., Garnaut, R., Fang, C. and Johnston, L. (eds), *China's Domestic Transformation in a Global Context*. Australian National University Press: Canberra; pp. 43–66.

Ma, G. and McCauley, R. (2013) Is China or India more financially open? *Journal of International Money and Finance* 39, 6–27.

Ma, G. and McCauley, R. (2014) Financial openness of China and India: Implications for capital account liberalization. In Song, L., Garnaut, R. and Fang, C. (eds), *Deepening Reform for China's Long-Term Growth and Development*. Australian National University Press: Canberra; pp. 295–314.

Ma, G. and Wang, Y. (2011) Why is the Chinese saving rate so high? *World Economics* 12(1), 1–26.

Ma, G., McCauley, R. and Lam, L. (2012) Narrowing China's current account surplus: The roles of saving, investment and the RMB. In McKay, H. and Song, L. (eds), *Rebalancing and Sustaining Growth in China*. Australian National University Press: Canberra; pp. 65–91.

Ma, G., Yan, X. and Liu, X. (2013) China's reserve requirements: Practices, effects and implications. *China Economic Policy Review* 1(2), 1–34.

Okazaki, K. (2007) Banking system reform in China. Occasional Paper, RAND Corporation, Santa Monica, CA.

Overholt, W.H. (2013) China's xi factor. Project Syndicate, December 16. Available at: https://www.project-syndicate.org/commentary/william-h–overholt-traces-the-origins-of-xi-jinping-s-rise-to-power-in-china

Overholt, W.H. (2015) The politics of corruption in China. East Asia Forum Quarterly, June.

PBOC (2014) Quarterly Monetary Policy Implementation Report, various issues.

Sheng, A. and Ng, C.-S. (2015) Bringing Shadow Banking into the Light: Opportunity for Financial Reform in China. Fung Global Institute Report.

CHAPTER 4

CAN THE CHINESE BOND MARKET SUPPORT A POTENTIAL GLOBAL RENMINBI?

A globally traded RMB needs to be underpinned by broad, sizable and deep financial markets. Although currencies make up the largest financial markets, trades typically involve bond purchases and sales. Thus, a liquid and actively traded currency is primarily one that is backed by a big and liquid bond market.

Markets for municipal and corporate bonds and stocks are also significant aspects of currency liquidity, but treasuries and policy bonds typically account for the bulk. China's bond market development faces significant challenges, including regulatory fragmentation, moral hazard, a relatively narrow investor base and still-low foreign ownership.

Bold policy initiatives can help overcome some of these impediments and could, in short order, double the size of the market for CGBs, or treasuries, by consolidating fragmented public-sector liabilities. This would lift CGBs into the top third of global treasuries markets. A combination of a bigger market and higher foreign ownership could increase CGB foreign holdings tenfold from now to 2020, reaching RMB2.3 trillion. Such bigger foreign holdings of CGBs would rival the Netherlands' entire treasury-bond market and easily be twice as big as the projected size of offshore RMB-denominated bonds globally.

This chapter provides an overview of China's domestic bond market, highlighting issuer and investor profiles and scale relative to international peers. We ask the question whether the bond market can facilitate an internationalizing RMB and focus more on the CGB market and its global ranking, discuss the possibility of public-sector debt consolidation that could overnight double the size of the market and also examine the policy-bank bond market.

OVERVIEW OF THE CHINESE BOND MARKET

If the RMB is to become a truly global currency – an SDR component, for example, or one of the top five most-traded currencies – then capital market development is crucial, especially for fixed-income securities. Currently, China's is the sixth-largest bond market defined broadly. It is about one-tenth the size of the US market and about the average size of the main euro member states (see Figure 4.1).

In relation to GDP, China's total outstanding domestic bonds rank lowest of the world's top ten markets. In this sense, Chinese bonds punch under their weight.

Nevertheless, China's overall leverage of government, non-financial corporations and households combined approaches 250% of GDP, which is high by international standards. This disparity mainly reflects the banking sector's dominance of China's financial sector, with its

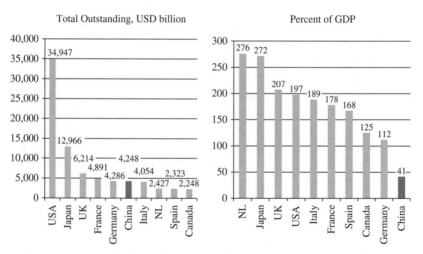

FIGURE 4.1 Top ten bond markets in the world, 2014
Notes: Bonds outstanding data as of June 2014; 2014 GDP. A broad definition is used in this chapter to measure the overall bond market size of the economies. NL = Netherlands.
Data Source: BIS

TABLE 4.1 Composition of domestic financing (percentage of total domestic financing, December 2013)

	CN*	HK	ID	JP	KR*	MY	PH	SG	TH**
Credit	63.3	14.9	39.1	47.5	36.2	34.2	28.5	22.0	34.5
Bonds	18.7	5.0	12.6	40.4	36.6	27.1	21.6	18.1	25.2
Equity	18.1	80.0	48.4	12.1	27.2	38.7	49.9	59.9	40.3

*CN = China; HK = Hong Kong; ID = India; JP = Japan; KR = Korea; MY = Malaysia; PH = Philippines; SG = Singapore; TH = Thailand.
**Korea and Thailand as of Q3 2014, China as of June 2013.
Data Source: Asian Bonds Online. http://asianbondsonline.adb.org/regional/data.php

debt-securities market still only a relatively small segment of the domestic credit market (see Table 4.1). Bank loans accounted for more than 60% of total domestic financing in 2013, while debt securities and equities captured less than 20%. This is in sharp contrast to the situation in most other Asian economies (see Table 4.1).

From this perspective, China probably will not continue leveraging up much further. Instead, a far larger fixed-income sector will have to be established and accompanied by considerable but incremental financial disintermediation (that is, taking funds from financial intermediaries, especially banks, to invest directly in capital markets). Thus, bank loans' relative share of total domestic financing will have to decline as bond markets grow. We expect the following four likely developments to drive the disintermediation process:

■ The new Basel III, soon to be more fully adopted by the CBRC, will impose more stringent capital requirements on China's commercial banks, thereby restraining their balance-sheet expansion. As a result, we expect China's debt-securities market growth to exceed that of bank lending over 2015–2020.
■ Policy measures to restrain bank lending to local-government financing vehicles (LGFVs) should see a big rise in municipal-bond issuance, replacing maturing bank and shadow-bank loans. The new Budget Law authorizes local-government bond issuance, with the State Council having promulgated detailed rules about the process. These also will cover a new scheme to swap LGFV bank and shadow-bank loans into municipal bonds.

- Sufficient improvement in China's regulatory frameworks may help spur a sizable pickup in the asset-backed securitization market, enabling banks to sell loans to investors in the form of bonds. Having offloaded those risks, banks could then take on new risk to provide more loans. Asset-backed securities have risen eightfold over the past two years – and this is probably just the start.
- Financial deregulation may force commercial banks to pay more attention to SMEs to maintain their net interest margins. As a result, blue-chip companies are likely to make more use of the debt-securities market. As the investment-grade area expands, high-yield segments may also pick up, although the lag may be considerable.

Thus, a deeper and more liquid bond market offers a viable alternative to bank loans – a "spare tire" in the search for finance (Greenspan, 1999). That will enhance financial stability through the facilitation of a more diversified credit market. By 2020, we expect China's domestic financing profile to have changed, reflecting bigger roles for debt and equities markets and a diminished one for banks. Depending on the pace of financial liberalization (and in light of the recent Japanese experience), we expect the bank-loan share of domestic financing to shrink from 63% in 2013 to 55% by 2020, while bond- and equity-securities financing should each increase from less than 20% to 22% (see Table 4.1).

China's domestic bond market has expanded sevenfold during the past decade. However, we highlight four striking institutional features of recent years (see Tables 4.2 and 4.3). First, domestic banks overwhelmingly dominate the market, both as issuers and investors (Huang and Zhu, 2007). They are also the biggest bond underwriters outside the treasuries segment of the primary market, which is not yet open to foreigners.

Second, most *bond issuers* are government-linked, giving rise to potential moral hazard. At times, these bonds – which include CGBs issued by the Ministry of Finance (MoF), government-supported bonds, PBOC bills and policy-bank and municipal bonds – have accounted for more than 70% of the total outstanding (Standard & Poor's, 2009). As well, most of the other segments – such as corporate and commercial-bank bonds – are often issued by SOEs and LGFVs. That China's domestic bond market experienced the first default by an SOE issuer only in 2015 suggests there remains significant moral hazard.

TABLE 4.2 Chinese domestic bond market by issuer (RMB bn, year-end)

	2010	Percentage of total	2014	Percentage of total	2015–2020 CAGR percentage	2020^e
Treasury (CGB)	5,963	29.6	8,553	29.8	10	15,152
PBOC bills	4,091	20.3	428	1.5	n.a.	0
Municipals	400	2.0	1,162	4.0	35	7,034
Financials	5,827	28.9	11,256	39.2	11	21,420
– Policy banks	5,160	25.6	9,957	34.7	12	19,653
– CDB bonds	3,680	18.2	6,266	21.8	12	12,368
Government-supported	109	0.5	1,103	3.8	10	1,954
Non-financials	2,810	13.9	5,005	17.4	8	7,942
Asset-backed	18	0.0	269	0.9	35	1,628
Others	975	4.8	954	3.3	9	1,600
Total	20,175	100	28,730	100	12	56,731

Notes: e refers to estimated and n.a. stands for not applicable. Savings bonds (electronic) issued by the MoF are included under Others rather than CGBs, because savings bonds are different from book-entry treasury bonds in that they are much smaller in scale, not liquid and only for retail bond investors. CDB = China Development Bank.
Data Sources: ChinaBond.com and CEIC

Government-linked bonds are spread across a number of segments with different regulators. This dilutes liquidity and makes for a shallow market. None has the weight to be a meaningful global asset class in its own right. When a liquidity pool is divided into two equal market segments, the liquidity of each can decline by as much as 80% or more.

Third, among *bond investors*, commercial banks and special institutions (mostly the PBOC, MoF and policy banks) hold a combined 70% of total outstanding domestic bonds (see Table 4.3). In 2014, the share held by all other non-bank financials – including insurers and pension and bond funds, which tend to trade more actively (Mu, 2006) – was a mere 23%. That compares with the two-thirds of UK gilts that are held by insurance companies and pension funds. Such a lopsided investor base is unlikely to nurture market liquidity. However, it points to the way forward.

Foreign holdings of onshore RMB bonds amounted to RMB672 billion in 2014, or about 2% of the total outstanding. That is far lower than in other Asian markets (see Table 4.6 later), but easily exceeds the entire global stock of so-called "dim sum bonds" – those denominated in RMB but issued offshore.

Fourth, the domestic bond market remains fragmented in terms of its regulatory framework across both instruments and trading platforms. At least five agencies (the MoF, the PBOC, the CSRC, the CBRC and the National Development and Reform Commission (NDRC)) supervise the various debt instruments that are traded mostly on two different exchanges, as well as the interbank bond-trading platform. For instance, the CGB benchmark yield curve comes under de facto PBOC supervision when the tenor is less than one year, but otherwise under the de facto purview of the MoF! Such fragmentation is not helping the bond market's development. It not only dilutes liquidity, but also results in regulatory arbitrage, inefficiency and higher financing costs (Bai, Fleming and Horan, 2013).

The next five years may see the emergence of four broad new forces that would particularly help shape the prospects of China's domestic bond market in 2020.

First, as noted above, expected incremental disintermediation would support the debt-securities market, especially municipals and securitization. An example is the 2015 swap scheme whereby RMB1 trillion official standardized municipals have been issued at the time of writing, to replace opaque thirty-party LGFV borrowings, often from banks and the shadow-banking sector.

TABLE 4.3 Chinese bond market by investor (RMB bn, year-end)

	2010	Percentage of total	2013	Percentage of total	2014	Percentage of total
Commercial banks	14,087.0	69.8	16,682	64.4	18,101	63.0
Special institutions	1,753.3	8.7	1,701	6.6	1,710	6.0
Non-bank financials	3,820.1	18.9	5,827	22.5	6,460	22.5
Non-financials	43.7	0.2	15	0.1	12	0
Overseas	n.a.	n.a.	400	1.5	672	2.3
– CGB*	n.a.	n.a.	136	1.7	222	2.6
– CDB	n.a.	n.a.	44	0.8	92	1.5
Others	470.8	2.3	1,286	5.0	1,774	6.2
Total	20,174.8	100	25,911	100	28,729	100

Notes: Municipals and others are not included due to limited data availability. Special institutions include the PBOC, MoF and policy banks.

*The share of overseas holding for CGBs (CDB bonds) is calculated as the amount of overseas holding of CGBs (CDB) divided by the onshore CGBs (CDB) outstanding.

Data Sources: China Central Depository & Clearing Co., Ltd and PBOC

Second, ongoing financial liberalization and market development may also help bring about a more efficient yield curve and broaden the derivatives market. Interest-rate deregulation is entering its final stages, with most rates having already been freed, in effect. The first full CGB benchmark yield curve was officially announced in November 2014. The latest relaunch of treasury futures is also a case in point (McCauley and Ma, 2015a). More fixed-income derivative instruments could also be launched.

Third, we expect the bond-investor base to diversify even more, with a heavier weight for pension and bond funds, as well as insurers. Further, steady capital-account opening could substantially increase foreign participation in the domestic bond market. In May 2015, 32 QFIIs, many of them global players, were allowed to enter the interbank bond market. This could easily double foreign holdings of onshore RMB bonds in a matter of months. A more diversified investor base tends to increase trading, thereby deepening market liquidity.

Fourth, a more consolidated regulatory regime and complementary policy measures could also benefit the bond market. In particular, a stronger and more transparent budgetary and debt-management framework could spur a significant rise in municipal-bond issuance. We also would hope to see a long-overdue integration of regulations across rival government agencies during the next few years.

Table 4.2 summarizes our baseline case of the prospects for the main bond-market components over 2015–2020. We expect the Chinese domestic bond market to expand by 12% per annum – faster than our baseline nominal GDP growth forecast of 10%. This reflects capital-market deepening and an enhanced role for direct financing in the economy. This should be driven mostly by continued CGB-market growth, fast expansion of policy-bank bond issuance and big jumps in municipals and asset-backed securities.

Over 2015–2020, we also expect the CGB market to grow organically in line with our baseline nominal GDP estimate, similar to the pace seen in recent years. Policy-bank bonds may expand at an average 12% per annum to fund affordable housing and shanty-town reconstruction projects, which are top government priorities. We also envision explosive increases in municipals and asset-backed securities, forecasting 35% growth per year over 2015–2020 for both – and for a number of good reasons.

First, the new Budget Law authorizes local-government bond issuance. Second, Beijing is encouraging swaps of municipals for the large overhang of maturing LGFV loans, which are often from shadow banking and tend to be shorter-term and carry higher interest rates. Third, a financing gap continues to arise from the need to provide services to rural migrants at local levels in the ongoing urbanization process. Fourth, more supportive policies and regulations are promoting securitization, in an attempt to ease pressure on bank capital.

However, we expect PBOC bills to be mostly phased out by 2020, due to a changing monetary-policy framework, a departure from sustained currency interventions and slower net capital inflows (or possibly even outflows). Also, the non-financial corporate-bond segment may grow fairly slowly, in part because a big chunk has been LGFV issuances, which will be curtailed or even replaced with municipals.

Nevertheless, thanks to reduced moral-hazard risk from implicit government guarantees, the corporate-bond segment will function more like a genuine credit market, facilitating more efficient credit pricing (Ma, Remolona and He, 2006). Four corporate-bond defaults in the first four months of 2015, including one by a central government-linked SOE, suggest the emergence of a slower but healthier corporate debt market.

CHINESE TREASURY MARKET IN INTERNATIONAL PERSPECTIVE

From the perspective of the RMB's internationalization, we focus in greater depth on one core segment of China's fixed-income market: the CGBs issued by the MoF and traded mainly among institutional investors on both the onshore interbank and exchange markets. We do so for the following five reasons.

First, the key question for policymakers is not so much whether the RMB will become more internationalized over time. It will. Of more importance is whether it can acquire meaningful global-currency status and, if so, when and how. Such a currency needs to be underpinned by global asset classes of its own. National, federal or central-government bonds ordinarily constitute the core of such asset classes. It is hard to imagine the RMB as a global currency while sitting on a minuscule CGB market.

Second, the size and liquidity of a government-bond market tend to be positively and highly correlated (McCauley and Remolona, 2000; McCauley, 2003). Without a big pool of assets, there would be no liquidity to speak of, although market size alone does not ensure this. A small and liquid CGB market would not suffice as a meaningful global asset class. Furthermore, a sizable CGB market would exert more pressure on the various regulators and trading platforms to become more integrated.

Third, as China further opens its capital account, a liquid and deep CGB market will better absorb shocks from potentially volatile cross-border capital flows – and boost the confidence of policymakers in the process. It would also encourage the authorities to further liberalize the primary and secondary CGB markets to domestic and foreign players, creating more diversified investor and market-maker bases and enhanced competition, all of which would boost liquidity. Moreover, a bigger onshore CGB market could only help the development of offshore "dim sum" markets. Any cross-border segmentation of the onshore and offshore RMB-bond markets would be of less concern if the overall market were sizable enough. Segmentation can arise from capital controls and differentials in tax and/or prudential rules. In short, a bigger and more liquid treasuries market would facilitate greater RMB convertibility, securing its place in the world.

Fourth, a better-functioning CGB market would provide a more robust benchmark yield curve and boost hedging vehicles that can support corporate- and municipal-bond markets (Committee on the Global Financial System, 1999a,b). By providing more efficient and reliable benchmarks for a fuller yield curve and credit spreads, as well as pricing fixed-income derivatives, a bigger and more homogeneous CGB market would also help reduce borrowing costs for the government in the long term. It would also ease the taxpayer burden and facilitate the development of the overall fixed-income market by providing more efficient and reliable benchmarks and trimming financial costs (BIS, 2002).

Fifth, central-government debt is typically a top asset class for global fund managers and a first choice for central-bank reserve-asset managers. Most central banks hold sovereign issues before moving down the credit spectrum to other fixed-income products. As a benchmark, foreigners hold 25% of US equities, 30% of corporate bonds and 60% of treasuries. Thus, a large and robust CGB market is crucial if the RMB is to become a meaningful reserve currency in the long term.

Simply put, size may not be everything, but it does matter, particularly in the long run. A sizable CGB market offers a crucial platform for a more diversified investor base, stronger competition, quality trading

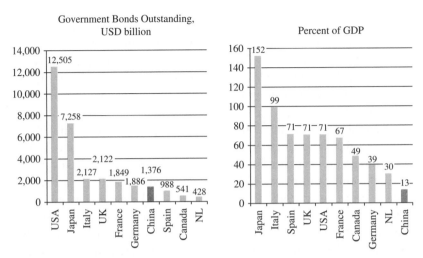

FIGURE 4.2 Top ten government-bond markets in the world, 2014
Notes: NL = Netherlands. Data only include debt securities issued by central governments.
Data Sources: SIFMA, Ministry of Finance Japan, UK Debt Management Office, Bank of Canada, Deutsche Bundesbank, World Bank, ChinaBond.com

infrastructure, greater market opening and better liquidity, serving as one central pillar supporting a structure in which the RMB functions as a potential global currency.

China's treasuries market is the world's seventh largest for national government bonds. It is about one-tenth the size of the US treasuries market and just ahead of those of Spain, Canada and the Netherlands (see Figure 4.2). Becoming a highly internationalized "small currency" such as the Canadian dollar (CAD) would not be worth the effort for Beijing to actively promote the RMB's external use. Equally, it would not be worth the commitment of resources by a global commercial bank to pursue RMB business opportunities.

To put the Chinese treasuries market in international perspective, we look at national government bond markets denominated in the currencies of the SDR's four components as benchmarks. Our baseline scenario entails the US treasuries market continuing in a class of its own in terms of size, depth and breadth over the next two decades. On that basis, the USD is unlikely to be challenged as the dominant global currency. Accordingly, our comparative study pays more attention to the markets of the SDR's three second-tier currencies: euro sovereigns, Japanese government bonds (JGBs) and UK gilts.

The euro area is the second largest global economy and trader, with a combined market for outstanding member-government bonds of some USD8 trillion, which is still well short of the US treasuries market's USD12.5 trillion, but ahead of the JGB market at USD7.3 trillion. Indeed, five of the top ten government-bond markets are euro-member states (see Figure 4.2).

Nevertheless, for the foreseeable future, the EUR is unlikely to challenge the dominance of the USD, mainly because of the limited fiscal integration backing the monetary union. Few fiscal arrangements cover the entire eurozone. Although the Stability and Growth Pact has been in effect since 1999, neither it nor other rules are always enforced. Also, fiscal centralization via the European Union budgetary system is limited. Yet these weak measures and the new European Stability Mechanism (ESM), under the governance of euro-area finance ministers, are all that bind the 19 diverse sovereign entities together. Thus, the euro sovereign-debt market remains fragmented.

Without a deeper and more permanent fiscal union, the huge aggregate euro-area government-bond market is just a collection of fragmented individual sovereign issues, despite a common central bank. Figure 4.3 shows the relative shares of the eight major euro sovereign-

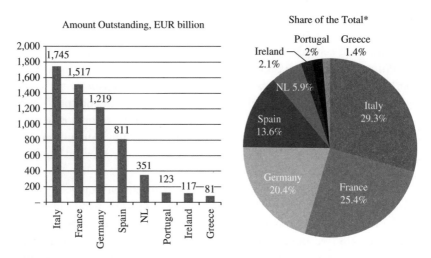

FIGURE 4.3 Main euro sovereign-bond markets, 2014
Note: NL = Netherlands.
* Total is the sum of the listed sovereigns in the left-hand side panel. Numbers include only central-government debt securities.
Data Source: Deutsche Bundesbank

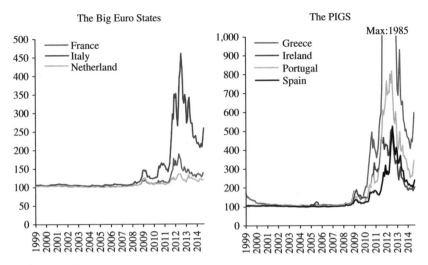

FIGURE 4.4   Ten-year sovereign-bond yield spreads over the bund (bps)
Note: PIGS = Portugal, Ireland, Greece and Spain.
Data Source: Datastream

bond markets. Given the substantial differentiation in credit risks across the euro area, the sovereign-bond markets look more like a group of municipal markets with distinct and variable credit and liquidity premiums, especially in times of stress (see Figure 4.4).

This situation is likely to continue for the foreseeable future, given the outlook for limited political union. The Greek-debt drama highlights the challenges. As well, the depth and liquidity of the national government bond markets in the euro area are questionable, with the exception of the mighty German bunds. The conclusion from this is that the EUR is underpinned by a collection of disparate sovereign bond markets under the 19 highly independent treasuries across the monetary union. This severely limits the liquidity required to back a common currency.

The JGB market is the world's second-largest central-government bond market, second only to that for US treasuries. However, less than one-tenth of total JGBs are held by foreigners because domestic private saving has so far been more than enough to cover the government's "dissaving." Furthermore, thanks to rounds of qualitative and quantitative easing (QQE), about one-fifth of total outstanding JGBs are held by the BoJ. Holdings of all government agencies account for about one-third of the total outstanding – a circumstance that, if prolonged, may depress both market-making and trading. In an extreme case, it could cause a market crisis. Another major QQE program may potentially further drain liquidity from the JGB market.

Moreover, if so-called "Abenomics" succeeds, interest rates may rise considerably, with worrying implications for debt-servicing dynamics in light of an extremely high outstanding JGB/GDP ratio. If the Japanese current-account surplus continues to shrink or even reverses into deficit, interest costs could rise further. As a result, the sizable JGB market could become an even less attractive global asset class. The footprints of the Japanese government are becoming so large that overseas institutions will increasingly see that market as risky and may even regard JGBs as less desirable than some emerging-market bonds as a major part of their foreign reserves.

Finally, although the UK gilt market is highly developed, it is only one-seventh the size of the US treasuries market. And it may have little room to grow, given the UK's high debt and servicing burdens. As well, over the longer term, the shadow of the Scottish-independence movement may continue to hang over the gilt market.

Thus, over the next decade, China needs to force its various regulatory agencies to adopt common national standards. If it succeeds in creating a more unified, larger and more efficient domestic bond market, liquidity in the CGB sector potentially can match those of the euro sovereign-debt and JGB markets. As a priority, China's leaders should aim to combine various policymaking and regulatory agencies during the next few years.

In terms of RMB internationalization, a key question is whether the CGB market can reach the threshold of a world-class national-government bond market by 2020. A simple illustrative projection of the 2014 top ten government-bond markets may provide some useful clues.

As a benchmark, we assume that outstanding national-government bonds for the top ten markets (as of 2014), except China, will each deliver a 5% annual growth rate over 2015–2020. This simple projection is aggressive and mostly for the purpose of illustration. As discussed, we also assume that CGBs outstanding will grow 10% annually over the same period.

Under our baseline scenario of 10% annual growth for the CGB market and 1.5% appreciation of the RMB against the USD per annum, total outstanding Chinese government bonds in nominal USD terms would double between 2015 and 2020. This would still amount to only about 16% of the US treasuries market and 27% of the JGB market by that time (see Figure 4.5). It may approach the size of the UK gilt market

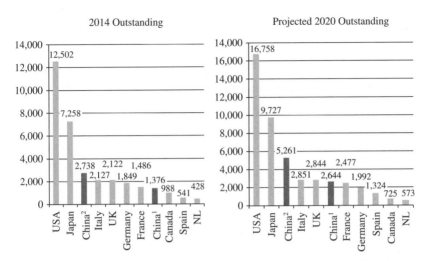

FIGURE 4.5 Top ten government-bond markets: 2014 vs 2020 (USD bn)

Notes: China[1] represents a scenario without public-sector liability consolidation, whereas China[2] represents a scenario with such a scheme, as discussed in the text. We assume a 10% average annual growth rate and 1.5% annual appreciation over 2015–2020.

Data Sources: SIFMA, Ministry of Finance Japan, UK Debt Management Office, Bank of Canada, Deutsche Bundesbank, ChinaBond.com and author's calculations

and slightly exceed the French treasuries market, but it would rise no higher than to be the fifth-largest national-government bond market. Even by 2030, the CGB market would be only about one-fifth the size of the US market under reasonable assumptions. Thus, trend expansion, while permitting the CGB market to progress, would be insufficient to elevate it to a top global ranking. Under reasonable assumptions, therefore, the size of the CGB market is unlikely to be big enough as an asset class to anchor the RMB as a top-three global currency by 2020. On top of this, the CGB market remains fragmented and far less liquid than those for US treasuries, JGBs or UK gilts and is partly restricted to foreign investors (see Table 4.4).

By 2020, under our baseline or business-as-usual scenario, the CGB market should gain ground, but it will achieve parity only with some individual core euro-sovereign debt and gilt markets. Thus, it would remain smaller than many of the sovereign-bond markets denominated in SDR-member currencies (see China[1] in Figure 4.5). To underpin the RMB as a serious global currency by 2020, the less-liquid CGB market would probably need to break into the top three national-government bond markets, as indicated by China[2] in Figure 4.5. But how?

TABLE 4.4 Turnover ratio of major government-bond markets

	UST	Gilts	JGB	CGB	CGB including futures	China's policy banks	CDB bonds	PBOC bills
2004	29.7	9.1	5.4	0.2	0.2	0.9	0.9	1.5
2005	30.2	9.1	5.1	0.4	0.4	1.0	1.0	1.8
2006	26.7	8.5	6.6	0.5	0.5	1.3	1.2	1.7
2007	28.5	8.1	8.8	0.6	0.6	1.2	1.0	2.7
2008	24.4	7.6	8.2	0.8	0.8	2.3	1.6	5.9
2009	14.6	6.0	6.1	0.8	0.8	4.4	3.0	3.2
2010	15.3	5.3	5.1	1.4	1.4	4.6	3.9	4.3
2011	14.3	6.5	5.1	1.4	1.4	3.4	2.9	4.0
2012	11.8	5.2	5.5	1.4	1.4	3.2	2.6	4.8
2013	11.4	n.a.	5.4	0.7	0.8	1.6	1.5	1.1
2014	10.0	n.a.	5.9	0.7	0.8	1.7	1.9	0.3

Notes: JGB = Japanese government bonds; Gilts = UK government bonds; UST = US treasury bonds; CGB = Chinese government bonds, CDB = China Development Bank. n.a. stands for not applicable. Turnover ratio is calculated as the annual total turnover divided by the average of outstanding amounts at the start and end of the year.
Data Sources: SIFMA, UK DMO, Japan Securities Dealers Association and ChinaBond.com

A DILEMMA AND A BOLD PUBLIC-DEBT CONSOLIDATION SCHEME

One way to expand China's treasuries market would be for the MoF to run larger current fiscal deficits to fund new spending programs and, thus, borrow more. Additional expenditure on pensions, healthcare and infrastructure are all worthwhile. However, borrowing excessively to fund wider government budget deficits while expanding the CGB market would damage China's fiscal position over the long term. Eventually, this would adversely affect its credit standing, widen risk premiums, crowd out private-sector investment and possibly even depress consumer spending.

Can the size of the CGB market be expanded meaningfully without running excessive fiscal deficits? In our view, this could be achieved by consolidating various, diverse public-sector liabilities at the central government level into the homogeneous and marketable CGBs.

One particular scheme involves PBOC–MoF liability swaps, in which the MoF would overfund its current financing needs by issuing more CGBs to the public and then deposit the proceeds from this issuance at the central bank. This short-term drain on reserves could be offset by a corresponding reduction in the currently high RRR. In essence, this would be a liability swap that transforms captive, non-tradable and illiquid central bank liabilities (mandatory deposits by commercial banks at the PBOC) into liquid and tradable MoF liabilities (CGBs). Table 4.5 sketches this proposed public-debt swap scheme, while McCauley and Ma (2015a) present a more analytical discussion of various public-sector liability consolidation schemes.

Lower RRRs would also mitigate the burden on Chinese banks. We illustrate the option here because we strongly believe that some version of this rebalancing would be extremely healthy for the economy. Indeed, we believe China's leadership may find the logic compelling. If adopted, it would greatly hasten the emergence of a truly global RMB.

China's RRR has been among the highest in the world, mainly because of the PBOC's need to fund and sterilize its massive FX-reserve build-up. That occurred mainly in the first decade of the 2000s (Ma, Yan and Liu, 2013). China's FX reserves rose more than 70-fold between 1994 and 2014 to a staggering pot of almost USD4 trillion. The increase in the required deposits by commercial banks at the PBOC funded some 85% of such FX-reserve accumulation over 2006–2014. The RRR was lifted from 6% in 2000 to a peak of 21% in 2011, before dipping back to 18% in April 2015. Nonetheless, the current level is still very high by world standards.

High reserve requirements tax financial intermediation, burden commercial banks, add to financing costs and encourage shadow-banking activities for regulatory arbitrage. Ironically, the implicit tax burden imposed by the RRR on commercial banks may have risen noticeably in an environment of more liberalized interest rates. In other words, the distortions from reserve requirements worsen after interest-rate deregulation. Thus, financial liberalization and such deregulation ought to be accompanied by a meaningful reduction of the currently excessive reserve requirements. Our proposed scheme of transforming the existing PBOC required deposits into CGBs therefore facilitates both capital-market development and financial liberalization.

TABLE 4.5 A possible scheme to consolidate public-sector liabilities in China

	PBOC		MoF		Memo
	Assets	**Liabilities**	**Assets**	**Liabilities**	
Status quo: End 2014	FX reserves	RMB22.7 trillion required reserves RMB8.6 trillion deposit by MoF PBOC bills	Deposit in PBOC	RMB8.6 trillion MoF bonds	Required reserves funded some 85% of FX accumulation 2006–2014
Swap scheme		+ RMB8.5 trillion deposit by MoF − RMB8.5 trillion required reserves	+ RMB8.5 trillion deposit in PBOC	+ New issue of MoF bonds: RMB 8.5 trillion	Policy actions: cut RRR from 18 to 9% and maintain excessive reserve at 2.5%
Results	FX reserves	RMB14.2 trillion required reserves RMB17.1 trillion deposit by MoF PBOC bills	Deposit in PBOC	RMB17.1 trillion MoF bonds	

Note: There can be a variety of similar schemes. For details, see McCauley and Ma (2015b).
Data Source: Author's calculations

As an example, if the current 18% RRR were to be halved to 9%, the liquidity thus released could be as large as RMB10 trillion and easily fund a doubling of outstanding CGBs from the RMB8.6 trillion at end 2014 to more than RMB17 trillion (see Table 4.5). CGBs would in short order become one of the top three sovereign-debt markets (see Figure 4.5). Still assuming 10% growth per annum, by 2020, it would almost triple to RMB24 trillion – equivalent to about one-third of the US treasuries market and some 60% of the JGB market. The CGB market would then be a serious contender as a global asset class.

This policy move offers a number of other distinct advantages, three of which we highlight here. First, it could consolidate fragmented, illiquid, non-tradable and captive public-sector liabilities into a homogeneous and large Chinese treasuries market, thereby enhancing bond-market liquidity. A bigger market would, in turn, enhance CGBs as an attractive global asset class for investors by accommodating more domestic and foreign players. As well, they would better absorb shocks arising from potential volatile cross-border capital movements in the context of a more open capital account.

Second, a large, integrated and liquid CGB market permits more regular benchmark issues of good size, which facilitates a more efficient and reliable benchmark yield curve. This would support the development of a new CGB futures market, in turn supporting the establishment of broader Chinese credit and derivatives markets such as interest rate swaps.

Third, the scheme also would help lessen the implicit tax burden of high reserve requirements on Chinese commercial banks (Ma *et al.*, 2013). China's RRR remains high even after a reduction to 9%. Therefore, a meaningful decline of reserve requirements would not only fund benchmark treasury issues traded publicly, but also help cushion the net interest margins of commercial banks in the wake of full interest-rate deregulation. That would lessen resistance to financial liberalization.

Of course, there are downside and upside risks to this scheme. We highlight two potential downsides below. First, implementation would require a strong political commitment from various government agencies to allow for policy coordination and sensible cost-sharing. The interest paid by the PBOC on required reserves is 1.62% – about half the prevailing one-year CGB yield. This increased payment by the consolidated public sector mirrors a de facto cut of implicit tax on banks in China. However, this cost can be offset in part by higher income tax because of stronger corporate earnings from lower interest payments and higher interest income.

Second, a higher level of headline gross sovereign indebtedness may concern ratings agencies. They tend to discriminate between central-bank liabilities and headline MoF liabilities, as well as worry more about gross than net debts. This was demonstrated in Europe by ECB President Mario Draghi's pledge to "do whatever it takes." This received a hugely positive market response at a time when additional finance-ministry borrowing was frowned on by the markets. Under our proposed scheme of transforming PBOC liabilities into MoF liabilities, gross – but not net – MoF debt would rise.

Thus, our baseline scenario assumes no policy innovation of this sort before 2020 and only organic 10% average yearly growth for the CGB market. A modest scale of fragmented, less-traded public liabilities is unlikely to attract international investors, let alone support China's dream of a global currency.

There are also potential upside risks to the scheme at the national-government level. The 18% RRR could be slashed all the way to 2% as part of financial liberalization and market development. In this case, the CGBs could triple in short order to a still manageable 40% of GDP.

In contrast, a combination of organic 10% growth and a doubling of CGBs through public-sector liability consolidation now would expand China's market by a factor of almost three by 2020. That would lift it into the ranks of the top three national-government bond markets (see Figure 4.5). Although it would still be only about one-third the size of the US treasuries market, it would be equivalent to more than 60% of the JGB market. This would help underwrite the RMB's bid to become a serious global currency. Indeed, unless Abenomics success-fully moderates the rise and concentration of JGBs, the RMB may by then seem a more appropriate global currency than the JPY.

Moreover, with a larger CGB market, Chinese policymakers may feel more comfortable with a rising share of foreign holdings. If by 2020 that share of an expanded CGB market were also to rise, from its current low of 2.6% to about 10% – comparable with current foreign ownership in the JGB market (see Table 4.6) – potential foreign holdings in the onshore CGB market would increase seven times under our base case (or ten times in the case of a bold scheme to consolidate public-sector liabilities). The increase would be from RMB222 billion (USD36 billion) in 2014 to RMB1.5 trillion (USD260 billion) in 2020 under our base case and to RMB2.3 trillion (USD413 billion) under the bold policy. The estimated 2020 foreign holdings of CGBs alone in the bold-

TABLE 4.6 Foreign holdings of domestic government bonds (percentage of total outstanding, year-end)

	Korea	Japan	Thailand	Malaysia	India
2008	6.1	6.9	2.9	13.7	16.7
2009	7.0	6.0	3.2	15.5	18.6
2010	9.9	6.4	7.2	24.4	30.5
2011	11.2	8.5	11.5	28.8	30.8
2012	9.5	8.6	16.4	32.3	33.0
2013	10.8	8.3	17.4	30.8	32.5
2014*	10.6	8.9	17.6	31.9	38.1

*As of Q3 2014.
Data Source: AsianBondsOnline. http://asianbondsonline.adb.org/regional/data
.php

policy scenario would rival the Netherlands' entire national government-bond market in 2014 (see Table 4.7).

If the offshore RMB-denominated bond market were also to expand faster, thanks to a bigger and more liquid onshore CGB market (which would alleviate concerns about the divided and diverted CGB-market liquidity), the onshore and offshore CGB markets together could be mutually reinforcing and further lift the potential scale of the investable CGBs in global-investor portfolios.

Even so, the fragmented bond market and still partly managed interest rates would in the short term impede the ability of traders and speculators to do the hedges and swaps that are essential to a world-class currency market. Above all (and absent the surprises discussed earlier), while there would undoubtedly be some increase in the use of the RMB for FX reserves, continuing liquidity limitations could be a drag in the next few years, potentially hampering the CGB market from becoming a global asset class capable of helping underpin an emerging global reserve currency.

GOVERNMENT-BACKED DEBT SECURITIES

Although sovereign bonds are typically the core of the fixed-income market, sovereign-backed or sponsored-agency debt securities are often

TABLE 4.7   Projections of the Chinese bond market and foreign holdings, 2020 (RMB billion (USD billion), year-end)

	Total outstanding		Foreign holding		Foreign share (2)/(1)
2014					
Total	28,730	(4,626)	672	(108)	2.3%
CGB	8,553	(1,377)	222	(36)	2.6%
CDB	6,266	(1,009)	92	(15)	1.5%
(A) 2020ᵉ – organic growth scenario					
Total	56,731	(9,918)	5,673	(992)	10%
CGB	15,152	(2,649)	1,515	(265)	10%
CDB	12,368	(2,162)	1,237	(216)	10%
(B) 2020ᵉ – bold policy scenario					
Total	65,231	(11,404)	6,523	(1,140)	10%
CGB	23,652	(4,135)	2,365	(413)	10%
CDB	12,368	(2,162)	1,237	(216)	10%

Notes: We assume average annual growth of 10% for CGBs, 12% for CDBs and 12% for the total bond market. Under the bold policy, the liability-consolidation scheme would increase CGBs outstanding by RMB8.5 trillion overnight. The RMB/USD exchange rate at the end of 2014 was 6.21 and will be about 5.72 by 2020, assuming 1.5% appreciation per annum.
Data Source: Author's calculations

also a major source of market liquidity. The Federal National Mortgage Association (Fannie Mae) and Federal Home Loan Mortgage Corporation (Freddie Mac), for example, play this role in the USA. This market segment of mortgage-backed securities historically far exceeded US treasuries prior to 2011 (see Table 4.8). These debt securities can be vast and often serve as an important asset class for foreign investors, including central banks and sovereign funds. Securities such as these have been a major source of market liquidity for the USD and, indeed, pillars of the US financial system, given their scale and depth.

Although the growth of China's asset-backed securities is set to accelerate in the years ahead, they have been lagging and are unlikely to be sizable enough to become a major fixed-income asset over the next decade. Instead, other government-sponsored agency debt securities figure more prominently in China's case (see Table 4.8). One such

TABLE 4.8 Comparison of CGB, China's policy-bank bond, UST and US MBS (amount outstanding, USD bn, year-end)

| | China | | | | | USA | | | |
| | CGB | | Policy-bank bond | | UST | | US MBS | | |
	Amount	Turnover ratio	Amount	Turnover ratio	Amount	Turnover ratio	Amount	Turnover ratio	
2004	292	0.2	166	0.9	3,944	33.1	6,289	8.6
2005	326	0.4	216	1.0	4,166	33.9	7,206	9.3
2006	359	0.5	286	1.3	4,323	30.0	8,376	8.2
2007	607	0.6	378	1.2	4,517	32.0	9,373	9.0
2008	689	0.8	528	2.3	5,774	27.1	9,458	9.2
2009	781	0.8	651	4.4	7,261	15.8	9,342	8.0
2010	881	1.4	762	4.6	8,853	16.3	9,221	8.6
2011	999	1.4	1,003	3.4	9,928	15.1	9,044	6.8
2012	1,120	1.4	1,245	3.2	11,046	12.4	8,815	8.0
2013	1,261	0.7	1,432	1.6	11,854	11.9	8,720	6.5
2014	1,376	0.7	1,602	1.7	12,505	10.0	8,729	5.2

Note: Turnover ratio is calculated as annual total turnover divided by the average of outstanding amounts at the start and end of the year.
Data Sources: SIFMA, ChinaBond.com

asset class consists of the bonds issued by the three main policy banks: the CDB, the Export–Import Bank of China (China Exim) and the Agricultural Development Bank of China. Fully backed by the national government, these bonds have expanded more than fivefold over the past decade. Similar to US agency bonds, they collectively rival and even exceed the sovereign CGB market. Of the three banks, the CDB is the biggest issuer and of special interest.

Some indicators suggest that the policy-bank bond market may be even more liquid than that for CGBs, as their turnover tends to be higher. There is a combination of possible reasons for this. First, the CGB-issuance system was designed mostly to fund budget shortfalls, with limited consideration of long-term market development. By contrast, CDB issues enjoy quasi-sovereign status, but have been more market-oriented.

Second, CDB bonds have been more innovative and market-oriented, offering a greater variety of instruments such as callable and puttable bonds, zero-coupon bonds, discount bonds, STRIPS and floating-rate bonds. Third, the higher issuance frequency of policy-bank bonds means greater availability of on-the-run issues, which are typically more liquid. Fourth, a bigger portion of policy-bank bonds is concentrated in the shorter and often more-liquid end of the yield curve than the CGBs.

Finally, interest income from CGBs is tax-free but not the capital gains. This encourages a buy-and-hold strategy, which depresses trading. These observations also point to possible measures to improve market liquidity for a given CGB market size.

Thus, the policy-bank bond market, especially for CDB bonds, represents a big and attractive alternative asset class within China. As discussed earlier (see Table 4.2), the size of the policy-bank bond market segment could double between 2015 and 2020, meaningfully adding to high-rated RMB fixed-income assets. If international investors' appetite for such bonds is the same as for the CGBs in 2020, their foreign holding could increase about 14 times by then, easily reaching RMB2 trillion (USD350 billion).

However, the CGBs and CDB bonds may also potentially compete and split the same pool of overall bond-market liquidity, resulting in a less robust benchmark yield curve. Historically, non-sovereign issues can also serve as the useful domestic benchmark yield curve, but not multiple and competing benchmark issuers at the same time.

CONCLUSION

A big, deep and liquid CGB and policy-bank bond market can facilitate the emergence of the RMB as a global currency by offering a big and liquid RMB fixed-income asset class. China's domestic bond market currently is the sixth-largest worldwide, although only one-tenth the size of the US market. Trend growth may bring the CGB market neck-and-neck with that of major euro sovereign markets by 2020, but that alone will not be enough to make it to a top-three treasuries market globally.

Financial liberalization, capital opening and a bold public-sector debt-consolidation scheme could boost the government-bond market by enhancing its integration and liquidity. This could lift CGBs to a top-three global market position, after those for US treasuries and JGBs, by 2020.

The policy-bank bonds could also be a sizable alternative RMB fixed-income asset class, rivaling both the scale and liquidity of the CGB market. However, Beijing must find a way to overcome the institutional weakness of market fragmentation and moral hazard.

If successful, by 2020 foreign holdings of CGBs and policy-bank bonds combined could reach RMB2.7 trillion (USD470 billion) under our baseline scenario and RMB3.5 trillion (USD620 billion) under a public-sector liability-consolidation scenario. This amounts to a rise of 9 times and 12 times, respectively, from their sizes in 2014. With further capital-account opening, China's bond market could become a big, investable RMB asset class, facilitating the potential emergence of a global RMB.

REFERENCES

Bai, J., Fleming, M. and Horan, C. (2013) The Microstructure of China's Government Bond Market. Federal Reserve Bank of New York Staff Report, No. 622.

BIS (2002) The development of bond markets in emerging economies. BIS Papers, No. 11.

Committee on the Global Financial System (1999a) Market liquidity: Research findings and selected policy implications. CGFS Working Group Reports, May 11.

Committee on the Global Financial System (1999b) How should we design deep and liquid markets? The case of government securities. CGFS Publications, October 13.

Greenspan, A. (1999) Do efficient financial markets mitigate financial crises? Speech at the 1999 Financial Markets Conference of the Federal Reserve Bank of Atlanta, October 19.

Huang, H. and Zhu, N. (2007) The Chinese bond market: Historical lessons, present challenges and future perspectives. Paper presented at the BIS– CEPR–HMKA conferences.

Ma, G., Yan, X. and Liu, X. (2013) China's reserve requirements: Practices, effects and implications. *China Economic Policy Review* 1(2), 1–34.

Ma, G., Remolona, E. and Jianxiong, H. (2006) Developing corporate bond markets in Asia: A synopsis of the Kunming discussions. In *Developing Corporate Bond Markets in Asia*, BIS Paper, No. 26, pp. 1–6.

McCauley, R. (2003) Unifying government bond markets in East Asia. BIS Quarterly Review, December, pp. 89–98.

McCauley, R. and Ma, G. (2015a) Consolidating public sector debts in China. Draft working paper.

McCauley, R. and Ma, G. (2015b) Transforming central bank liabilities into government debt: The case of China. *China and World Economy* 23(4), 1–18.

McCauley, R. and Remolona, E. (2000) Size and liquidity of government bond markets. *International Banking and Financial Market Developments* Nov, 52–58.

Mu, H. (2006) The development of China's bond market. In *Developing Corporate Bond Markets in Asia*, BIS Paper, No. 26, pp. 56–60.

Standard & Poor's (2009) *Chinese Bond Markets – An Introduction.*

CHAPTER 5

WAXING AND WANING OF THE CHINESE STOCK AND BANKING MARKETS

This chapter examines two major sectors of the domestic RMB market: A-shares and onshore banking. Both have experienced a remarkable transformation and will continue expanding during 2015–2020, although at different rates. We expect the stock market to grow faster than GDP, but the banking sector slower as it becomes less dominant and the overall economy reduces its leverage. By 2020, both promise to be more attractive for global investors, due to a combination of expanding domestic markets and higher foreign ownership.

Foreign holdings of A-shares could increase 14-fold by then, approaching RMB8 trillion (USD1.3 trillion), which would be far greater than Singapore's current entire market cap. Meanwhile, non-resident onshore deposits could more than triple to RMB10 trillion (USD1.7 trillion), easily twice as large as the forecast total offshore RMB deposits. Like the RMB bond market, the game will decisively be onshore.

CHINESE STOCK MARKET: GROWING DESPITE IMMATURITY FLAWS

The already huge A-share market continued to expand rapidly through early June of 2015, becoming a major bubble, and then crashed. Despite its large size, due to major flaws it remains underweight in terms of both fundraising ability and global benchmark indices. A large, deep and efficient stock market is vital to China's ongoing economic transition.

Market-based reforms, the rule of law, enhanced regulation and further opening will all help it develop into a global RMB asset class.

Fast-Growing But Under-Represented

China's modern market dates from the early 1990s, with the establishment of the Shanghai and Shenzhen exchanges (SSE and SZSE). This followed chaotic experiments with joint-stock corporations and street-trading of their shares in the late 1980s. The SSE and SZSE are now among the world's top ten exchanges by market capitalization (see Figure 5.1, left panel). In just 25 years, the A-share market has expanded massively. Its total market cap of more than USD6 trillion in 2014 makes

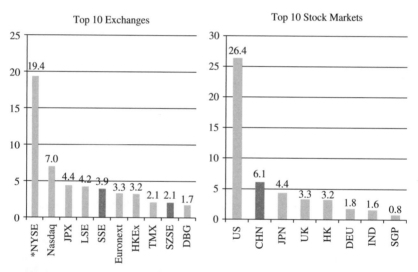

FIGURE 5.1 Top ten exchanges and stock markets in the world (by 2014 market capitalization, USD trn)

Notes: (1) NYSE and Euronext merged into NYSE Euronext in 2007, but we list them separately, as if there had been no merger. (2) LSE refers to London Stock Exchange Group data and includes Italy Stock Market. (3) JPX stands for Japan Exchange Group, LSE for London Stock Exchange, SSE for Shanghai Stock Exchange, HKEx for Hong Kong Exchanges and Clearing Limited, TMX for Toronto Stock Exchange, SZSE for Shenzhen Stock Exchange and DBG for Deutsche Börse Group.

Data Sources: CSRC, NBS, HKEx website, Japan Exchange Group, Taiwan Stock Exchange, SSE annual report, Hong Kong Securities and Futures Commission, CEIC and FGI analysis

TABLE 5.1 Key indicators for the SSE and SZSE (2004–2014) (RMB bn)

	Full market cap		Free-float market		Capital-raising		Listed firms (number)	
	SSE	SZSZ	SSE	SZSE	SSE	SZSE	SSE	SZSE
2004	2,601.4	1,104.1	735.1	433.8	45.7	19.7	837	536
2005	2,309.6	933.4	675.5	387.6	3.0	3.0	834	544
2006	7,161.2	1,779.2	1,642.8	857.5	211.6	49.0	842	579
2007	26,983.9	5,730.2	6,453.2	2,853.2	670.1	117.5	860	670
2008	9,725.2	2,411.5	3,230.6	1,290.8	223.8	123.4	864	740
2009	18,465.5	5,928.4	11,480.5	3,645.4	334.3	171.3	870	830
2010	17,900.7	8,641.5	14,233.7	5,077.3	553.2	408.4	894	1,169
2011	14,837.6	6,638.2	12,285.1	4,207.0	320.0	448.3	931	1,411
2012	15,869.8	7,165.9	13,429.4	4,736.4	289.0	204.6	954	1,540
2013	15,116.5	8,791.2	13,652.6	6,305.3	251.6	176.2	953	1,536
2014	24,397.4	12,857.3	22,049.6	9,512.8	396.3	423.0	995	1,618

Notes: See notes to Figure 5.1. The sum of capital-raising from the SSE and SZSE differs from the national total domestic capital-raising estimated by the CSRC due to statistical adjustments by CSRC.
Data Sources: SSE and SZSE annual reports

it the second largest in the world – ahead of Japan, although only one-quarter the size of the US equity market (see Figure 5.1, right panel).

The two exchanges jointly hosted more than 2,600 listed companies in 2014, which doubles the number in 2004 (see Table 5.1). Although the SSE's market cap was twice that of the SZSE at the end of 2014, Shenzhen rivals and sometimes even beats Shanghai for net equity-capital raising. It also lists more companies, given its strength in small and mid-caps, as well as growth firms.

A so-called "new third board" (National Equities Exchange and Quotations) was launched in late 2012. Similar to the US OTC Bulletin Board, or pink-sheets trading system, it was hosting more than 2000 companies by early 2015 and has been expanding explosively.

China's domestic market comprises not only RMB A-shares, which easily account for the bulk, but also a tiny portion of B-shares, denominated in HKD or USD.

TABLE 5.2   China's stock market: key indicators (2004–2014)

	Total market cap		Free-float market cap		Domestic capital-raising	
	Value (RMB bn)	Ratio to GDP (%)	Value (RMB bn)	Ratio to GDP (%)	Value (RMB bn)	Ratio to GDP (%)
2004	3,705.6	23.1	1,168.9	7.3	87.8	0.5
2005	3,243.0	17.4	1,063.1	5.7	33.9	0.2
2006	8,940.4	41.1	2,500.4	11.5	237.9	1.1
2007	32,714.1	122.1	9,306.4	34.7	789.8	2.9
2008	12,136.6	38.3	4,521.4	14.3	353.5	1.1
2009	24,393.9	70.6	15,125.9	43.8	499.6	1.4
2010	26,542.3	64.9	19,311.0	47.2	895.5	2.2
2011	21,475.8	44.4	16,492.1	34.1	507.3	1.0
2012	23,035.8	43.1	18,165.8	34.0	312.8	0.6
2013	23,907.7	40.7	19,958.0	33.9	280.3	0.5
2014	37,254.7	58.5	31,562.4	49.6	485.6	0.8

Notes: Domestic capital-raising includes capital-raising from A- and B-shares, but excludes that from H- and N-shares. Domestic capital-raising is calculated as the sum of IPO-raising and secondary placement of A- and B-shares. Data Sources: CEIC, NBS and CSRC

As of 2014, the domestic market cap amounted to almost 60% of GDP, compared with 23% a decade earlier. The free-float market cap – excluding non-tradable and restricted shares – has also increased rapidly, from 7% of GDP in 2004 to 50% by 2014 (see Table 5.2). As a share of GDP, the overall market cap is higher than that of Germany but below that of India. The market may expand faster than nominal GDP, partly due to forecast bank disintermediation and deleveraging.

Nonetheless, net capital-raising has been meager at less than 1% of GDP in recent years. We examine this in more detail later. For now, we simply note that this is consistent with the relatively low equity share in China's domestic financing (see Chapter 4 on the bond market).

As well, the equity market is under-represented in global investors' portfolios. Although it contributes 9% to the estimated world market cap (see Figure 5.2), it is not included in either of the two major benchmark indices (MSCI and FTSE). However, China accounts for a dominant

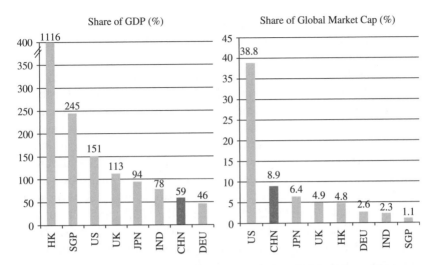

FIGURE 5.2 Stock markets by market cap to GDP and global share, 2014
Notes: (1) China's market cap is the same as the full market cap in Table 5.2.
(2) Singapore's market cap is represented by the Singapore Exchange. (3) The
US market cap is the sum of NYSE Euronext and NASDAQ. (4) The UK
market cap is represented by the London Stock Exchange (Main Board and
AIM). (5) India's market cap is represented by the Bombay Stock Exchange.
(6) Germany's market cap is represented by the Frankfurt Stock Exchange.
Data Sources: World Federation of Exchanges, CSRC, NBS, HKEx website, Japan
Exchange Group, Taiwan Stock Exchange, SSE annual report, Hong Kong Securities and
Futures Commission, CEIC and FGI analysis

19% of the MSCI Emerging Market Index, based on the value of its
overseas-listed companies and onshore B-shares alone. While the FTSE
has devised two new transitional indexes to include A-shares in a staged
process, the MSCI is also reportedly considering a possible phased
inclusion of A-shares in its Emerging Market Index (MSCI, 2014).

There are four key reasons why A-shares have been excluded from the
global benchmark indices: free-float limitations on the multiple-share
structure of A-share companies; restricted foreign access to the onshore
stock market; FX controls that hamper hedging and arbitrage; and
concerns about settlements, investor protection and corporate governance.

The planned phased inclusion in both major equity benchmarks
would enhance the potential of A-shares as a global asset class, in much
the same way as the RMB's addition to the IMF's SDR basket.
Following the 2005 non-tradable share reform of China's multiple-share
structure, the first barrier is disappearing. Most A-shares have become

tradable, with the free-float portion of the overall market cap rising from below one-third in 2004 to 85% by 2014. So, the first impediment has mostly been removed.

As for the second barrier, foreign access to the A-share market has been controlled via managed cross-border portfolio investment schemes such as QFII, RQFII, the Shanghai–Hong Kong Stock Connect and the forthcoming Shenzhen scheme (see Chapter 3). The foreign-ownership limit for a listed company is now 10% for any single foreign investor and a total of 30% for all foreign investors in the market. However, the cross-border investment quotas of these schemes have increased substantially and become less onerous, as evidenced by rising QFII and RQFII quotas on inward flows. Combined, they exceed the QDII quota on outward flows (see Figure 5.3). Further, the utilization of the Shanghai–Hong Kong Stock Connect daily quota has been low, except for a sudden and brief surge into Hong Kong in April 2015.

As well, the FX barrier has become less restrictive. We envision significant capital-account and FX liberalization in the coming years (see Chapters 3 and 6). Since April 2015, QFII investors have been able to move funds in and out on a daily, rather than a weekly, basis. Moreover, the fast-growing offshore RMB (CNH) market facilitates hedging for foreigners – although the hedging ratio of emerging-market equity portfolios tends to be low in practice, anyway.

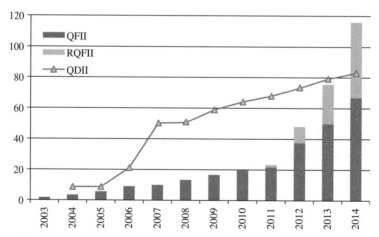

FIGURE 5.3 Quotas outstanding for QFII, RQFII and QDII (USD bn)
Note: The RQFII quota is denominated in RMB and converted into USD using the year-end exchange rate.
Data Sources: CEIC, PBOC

Finally, the CSRC has stepped up its efforts to strengthen investor protection and corporate governance, as well as to crack down on self-dealing and insider trading, improve disclosure and accounting standards, and toughen disciplinary actions such as delisting (Allen *et al.*, 2014). Over time, these measures should enhance the institutional quality underpinning the A-share market.

In summary, foreign investment in the domestic market is becoming easier, which will boost the chances of A-share inclusion in the MSCI and FTSE before long. In turn, this should increase the market's weight in global investors' portfolios, making it more attractive as a potential global equity asset class and thus expanding investable RMB assets.

Immaturity Flaws

Nevertheless, the A-share market punches below its weight, both internationally and in terms of domestic financing. As discussed in Chapter 4, commercial banks dominate the financial system, with the bond and stock markets playing only a secondary role. Net capital-raising from the onshore public-equity market has averaged a tiny 0.8% of GDP in recent years (see Table 5.2). That compares with 1.5–1.8% for the USA. Capital controls alone are probably not to blame.

Indeed, the anemic capital-raising capacity of China's public-equity market has been a major cause of its high and rising corporate leverage. By definition, bank loans and bonds are debt financing. China needs a stock market with much stronger fundraising capability to manage its tricky deleveraging process. Also, fundraising is particularly important for new firms, emerging industries and industrial upgrading. It helps improve capital allocation and would facilitate the much-needed transformation of China's economy toward a more sustainable growth model.

Why then is the market's capacity so poor, despite a sizable market cap? One major reason is probably the conflicting roles of the government (Chen, 2013). A hallmark of modern corporations is the ability to issue tradable equity shares to outside investors, while ensuring they face only limited liability. This separation between ownership and control requires extensive supporting legislation and institutions to protect the interests of outside shareholders.

Moreover, most public companies in the West were initially privately owned, with the exception of a few privatized state companies. By contrast, most Chinese listed companies were initially state-owned or -controlled, especially those floated in the first decade of the A-share market. Indeed, the market was established mainly to reform and fund the financially troubled SOEs. Thus, from the start, the government has played conflicting roles: controlling shareholder of listed SOEs; rules-maker for the market; regulator of its operations; and arbitrator of disputes between itself as controlling shareholder and minority interests. China's lack of judicial independence does not help. In short, the creation of the Chinese stock market had little to do with enabling private firms to raise capital from the public, but instead was initially intended to accommodate SOEs.

This fundamental flaw helps explain: why the market has histori-cally catered mostly to SOEs; why its approval-based IPO process has been so bureaucratic and political; and why investor protection has been so toothless. From the start, the government had strong incentives to restrict IPO approvals to ensure demand was strong for any new listings.

During the market's first decade, in particular, the number and size of IPOs were subject to quotas negotiated among the likes of the CSRC, the NDRC, local governments and relevant ministries. As with "policy lending" in the banking sector, many listings were, in effect, "policy IPOs" until the launches of the SME Board (2004) and the ChiNext Board (2009), which we discuss later.

Moreover, until the non-tradable share reform of 2005, the multiple-share structure of SOEs (divided between the state, the company as a "legal person" and public investors) was designed to ensure state control over the listed entities.

The consequence of these flaws is a malfunctioning market. Until recently, most of the capital raised from listings went to favored SOEs. Thus, the IPO process has been political, costly and corrupt – partly because of rent-seeking. IPO shares have often been priced too high or too low, leading to volatility in the secondary market. Then, in a bid to revive the depressed secondary market in 2013, the CSRC began issuing informal guidance to artificially cap IPO prices below a 23× price/earnings ratio. Thus, prices were unlikely to reflect prevailing market demand and supply, which risked turning IPOs into lotteries.

Political ideology also constrains any substantial selling down of the existing shares of public SOEs. This restricts the effective free float, leaving the share structures of many such companies heavily concen-trated, even after the 2005 reform. The limited numbers of tradable shares are more like gambling chips, attracting retail investors and contributing to speculative booms and busts, while discouraging value investors.

Indeed, China's stock market functions so poorly that many companies – both state and private – have listed in Hong Kong because of its superior legal, institutional and market infrastructure. That has been a major driver of H-shares (Hong Kong-listed shares of China-registered companies) and "red-chips" (Hong Kong-listed shares of Chinese firms incorporated overseas). Increasingly, Chinese companies have ventured to more distant offshore stock markets such as New York, London, Toronto, Singapore and Frankfurt.

In 2005, Beijing itself bypassed both Shanghai and Shenzhen for the first IPO of a major state commercial bank. Its decision to list all of its top four state-controlled banks (China Construction Bank, Bank of China, Industrial and Commercial Bank of China and Agricultural Bank of China) in Hong Kong first was a vote of no confidence in the A-share market. Over the years, many flagship state and promising private firms have listed overseas, although some are now cross-listed in both the A- and H-share markets. The estimated market cap of Chinese companies listed offshore is now about one-third that of all Chinese listed companies. This is testimony to the constraint that the underdeveloped A-share market has put on economic growth and reforms, let alone RMB internationalization.

While all this highlights the weakness of the institutions that underpin the domestic market, it also underscores the massive potential if these flaws can be remedied. However, it will not be easy. The following three important reforms would provide a starting point.

First, SOEs need substantial ownership diversification. Some form of hybrid structure, as has been suggested recently, would be a small step in the right direction.

Second, disclosure, auditing and investors' rights must be strengthened.

Third, the approval-based IPO regime must be replaced with the sort of registration-based process used by most exchanges. In mature exchanges, any company that satisfies objective economic criteria may list. Securities Law revisions tabled at the National People's Congress in March 2015 are encouraging.

However, these proposed revisions would transfer IPO approvals from the CSRC to the two stock exchanges – which are both subsidiaries of the CSRC rather than membership-based or corporate entities. Thus, there is a clear risk that the proposed registration-based regime would simply hand control of the process from central-government authorities to lower-ranking bureaucrats.

Greater SOE-ownership diversification could also be hastened by reforms of local-government finances in that they may trigger a wave of sell-downs of government stakes. As well, mooted transfers of government-held SOE shares to underfunded pensions and social security schemes could broaden ownership. However, it is far from clear how willing the government is to loosen its controlling stakes.

Finally, with the private sector now accounting for more than two-thirds of all new jobs, the government may at last become more even-handed in its approach to the stock market. Rather than using it as a policy instrument to bail out troubled SOEs, Beijing may allow more SMEs and private firms access. Of course, while market institutions remain weak, that alone would not guarantee that capital would flow to the more efficient and attractive private firms.

Promising Signs, Yet Some Hurdles Ahead

Two new boards established by the SZSE in the 2000s are encouraging. The SME Board caters mostly to small and mid-caps, while the ChiNext Board is mainly for technology and new growth firms. They have helped allocate a bigger share of newly raised funds to the more productive and capital-hungry private sector and startups.

The combined market cap of the two boards has risen from less than 5% of the SZSE total in 2004 to more than 50% by 2014 (see Table 5.3). Their share of China's total market cap has risen from 1% to 20% over that time. More importantly, the net equity capital-raising from the two boards has gone from 10% of the national total in 2004 to 45% in 2014.

The SME and ChiNext boards represent both an opportunity and a challenge, however. Their success has inspired the SSE to plan an emerging-industry board in the coming years to meet the needs of enterprises in fast-growing new industries. As well, the nascent "third board" discussed earlier could help fund startups and other more promising growth drivers. On the downside, both SZSE boards appear to have experienced bubbling valuations lately, with lots of abnormalities and an average P/E ratio exceeding 50× (see Figure 5.4). By comparison, the average for the NASDAQ is about 20×.

Such abnormalities derive in large part from the composition of the market participants – both investors and intermediaries. Stock ownership is heavily concentrated in the hands of controlling or major shareholders, but retail investors dominate in secondary trading. Mutual funds, for

TABLE 5.3   Indicators for the SME and ChiNext boards at SZSE

	As a share of SZSE total (%)			As a share of national total (%)		
	Market cap	Capital-raising	Turnover	Market cap	Capital-raising	Turnover
2004	3.7	46.3	5.2	1.1	10.4	1.9
2005	5.2	96.0	9.7	1.5	8.6	3.8
2006	11.3	36.6	9.4	2.3	7.5	3.4
2007	18.6	38.2	10.4	3.3	5.7	3.5
2008	26.0	34.8	19.2	5.2	12.1	6.2
2009	31.2	45.6	26.4	7.6	15.6	9.3
2010	49.4	81.1	42.1	16.1	37.0	18.6
2011	52.5	50.8	47.8	16.2	44.9	20.8
2012	52.4	55.8	56.8	16.3	36.5	27.1
2013	59.4	34.9	63.5	21.9	22.0	32.3
2014	56.7	52.0	62.8	19.6	45.3	30.9

Note: National total capital-raising refers to national total domestic capital-raising.
Data Sources: CSRC, NBS and SZSE

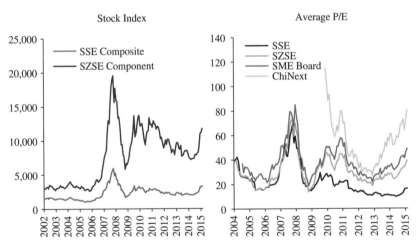

FIGURE 5.4   Stock index and P/E of different stock market boards
Note: SSE stands for Shanghai Stock Exchange, SZSE for Shenzhen Stock Exchange.
Data Source: CEIC

TABLE 5.4   Investor profile at SSE (as a share of SSE total, 2013)

	Hold account (%)	Hold value outstanding (%)	Turnover (%)
Corporation investors	0.1	63.6	2.5
Individual investors	99.8	21.8	82.2
Institution investors	0.1	14.6	15.3
– Investment funds	0.0	4.5	6.2

Data Source: SSE Statistical Yearbook 2014

example, held less than 4% of the combined bonds outstanding and stock-market cap at the end of 2014.

In 2013, retail investors had 99% of the total stock accounts on the SSE and held 20% of the full market cap. But they accounted for more than 80% of the total market turnover (see Table 5.4). By contrast, fewer than 0.2% of investors were corporate entities – that is, controlling shareholders – yet they held two-thirds of the total market cap and traded rarely. Institutional investors – including securities firms, investment-fund and asset managers, the National Social Security Fund, insurers and QFIIs – held 15% of the full market cap and accounted for only about as much of the total SSE turnover. Such a combination is unlikely to be conducive to efficient market valuations and robust corporate govern-ance. More likely, it fuels short-term, speculative trading and excessive volatility. Indeed, some observers liken the Chinese stock market to a casino.

Thus, the A-share market is highly liquid and even hyper, with high turnover ratios. In 2014, shares changed hands more than twice on average (see Table 5.5), compared with 0.7 times in Hong Kong, 1.3 times in the USA and 1.4 times in Japan. This is more likely to reflect excessive speculation than healthy liquidity.

Foreign A-shares ownership was 1.5% of the full market cap in 2014, which is low by global standards. To access the market, foreign funds managers must form joint ventures with local partners, subject to a 49% ceiling. Rising quotas of QFII, RQFII and the two connect schemes of stock exchanges are likely to continue lifting foreign holdings. Inclusion in the MSCI and FTSE, as noted above, would also boost A-shares as a potential global investable asset class. As a result, we expect foreign ownership to rise from the current low of 1.5% toward 9%

TABLE 5.5   Stock market turnover in China (2004–2014)

	Turnover (RMB bn)	Turnover ratio (full market cap, %)	Turnover ratio (free-float cap, %)	Ratio over GDP (%)
2004	4,233.4	114.2	362.2	26.3
2005	3,166.5	97.6	297.9	17.0
2006	9,046.9	101.2	361.8	41.6
2007	46,055.6	140.8	494.9	171.8
2008	26,711.3	220.1	590.8	84.3
2009	53,598.7	219.7	354.4	155.1
2010	54,563.4	205.6	282.6	133.4
2011	42,164.5	196.3	255.7	87.1
2012	31,466.7	136.6	173.2	58.9
2013	46,872.9	196.1	234.9	79.7
2014	74,391.3	199.7	235.7	116.9

Note: Turnover ratio is computed as the ratio of annual turnover over the year-end full or free-float market capitalization.
Data Sources: CEIC, NBS and CSRC

by 2020. By comparison, foreign ownership in the public-equity market in the USA reached 16% and in Japan 28%.

China's securities brokerage industry is highly decentralized, but still partly protected from foreign competition. As of 2014, there were 120 securities firms. The top ten domestic companies accounted for 40–50% of revenue and net profits. The sector is highly competitive and may even be crowded, suggesting the possibility of a painful medium-term consolidation.

Foreign investment banks and brokers also can gain exposure only via joint ventures with a 49% ceiling (up from one-third initially). Currently, there are a dozen joint-venture securities firms, involving top global investment banks such as Goldman Sachs, Morgan Stanley and UBS. Most joint ventures reportedly suffer low market share and poor earnings. One key reason is that their business scope is often more restricted, with only a handful having full business licenses. However, ownership above 50% for Hong Kong brokerages has now been allowed.

The A-share market also has a long way to go in terms of product sophistication. Same-day trading is still banned, for example, and coverage of short-selling and stock-index futures has only cautiously been expanded. The government scrapped T + 0 trading in 1995 and has maintained a T + 1 system since, although a same-day trading pilot is planned. Margin-trading and short-selling were introduced only in 2008. However, investors can short only 700 of the more than 2,600 stocks listed on the SSE and SZSE, and only 20 of the 120 brokerages can borrow shares from China Securities Finance. The Shanghai–Hong Kong Stock Connect has enabled foreign investors to short A-shares for the first time, but subject to complex rules and strict daily limits. China's first ETF-based equity option was finally introduced in early 2015. Currently, only three stock-index futures trade in Shanghai. In short, China's stock markets are still emerging markets – but they have been emerging quickly.

The Boom and Bust of 2014–2015

A stock-market bubble in the latter half of 2014 and early 2015, and the bubble's collapse in June/July of 2015, displayed both the immaturity of China's stock markets and the limits of the Chinese leadership's willingness to accept market outcomes. Regulators tolerated an extraordinary build-up of margin debt for stock purchases and senior financial officials encouraged investors to believe that the bull market was just beginning. Margin loans rose from RMB400 billion in July 2014 to more than RMB2 trillion. As late as April 2015, when the market valuations were far above any reasonable level, financial leaders and Party media organs were encouraging the public to continue to buy into the market and even stating that the bull market had just begun. Given the history of official management of the market, this encouragement was decisive; people, most of whom were unsophisticated investors, believed that if the government backed the market it would go up.

On June 13, 2015, the market regulator, CSRC, tightened the rules on margin lending. The subsequent crash was managed by a truly extraordinary set of interventions: reducing bank capital requirements, reducing interest rates, weakening constraints on margin purchases of stock, more than quadrupling the capital of the institution (China Securities Finance Corporation, or CSF) that provides most official funding for margin finance, helping CSF to raise other funds, encouraging CSF to borrow more than RMB1 trillion from commercial banks for stock purchases, loosening previously tightened rules on margin finance, intervening to get banks to stretch out the maturities of margin loans, ordering brokerages to provide RMB120 billion to CSF for stock purchases, instructing CSF to provide the brokerages with RMB260 billion of margin finance, cutting stock-market transaction fees, allowing pension funds to invest in the stock market, curtailing IPOs, instructing big holders of stock not to sell, getting 21 big securities companies to promise to buy stocks of state enterprises, allowing about one-third (700) of listed companies to suspend trading based on flimsy excuses, telling big companies not to sell their own shares, banning short sales and warning journalists that "speculative reports" must be cleared by the CSRC before publication. Officials criticized Morgan Stanley for having reported (correctly) that the market had risen too high and was a sell, suggested foreign conspiracies and launched an investigation into "malicious short sellers," defined as spreading rumors to induce selling, taking advantage of inside information to dump shares, colluding with others to drive down prices and using related accounts to buy and sell shares of the same company in order to rig prices.

The market lost only a fraction of what it had gained in the previous year, but many individuals and other investors had joined the party just before it ended and had bought on margin, borrowing more than they could afford. Disruption of market processes was extreme. As one commentator, Song Ma, posted, "11:10 a.m. on July 7, 2015 was a dark moment that will inevitably be written into the history of the A-shares market, not because the Growth Enterprise Index was down 5.71 percent, but because 51 out of 100 stocks on the index halted trading, and 48 were stopped because they dropped the maximum allowed. Only Lepu Medical, which was down 8.97 percent, hasn't stopped trading. Only a company that treats mental illness hasn't stopped trading . . ." (Ramzy, 2015).

The bubble's inflation and partial deflation could give opponents of market reform leverage to slow further reforms. The market's rise was referred to as the "reform bull market" and its demise may damage the image of reform, although neither the inflation nor the deflation was caused by market liberalization. The powerful interventions to halt decline achieved early success at a very heavy price. Telling market participants that they cannot sell or must buy necessarily deters some future participation in the market. Strong government management of the market encourages current and potential market participants to focus on government policy rather than fundamental valuation. Curtailing IPOs means the main markets continue to be dominated by state enterprises, while the leadership's desire for more innovative and dynamic companies to have access to the market gets postponed.

Bottled-up selling pressure is likely to emerge gradually, possibly keeping large parts of the market subdued for an extended period.

Internationally, MSCI is less likely to see the A-share market as ready for incorporation into global indices. Importantly for the purposes of this book, the strong intervention gives ammunition to those who argue that the RMB is not ready for inclusion in the SDR because, if financial instruments are subject to drastic government intervention in a crisis, they are seen as unsuitable for a major role in national reserves; reserves are by definition held mainly for the purpose of liquidity in a crisis. If stock markets are subject to such drastic intervention, then most international participants will assume the currency remains equally susceptible.

As this book goes to press, the consequences of the rise and fall of the stock-market bubble for the scope and pace of reform remain unclear, but they certainly include a heightening of controversies about financial liberalization. Five years hence, the crash of 2015 may be seen as a blip that did not disrupt underlying trends, as momentary crashes have passed in many other markets, or it may be seen as having slowed market reforms. We will make projections based on the trends that have been driving the market, while noting that those trends could be slowed or disrupted.

A More Internationalized A-Share Market in 2020

A growing and more open domestic public-equity market is crucial for efficient allocation of capital, a balanced financial system, orderly deleveraging and expansion of investable RMB assets for global investors. All these would help underpin a global RMB. To achieve this, many wide-ranging reforms are required, including SOE-ownership diversification, a registration-based IPO regime, a stronger regulatory and legal framework, market opening and capital-account liberalization.

Given the inherent volatility, the medium-term outlook for China's stock-market cap and fundraising is highly uncertain. Nevertheless, it is reasonable to expect that, with strong reform momentum, steady growth, further opening of the market and the expected inclusion of A-shares in the MSCI and FTSE, the overall market cap could grow at 15% a year over 2015–2020. That would be on a par with our baseline nominal GDP growth. At such a pace, the market cap by 2020 could easily more than double its 2014 value, reaching RMB86 trillion (more than USD13 trillion). This would still be only half that of the USA in 2014, but three times that of Japan. A much larger public-equity market and a slower banking sector could also assist an orderly deleveraging in the Chinese economy.

Also, by 2020 the full and free-float market caps should have more or less fully converged as the legacy of restricted shares becomes negligible. More importantly, we expect that net capital-raising could more than double from a mere 0.8% of GDP in 2014 to 2.0% by 2020.

Finally, we expect that the steady pace of capital opening could bring about a sixfold rise in foreign ownership, from 1.5% of market cap in 2014 to 9.0% by 2020. Combining an expected bigger underlying market and a higher foreign-ownership share, foreign A-share holdings could increase by a factor of 14 between 2015 and 2020, approaching RMB8 trillion (USD1.3 trillion). This foreign holding of A-shares would far exceed Singapore's entire market cap in 2014 and equal that of Malaysia, the Philippines and Thailand combined. Such a pool would provide a substantial boost to a globalizing RMB.

Again, if the market crash increases the influence of those who oppose market reforms, these projections could prove to be much too optimistic.

A MASSIVE CHINESE BANKING MARKET OPENING

China's banking market is by far the world's largest and amounts to the single biggest RMB financial asset class. Although foreign-bank penetration remains low, we expect that by 2020 non-resident onshore RMB deposits will be twice that of forecast total offshore deposits.

The Core of the Chinese Financial System

Banks overwhelmingly dominate China's financial system. Indeed, it has one of the highest bank assets-to-GDP ratios among the major economies (see Table 5.6). In 2013, banks accounted for two-thirds of total domestic financing (see Chapter 4 on the bond market). They are the biggest investors in and underwriters of the bond market, as well as being the biggest players in the onshore interbank FX market. Total banking assets are three times the combined domestic stock-market cap and bonds outstanding, while the value of domestic bank loans is about twice as big. The health and openness of the sector are significant for the prospects of RMB internationalization.

At least one Chinese bank is among the world's top ten listed companies by market cap. Overseas expansion in recent years has facilitated the development of offshore RMB markets, trading, dealing and clearing, thus establishing a global trading network (see Chapter 7 on offshore markets). In summary, a strong and efficient Chinese banking sector supports economic growth, facilitates financial stability and promotes external uses of the RMB.

The banking sector has experienced marked turnaround over the past 15 years, from the brink of technical insolvency to a strong expansion. Initially, virtually all domestic banks were wholly state-owned, apart from a small number of rural credit cooperatives controlled by town and village administrations. They served largely as "tellers" for the fiscal authorities, with little commercial spirit or risk-management. Policy lending gave rise to a large overhang of non-performing loans, which brought the whole banking system to the brink of collapse (Ma and Fung, 2002).

That began to change in the late 1990s, first with the introduction of national laws governing commercial and central banks. Second, supportive government policy facilitated a steady rise in the number of commercial banks at both national and regional levels, introducing real competition for the first time. As a result, the market share of big state-controlled banks has since declined noticeably (see Table 5.6). Third, China's 2001 WTO accession required partial opening of the sector to foreign banks, many of which bought strategic stakes in local firms and established their own representative offices, branches and subsidiaries. Finally, large-scale cleansing of bad loans and recapitalization were successfully conducted during the early 2000s, ahead of most of the major banks' listings (Ma, 2007). The results are that today, China's banks are far more sophisticated, profit-oriented and generally efficient (Xu, van Rixtel and van Leuvensteijn, 2013).

Although the transformation has paid off handsomely, there is still much more to be done. Balance sheets have improved significantly from the early 1990s, when many banks were on the brink of technical insolvency. Their capital base is much stronger and provisions rival those of top banks in the advanced economies. This will help contain the risks associated with a cycle of rising bad debt, underpin the continued overseas expansion of China's banks in the years ahead and, in turn, support RMB internationalization. The profitability of most banks has increased massively during the past 15 years, with the sector expanding at a double-digit pace (see Table 5.6). Corporate governance and

TABLE 5.6 The Chinese banking sector by assets (2005–2014)

	Total bank assets		Share of total bank assets			
	RMB trillion	% of GDP	Big 5	Policy banks	Foreign	Others
2005	37.5	201.6	56.1	7.8	1.9	34.2
2006	43.9	201.9	55.1	7.9	2.1	34.8
2007	53.1	198.2	53.7	8.1	2.4	35.9
2008	63.2	199.4	51.6	8.9	2.1	37.3
2009	79.5	230.1	51.3	8.7	1.7	38.3
2010	95.3	233.1	49.2	8.0	1.8	40.9
2011	113.3	234.0	47.3	8.2	1.9	42.5
2012	133.6	250.2	44.9	8.4	1.8	44.9
2013	151.4	257.4	43.3	8.3	1.7	46.7
2014	172.3	270.8	41.2		1.6	

Notes: "Big 5" refers to the Bank of China, Industrial and Commercial Bank of China, Construction Bank of China, Agriculture Bank of China and Bank of Communications. "Others" includes share-holding banks, city and rural commercial banks and rural and urban credit cooperatives.
Data Source: CEIC

supervisory capacity are also being strengthened, as the CBRC implements the Basel III rules more forcefully.

Although the sector weathered the GFC reasonably well, it has since experienced difficulties, including fallout from aggressive borrowing by LGFVs and the expansion of under-regulated shadow banking (Sheng and Ng, 2015). High leverage could also weigh on the economic-growth momentum and poison banks' asset quality, because earnings are expected to slow considerably in the coming years. The state remains the controlling shareholder of all the major banks and reserve requirements remain punitively high by international standards (Ma, Yan and Liu, 2012; McCauley and Ma, 2015). The official non-performing ratio of below 2% may be understated; some foreign analysts believe that, using international standards, the level was several times higher even before the stock-market crash. Interest-rate deregulation and easier market entry may also intensify competitive pressure and further squeeze margins. The downswing in China's business cycle could also add to asset-quality woes. Indeed, we are likely to witness gradual disintermediation and possible outright deleveraging in the economy over the coming decade.

Thus, there are real questions about whether the domestic banking sector still offers attractive opportunities to foreigners and, equally, whether local banks can continue expanding overseas. Both matter to the pace and extent of RMB internationalization. Japan's banking crisis of the early 1990s, for example, might have derailed the process for the JPY (Takagi, 2012).

How Open is China's Banking Sector?

A key indicator of a market's openness is the involvement of foreign players. By that measure, China's banking sector does not fare well. Foreign involvement or penetration has consistently been low. Foreign banks' share of the market, as measured by bank loans or deposits, has been mostly below 2% over the past decade (see Table 5.6).

The GFC is partly to blame for the low penetration of foreign banks in the Chinese banking market, as measured by the share of either loans or deposits. China's massive RMB4 trillion stimulus response resulted in a surge in bank credit over 2009–2010. However, most new loans were to fund local-government investment projects and local banks were the major beneficiaries of this business. As well, the balance sheets of many major international banks were badly hit by the crisis. Combined with the introduction of tighter rules by regulators in their home markets, this dampened both their risk appetite and their capacity to expand in emerging markets, including China.

However, China's capital controls have also contributed to the small share of foreign banks in China's home market. Given their limited branch networks in China, foreign banks often depend heavily on offshore funding. Thus, capital controls and FX regulations have impeded their ability to efficiently and flexibly operate (Ma and McCauley, 2013, 2014). Foreign-debt and -guarantee quotas, as well as rules on loan-to-deposit ratios and net open foreign-currency positions, have proved onerous for foreign banks. Among other things, these restrict offshore-funding flows and require local deposits to form a major part of overall funding. It was not until 2011 that foreign banks finally received regulatory treatment similar to their domestic competitors.

On top of this, foreign banks faced heavy capital requirements for opening new branches, as well as tight ceilings on ownership in local banks. (The heavy capital requirements will be phased out in 2015.) As of September 2014, only a total of 51 foreign banks operated 42 legal entities, 92 branches and 187 representative offices in China.

TABLE 5.7 Deposits and loans of domestic and foreign banks in China

	Deposits (RMB bn)			Loans (RMB bn)		
	Foreign banks	China total	Foreign banks' share (%)	Foreign banks	China total	Foreign banks' share (%)
2005	179	30,021	0.6	321	20,684	1.6
2010	968	73,338	1.3	848	50,923	1.7
2011	1,220	82,670	1.5	947	58,189	1.6
2012	1,307	94,310	1.4	1,126	67,287	1.7
2013	1,511	107,059	1.4	1,198	76,633	1.6
2014	1,573	117,373	1.3	1,320	86,787	1.5

Data Source: CEIC

In summary, more than a decade after China was granted entry to the WTO, foreign banks' market penetration, as measured by the foreign share of bank loans or deposits, is only less than 2%. By many other measures, its banking sector is far from open – even when compared with other emerging markets, including India (Ma and McCauley, 2013, 2014). Nonetheless, as shown in Tables 5.7 and 5.8, the foreign share of China's banking sector is larger than in Japan, in terms of both deposits (1.2% of the Japanese total in 2013) and loans (1.5%). As well, the decline in foreign banks' share of business in Japan during the past decade has been

TABLE 5.8 Domestic and foreign banking deposits in Japan

	Deposits (JPY bn)			Loans (JPY bn)		
	Foreign banks	Japan total	Foreign banks' share (%)	Foreign banks	Japan total	Foreign banks' share (%)
2005	15,725	544,635	2.9	10,411	430,128	2.4
2010	4,398	585,569	0.8	7,841	458,173	1.7
2011	5,460	601,615	0.9	6,459	462,585	1.4
2012	5,923	615,711	1.0	5,913	477,689	1.2
2013	7,729	649,438	1.2	7,352	492,533	1.5
2014	8,424	670,877	1.3	8,166	511,984	1.6

Data Source: CEIC

sharper than in China. One reason for the low penetration in both economies may be that they have been surplus economies and, thus, have had less need for offshore funding and foreign financing.

In contrast, China's RMB deposit base, amounting to about 180% of GDP, offers a potentially huge asset class for non-residents. By the end of 2014, non-resident onshore RMB deposits reached RMB2.5 trillion, which were only 2.32% of total onshore deposits but exceeded the total offshore deposits estimated at about RMB2 trillion. With further capital-account opening, non-resident onshore deposits should increase substantially and far outpace the offshore deposits that attract so much media attention (see Chapter 7 on offshore markets).

Outlook: Challenges and Opportunities

Foreign banks' business strategies in China naturally enough have been skewed toward their perceived advantages. Thus, they tend to focus more on corporate than retail clients, for example. (It would be difficult for them to compete with the local banks' huge networks, some of which encompass more than 10,000 branches.) Trade finance is another important segment, given their international networks and China's status as a major trading nation.

Interestingly, some foreign banks have ventured into SME lending. Big Chinese state banks may not have a strong edge in this new field, despite the government policy to promote SME loans. The Bank of East Asia, for example, claims that its small and micro-enterprises business may come to account for as much as 20% of its profit in China over the next few years. Meanwhile, Standard Chartered Bank recently raised RMB5 billion to support its small and micro-loan business.

Nonetheless, foreign banks may face an uphill battle because of slower trade growth, increased market competition, a disadvantage in the vast retail-banking field and growing domestic incursions into the wealth-management business.

With trade financing a major source of income for most foreign banks in China, their revenue is likely to be significantly affected by the current downturn in China's trade. Indeed, slower trade has been a major factor in their decreasing profits since 2011. The subdued global-trade outlook (Constantinescu, Mattoo and Ruta, 2014) is likely to exacerbate this.

Competitive pressure is also set to intensify. With more than 40 foreign banks chasing a market share of only about 2% of the total, the competition is fierce – not only among themselves, but also against dominant local players. Foreign banks also face higher operating costs and may experience thinner margins in the wake of further interest-rate liberalization and an increase in the number of banks because of Chinese official policy for increased market entries. Banking scandals and controversies around the world do not help.

Retail banking in China is particularly challenging for foreigners, given the local banks' vast branch networks. As of July 2013, only HSBC, Standard Chartered Bank and possibly Bank of East Asia had more than 100 branches and offices in China. Royal Bank of Scotland sold its whole Chinese retail-banking business in 2009.

Finally, foreign banks' wealth-management niche is coming under pressure. Capital-account controls have always restricted the potential to fully service high-wealth individuals. However, domestic banks have also begun to expand rapidly into private banking for their large customer base in China, as well as expanding their networks overseas. Moreover, a significant proportion of foreign banks' wealth-management products suffered big losses during the GFC, further undermining the confidence of Chinese investors in foreign banks.

Despite the many challenges, we see some opportunities ahead for foreigners pursuing RMB-banking business. The most important factor is the size and still robust pace of the economy. China's per capita GDP now exceeds USD7,500, highlighting an emerging but significant middle class of consumers. The country's exceptionally high savings rate offers significant potential for investment services, as well as decent purchasing power once the savings rate normalizes. The fast pace of urbanization and rising living standards will increase demand for banking services. Advances in information technology and government policies favoring innovation may yet offer a way to overcome the current disadvantage of limited branch networks.

In addition, the regulatory regime has become less restrictive for foreign banks. Late in 2014, for example, the CBRC started removing the minimum operational capital requirement for foreign- or joint-bank branches, a policy that will be implemented fully in 2015. It has also made it easier for foreign banks to apply for RMB-business licenses for branches in China.

Moreover, interest-rate deregulation, capital-account opening and RMB internationalization will also spur new opportunities. Cross-border business plays to foreign banks' natural advantage. Meanwhile, Chinese banks can use offshore RMB business to help their overseas ventures.

Thus, further RMB internationalization and capital-account liberalization will provide more business opportunities for both Chinese and foreign banks. Similarly, in a more liberalized interest-rate environment, customers will be more willing to use financial derivatives to hedge risks. Foreign banks are more experienced in designing such products, although domestic banks have plenty of incentive to learn quickly.

The two-way, cross-border RMB cash-pooling scheme started in late 2014 is proving to be popular with both foreign and Chinese multinationals because it enables them to centralize their RMB credit and debit positions among their onshore and offshore subsidiaries in whatever way benefits them most. There are two versions of the scheme. One applies only to the SFTZ and the other nationwide. With three more free-trade zones to be fully operational in 2015, these two versions of the RMB cash-pooling scheme are set to expand and converge quickly. They offer huge business potential for foreign banks, which enjoy a natural edge in managing cross-border transactions. Nevertheless, Chinese banks are actively participating as they follow their customers and beef up their overseas capabilities.

As of late 2014, there were 45 bank branches in the SFTZ, of which 23 belonged to foreign banks. Some 20,000 companies (of which 1,200 were foreign-funded enterprises) are registered in the SFTZ, with 3,000 having already set up the special RMB accounts required for cross-border cash pooling. From April 2015, these accounts could also handle foreign-currency transactions. We expect these to increase significantly in the next few years.

Finally, China's "One Belt, One Road" strategy aims to promote infrastructure investment, enhance communications and deepen financial cooperation across the Asia-Pacific region. This is likely to promote RMB internationalization and provide new business opportunities for Chinese and foreign banks along strategic routes, both onshore and offshore. China is also driving the AIIB and has set up a USD62 billion Silk Road Fund, as well as injecting a further USD62 billion of its FX reserves as entrusted debt for equity into the policy banks of CDB and China Exim Bank. They are expected to play a key role in supporting domestic and overseas infrastructure projects, which is likely to also boost offshore use of the RMB.

Nevertheless, our baseline case for 2020 is that China's banking sector will slow noticeably due to a mixture of disintermediation, asset-quality challenges and compressed margins. As an indication, we expect total onshore RMB deposits to grow at an 8% annual rate over

2015–2020, compared with 10% for nominal GDP and 12% for the bond market. We also expect the deposit and loan shares of foreign banks operating in China to rise slightly, with both likely reaching 3% by 2020, compared with an average of less than 2% over 2010–2014.

More importantly, we expect non-resident onshore RMB deposits as a proportion of the total to rise from 2.1% in 2014 to 5.0% of the total by 2020. That will be the result of a much more open capital account. Total non-resident onshore RMB deposits could therefore more than triple to almost RMB10 trillion (USD1.7 trillion) by 2020 – easily twice that of the expected total offshore RMB deposits at that time. In short, the weight of investable RMB financial assets will remain onshore.

CONCLUSION

Despite its rapid expansion, China's modern stock market remains plagued by fundamental flaws, given the government's dominant but conflicting roles and weak institutions. A functioning stock market would enhance capital-allocation efficiency while rebalancing the country's financing structure and assisting much-needed deleveraging. A fast-growing and open Chinese equity market could see foreign holdings increase tenfold by 2020, serving as a potential global asset class and supporting RMB internationalization.

China's banking sector has undergone major transformations over the years, and today still dominates the nation's financial system. The sector still accounts for the single largest RMB financial asset globally, but is expected to slow over the next decade, mainly due to deleveraging, disintermediation and compressed margins. By 2020, we expect non-resident onshore RMB deposits to be twice the size of total offshore RMB deposits.

REFERENCES

Allen, F., Qian, J., Shan, S. and Zhu, J. (2014) Explaining the underperformance of the Chinese stock market. Draft.

Chen, Z. (2013) Capital freedom in China as viewed from the evolution of the stock market. *Cato Journal* 33(3), 587–601.

Constantinescu, C., Mattoo, A. and Ruta, M. (2015) The global trade slowdown: Cyclical or structural? IMF Working Paper, 15/6.

Ma, G. (2007) Who pays China's bank restructuring bill? *Asian Economic Papers* 6(1), 46–71.

Ma, G. and Fung, B. (2002) China's asset management corporations. BIS Working Papers, No. 115.

Ma, G. and McCauley, R. (2013) Is China or India more financially open? *Journal of International Money and Finance* 39, 6–27.

Ma, G. and McCauley, R. (2014) Financial openness of China and India – implications for capital account liberalization. In Song, L., Garnaut, R. and Fang, C. (eds), *Deepening Reform for China's Long-Term Growth and Development*. Australian National University Press: Canberra.

Ma, G., Yan, X. and Liu, X. (2012) China's reserve requirements: Practices, effects and implications. *China Economic Policy Review* 1(2), 1–34.

McCauley, R. and Ma, G. (2015) Transforming central bank liabilities into government debt: The case of China. Draft working paper.

MSCI (2014) Consultation on China A-Shares Index Inclusion Roadmap, March.

Ramzy, A. (2015) Plunge in Chinese stocks leads to bull market for gallows humor. *New York Times*, July 15.

Sheng, A. and Ng, C.-S. (2015) Bringing Shadow Banking into the Light: Opportunity for Financial Reform in China. Fung Global Institute Report.

Takagi, S. (2012) Internationalizing the yen, 1984–2003: Unfinished agenda or mission impossible? Currency internationalization: Lessons from the global financial crisis and prospects for the future in Asia and the Pacific. BIS Papers, No. 61, pp. 75–92.

Xu, B., van Rixtel, A. and van Leuvensteijn, M. (2013) Measuring bank competition in China: A comparison of new versus conventional approaches applied to loan markets. BIS Working Papers, No. 422.

CHAPTER 6

RISING FX TURNOVER OF THE RMB

By definition, a major international currency is widely and actively traded in the FX market globally and used extensively among non-residents offshore. This chapter examines the RMB FX market that extends well beyond the still partially closed onshore RMB market. In terms of global FX-turnover ranking, the RMB is rising rapidly, but at number 9 is still grossly underweight. The next chapter will show that Beijing has been tapping offshore RMB markets to promote external use of the RMB, given its concerns about a more open capital account and the associated more volatile capital flows, with Hong Kong as the premier offshore RMB center.

FX-market turnover is both a cause and a consequence of the more international RMB. By 2020, we believe that RMB daily turnover could increase eightfold to about USD1 trillion, which would place it among the world's five most-traded currencies – after the JPY and ahead of the GBP. This projected rise in the RMB FX trading is principally driven by China's rising weight in world GDP and trade, more flexible exchange rate policy and considerably more open capital account, which should give rise to larger and more volatile capital flows as well as an expanded international balance sheet of assets and liabilities.

COULD THE MARKET ACCOMMODATE MORE GLOBAL CURRENCIES?

To be meaningful globally, a currency must trade actively against most others in the FX market and across all trading zones and be used widely abroad for the likes of commerce, investment, positioning and hedging.

If thinly traded, a currency is unlikely to be meaningful for even commercial settlements or invoicing, let alone for investment or as a reserve currency.

As measured by trading volume, FX is easily the biggest global financial market. For an international currency, its market operates onshore and offshore as well as across borders, linking to both commercial and financial transactions and involving a wide range of financial markets, from the bond market, stock market and money market to their derivatives. According to the BIS 2013 Triennial Central Bank Survey of Foreign Exchange and Derivatives Market Activity (BIS, 2013), global daily FX turnover reached USD5.3 trillion in 2013, dwarfing the stock-market daily average of "only" USD220 billion.

Yet, in reality, FX-market liquidity is concentrated within only a few major currencies. This is mainly to avoid the major inefficiencies of trading more than a few currencies, along with market inertia and the strong positive externalities related to network effects in the currency market. A currency is widely used in part because everyone else uses it.

The USD is by far the dominant global currency, accounting for more than 40% of global FX turnover. When added to the EUR and JPY, this rises to 75% of the global FX turnover (see Figure 6.1). The remainder of the aggregate FX turnover is divided among 60 other currencies, according to the BIS survey. The RMB accounts for a tiny 1% of global FX turnover. Therefore, currency traders call the USD a "vehicle" currency, since it is often cheaper and faster for the Mexican peso (MXN) and the Philippine peso (PHP), for instance, to exchange through two separate legs of USD/MXN and PHP/USD rather than for the two pesos to trade directly against each other.

The FX market currently has three tiers of currencies, with the USD at the top, then a small group of three to five currencies, and far below about 60 other currencies (Figure 6.1). We designate the top two tiers as "global currencies" here. Some of the smaller currencies may be actively traded, but are not meaningful globally for our purposes. This three-tier structure in the global FX market has been broadly stable over the past three decades. As a baseline scenario, we expect the USD to continue to dominate over the next two decades. A multipolar-currency regime is possible by 2030, but most unlikely before 2020.

Is there scope for additional global currencies or is the FX market already too crowded? New international currencies offer potential benefits in terms of portfolio diversification, but managing the resulting risks may be too costly. Given the heavy concentration of

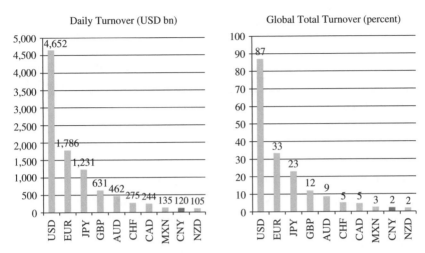

FIGURE 6.1   Top ten most-traded currencies globally, 2013

Notes: The shares of all currencies add up to 200%. USD = US dollar, EUR = Euro dollar, JPY = Japanese yen, GBP = British pound, AUD = Australian dollar, CHF = Swiss franc, CAD = Canadian dollar, MXN = Mexican peso, CNY = Chinese RMB, NZD = New Zealand dollar.

Data Source: BIS

FX-market liquidity, the higher hedging costs of less-traded currencies could even outweigh the potential diversification gains, and as a result, traders may see diminishing returns (Ma and Villar, 2014).

Therefore, a more germane question is whether the RMB can achieve second-tier status by 2020, joining the EUR, JPY and GBP. A global portfolio can accommodate only so many currencies, typically weighted toward the few that are already widely used and actively traded. For the RMB to join those ranks, it would have to either share the same liquidity pool or displace one or more second-tier currencies. An expanded FX market could, of course, create room for additional global currencies.

Is the RMB then capable of capturing any such additional turnover? Assuming that rapid reform continues, it seems promising, based on its recent record. Between 2007 and 2013, the key emerging-market currencies' share of global FX turnover rose from 12% to 17%. The RMB appears to have captured a significant portion of this gain (see Table 6.1). As discussed earlier, we estimate that RMB turnover globally at the end of 2014 had doubled from the April 2013 level of USD120 billion reported by the last BIS FX survey.

TABLE 6.1 Emerging-market currency OTC FX turnover, by currency

(USD bn, daily)	2007	2010	2013	2010–2013 growth (%)	2013 global share (%)
EM currencies	415.7	587.5	1,006.6	71.3	18.8
Emerging Asian currencies	236.0	332.9	468.2	40.6	8.8
Chinese RMB	15.0	34.3	119.6	248.7	2.2
HK dollar	89.9	94.0	77.4	(17.7)	1.4
Singapore dollar	38.8	56.3	74.6	32.5	1.4
Korean won	38.4	60.3	64.2	6.5	1.2
Indian rupee	23.6	37.7	52.8	40.1	1.0
Latin American currencies	63.7	90.4	220.9	144.4	4.1
Mexican peso	43.6	49.9	135.3	171.1	2.5
Other EM currencies	116.0	164.2	317.5	93.4	5.9

Note: "Net/net" basis; the global total adds up to 200%.
Data Source: BIS

WHAT DETERMINES THE FX LIQUIDITY OF THE RMB?

What would it take for the RMB to become one of the five top global currencies by 2020? Currently, it ranks ninth, after the MXN and ahead of the NZD, having risen from number 17 in 2010 (see Figure 6.1). Although its share of global FX turnover is only about 1%, trading volume surged by 250% between 2010 and 2013 – an average pace of 50% per annum (see Table 6.1 and Figure 6.2). This is no more than a simple catch-up to its potential, given China's income level and trade volume.

Three key influences on the RMB's share of the global currency market are as follows: China's expanding contribution to global GDP and trade; its evolving exchange-rate policy; and the extent of its capital-account opening. Although the relative size of China's economy and global trade have been growing (see Figure 6.3), two hurdles have kept the RMB punching below weight in terms of its share of global FX-trading turnover.

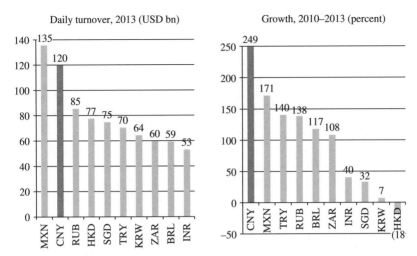

FIGURE 6.2 Top ten traded emerging-market currencies
Notes: MXN = Mexican peso, CNY = Chinese RMB, RUB = Russian
ruble, HKD = Hong Kong dollar, SGD = Singapore dollar, TRY = Turkish
lira, KRW = Korean won, ZAR = South African rand, INR = Indian rupee.
Data Source: BIS

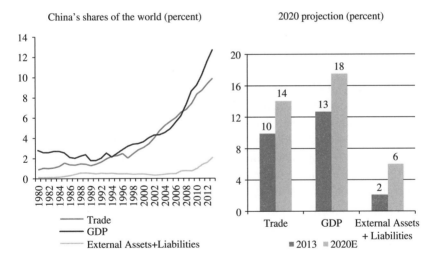

FIGURE 6.3 China's shares of world total
Notes: The 2020 projections are based on the following assumptions (all
expressed in CAGR). (1) Trade, 6.5% for the world and 12% for China. (2)
Nominal GDP in USD: 6% for the world and 11% for China. (3) External
balance sheet: 8% for the world and 25% for China.
Data Sources: BIS, IMF and author's calculations

The first is China's exchange-rate policy. The RMB exchange rate has been heavily managed over the past 20 years. The USD peg introduced in 1994 initially served the Chinese economy well by providing a credible nominal anchor. This became more rigid during the Asian financial crisis. However, in the early 2000s, amid big productivity gains and a weaker USD, the peg began driving significant undervaluation of the RMB, widening China's current-account surplus to a peak of 10% of GDP in 2007. To defend the peg, the PBOC undertook massive USD purchases. Of course, a heavily managed RMB discouraged trading – speculative or otherwise – because no one would want to bet against a determined central bank armed with heavy capital controls and a massive war chest of reserves. Furthermore, Chinese corporations find hedging less rewarding with a highly predictable RMB/USD exchange rate.

The second and more important barrier is China's limited capital-account convertibility. If cross-border financial flows are free, a currency may still be actively traded even under a tight USD peg, as occurs with the HKD. This is in part because the international assets and liabilities of the economy in question would be much larger than otherwise. As discussed in Chapter 3, China's capital controls were among the tightest in the world until quite recently. This limits cross-border capital flows and retards the external balance sheet, thus reducing exposure to currency risk and diminishing hedge needs, thereby dampening RMB trading.

As a result, China's balance sheet of foreign assets and liabilities is miniscule relative to both its trade volume and economic size. Its contribution to global GDP, for example, doubled to 10% over 2003–2013, while its share of global trade trebled to 13% (see Figure 6.3). Although its share of global assets and liabilities increased fivefold over that time, by 2013 this still represented only 2% of the world total. In other words, China has a tiny external balance sheet, which naturally implies relatively low RMB global FX-trading volume, especially if we exclude the huge official foreign-reserve assets from external financial claims.

Thus, a combination of heavy capital controls and a tightly managed exchange rate depresses RMB trading. In April 2013, for example, the RMB was the second-most traded emerging-market currency after the MXN. But considering China's rising income levels and expanding trade flow, RMB turnover remains well below its potential (see Figure 6.4). Indeed, it is even less actively traded than the INR after allowing for trade activity and income level. In summary, such thin trading and heavy management are not conducive to the RMB achieving the status of a meaningful global currency.

2010   2013

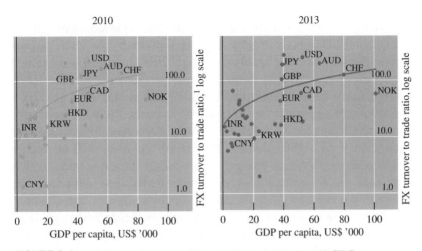

FIGURE 6.4 Ratio of foreign-exchange turnover to trade and GDP
Notes: Foreign-exchange turnover includes not only over-the-counter but
also exchange-traded turnover, which is most significant for the Brazilian
real, the Indian rupee and the Korean won. The estimated relationship,
common to the whole sample (2010 and 2013), is:
$y = 0.492(5.621) + 0.029(5.275) \times -1.96E - 07(-2.754) \times 2$;
Adj $R^2 = 0.41$, total number of observations $= 99$. With $y =$
log(FX turnover/trade) and $x =$ GDP per capita; t-statistics in parentheses.
Data Sources: McCauley and Scatigna (2011); author's estimates

However, it has been catching up fast in recent years, coming ever
closer toward fulfilling its potential (see Figure 6.4). We expect continued substantial increases in RMB trading until 2020, thanks to the past
hurdles turning into new drivers.

First, economic fundamentals and size still favor a more actively
traded RMB globally. China's annual growth should average 6.5% over
2015–2020, while its trade sector may expand 6–8% a year. Although
slower than previously, this will be about twice as fast as the rest of the
world. It will comfortably lift its contribution to global GDP from 13% in
2013 to about 18% by 2020, with its share of global trade rising from
10% to a range of 12–14%. Size may not be everything, but it matters in
the long term (see Figure 6.3). Accordingly, the RMB's share of global
FX turnover is likely to also rise, other things being equal.

Second, the RMB has become more flexible and will become even
more free-floating in the years ahead. Since 2005, it has been managed in
reference to a currency basket, albeit weighted toward the USD (Ma and

McCauley, 2011). Its daily trading band has widened from $\pm 0.5\%$ against the USD initially to $\pm 2\%$. FX interventions by the PBOC appear to have diminished considerably since early 2014. Indeed, having gained over 50% in real (REER) terms over the previous decade, the RMB became fairly valued (confirmed by IMF) and in late 2014 and 2015 overvalued. It weakened for the first time since the PBOC loosened the peg in 2005 and in 2015 PBOC actively intervened to stabilize and strengthen it by selling dollars. Henceforth volatility will be higher and two-way rather than one-way. This makes the carry trade (which depended on a constantly strengthening RMB) less attractive and increases the need for hedging and the opportunities for speculation.

As well, more players, such as non-bank financial institutions, have been allowed to trade RMB onshore, adding to diversity. Furthermore, a fast-growing offshore RMB market, to be discussed in Chapter 7, means that market sentiment may play a bigger role in shaping the dynamics of the exchange rate, both onshore and offshore, thus likely lifting currency volatility. Finally, Beijing has promoted direct bilateral trades of the RMB against more currencies, including the EUR, JPY, GBP, AUD, NZD, SGD, KRW and MYR, albeit with limited success.

Fewer interventions, more-balanced expectations and greater FX-trader diversity all point to a more flexible (or volatile) RMB in the years ahead. That, in turn, should give rise to more diverse market views and greater hedging needs – both of which bode well for growing RMB trade. One major challenge in achieving a more market-oriented exchange rate remains how daily fixing of the RMB can become less policy-driven.

Third, over the past few years China has achieved incremental but quite rapid capital opening via an expansion of more-liberal cross-border capital-flow management schemes (see Chapter 3 for more details). This will increase cross-border flows and expand China's international balance sheet. Hence, underlying currency exposure and the corresponding hedging needs of both Chinese and foreign investors are likely to increase considerably.

Thus, we expect an expanding Chinese economy, a more volatile or flexible RMB, greater two-way cross-border capital flows, a bigger external balance sheet and a more convertible capital account. All of these will work in concert to boost the RMB's FX turnover. Indeed, we expect the RMB turnover to rise much faster than those for the overall global FX market, and emerging-market currencies in particular, on the back of stronger cross-border flows and further expansion and deepening of offshore RMB markets that have been rapidly spreading around the globe.

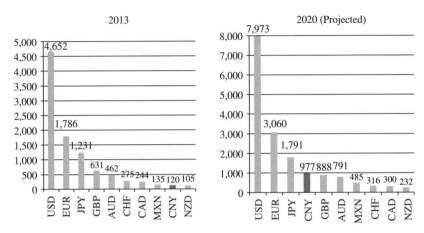

FIGURE 6.5   Top ten traded currencies (daily turnover, USD bn)
Notes: USD = US dollar, EUR = euro, JPY = Japanese yen, GBP = British pound, AUD = Australian dollar, CHF = Swiss franc, CAD = Canadian dollar, MXN = Mexican peso, CNY = Chinese RMB, NZD = New Zealand dollar.
Data Source: BIS

We have reason to believe that RMB trading has already surged since the BIS 2013 survey. Based on our market intelligence and estimates, between April 2013 and the end of 2014, daily turnover in Hong Kong rose 150%, while that in both London and Taipei increased by 90%. In other words, the combined daily turnover of these three offshore centers alone by end-2014 could have far exceeded the RMB's global daily turnover in April 2013. We estimate that by end-2014, global RMB daily turnover may have more than doubled from the USD120 billion reported in the BIS 2013 survey.

Our 2020 projection sees the RMB's average daily FX turnover rise from USD120 billion in 2013 to about USD1 trillion – an eightfold increase or 35% average annual growth rate. The RMB's share of global FX turnover should more than quadruple over that period, from 2% to 10%, if the global total sums to 200% (see Figure 6.5 and Table 6.2).

POTENTIAL FOR RISING RMB TURNOVER BY MARKET SEGMENT

We now examine the outlook for RMB turnover by instrument and geography. Globally, FX derivatives represent 70% of all FX trade, while spot captures 30% (Table 6.3). Recent trends suggest that over

TABLE 6.2 Daily FX turnover of top ten currencies

	2013		Projection 2013–2020			
	(USD bn)	Share (%)	2010–2013 CAGR (%)	2013–2020 CAGR (%)	2020 (USD bn)	2020 share (%)
USD	4,652	87.0	11.3	8.0	7,973	87.0
EUR	1,786	33.4	4.8	8.0	3,060	33.4
JPY	1,231	23.0	17.7	5.5	1,791	19.6
GBP	631	11.8	7.3	5.0	888	9.7
AUD	462	8.6	15.3	8.0	791	8.6
CHF	275	5.2	3.2	2.0	316	3.5
CAD	244	4.6	5.2	3.0	300	3.3
MXN	135	2.5	39.4	20.0	485	5.3
CNY	*120*	*2.2*	*51.7*	*35.0*	*977*	*10.7*
NZD	105	2.0	18.3	12.0	232	2.5
Total	**5,345**	**200.0**	**10.4**	**8.0**	**9,160**	**200.0**

Notes: "Net/net" basis – adjusted for local and cross-border inter-dealer double-counting. USD = US dollar; EUR = euro; JPY = Japanese yen; GBP = British pound; AUD = Australian dollar; CHF = Swiss franc; CAD = Canadian dollar; MXN = Mexican peso; CNY = Chinese yen; NZD = New Zealand dollar.
Data Sources: BIS and author's calculations

2015–2020, FX derivatives are likely to be the main driver behind the expected eightfold rise in turnover over 2013–2020. We suggest the following three reasons.

First, FX derivatives (such as forwards, swaps, options and futures) have been the main drivers behind the recent rapid increase in market turnover in emerging-market jurisdictions (see Table 6.3). As global investors increase their exposure to emerging-market assets, the need to position and hedge naturally also increases.

Next, high-frequency trading, which is important for the spot market, matters less for emerging-market currencies. Thus, derivatives would provide the main source of FX turnover growth for them (and the RMB). The new IMF criteria for inclusion in the SDR, however, happen to focus more on spot than derivatives.

Finally, with a bigger balance sheet of both external assets and liabilities, as well as larger and more active two-way cross-border capital

TABLE 6.3 OTC FX market turnover in emerging markets, by instrument

(USD bn, daily)	2007	2010	2013	2010–2013 growth (%)	Share in EM FX market 2013 (%)
Spot	187.9	202.8	236.8	16.8	30.7
FX derivatives	299.2	380.3	535.5	40.8	69.3
Outright forwards	46.7	73.0	105.8	44.9	13.7
FX swaps	230.6	276.8	373.0	34.8	48.3
Currency swaps	4.0	6.8	8.8	29.4	1.1
Options and others	17.8	23.8	47.9	101.3	6.2
FX market	487.1	583.1	772.3	32.4	100.0
Derivative-to-spot ratio	1.6	1.9	2.3	n.a.	n.a.

Notes: n.a. refers to not available; "net/net" basis; "emerging markets" refers to emerging-market jurisdictions.
Data Source: BIS

flows, both Chinese and foreign investors may see a greater need to hedge against the currency risks associated with a less-managed RMB. If recent trends in emerging markets are any guide, FX swaps, options and futures could lead the way in the expected rise in RMB turnover in the coming years.

We now consider the *geographic location* of RMB trading. Is the RMB likely to be mostly traded onshore or offshore in the coming years? And if offshore, in the likes of London or Asian financial centers? Although the onshore FX market is likely to expand substantially, offshore trading may still dominate RMB turnover. This is not surprising, as a majority of euro trading takes place in London.

We estimate that the global spot share of the RMB turnover in 2013 was 28% and that of FX derivatives was 72% (see Table 6.4). This offshore share of global RMB turnover is higher than those for many emerging-market currencies. One important reason is China's strict requirement of underlying export or import documents for hedging RMB onshore. This discourages pure positioning onshore and, in turn, boosts offshore hedging and positioning, thereby encouraging trading FX derivatives outside the Chinese mainland.

TABLE 6.4 Offshore trading of emerging-market currencies

(USD bn, daily, 2013)	Offshore turnover	Share of global turnover (%)	Shares (%)				
			Regional centers	London	New York	Eurozone	Other
EM currencies	678.7	67.4	—	29.9	16.4	4.6	3.9
Emerging Asian currencies	277.2	59.2	25.3	18.8	8.4	2.6	2.8
Chinese RMB	86.1	72.0	43.7	18.0	5.8	1.5	1.2
HK dollar	40.7	52.6	8.1	22.9	8.9	5.1	5.0
Singapore dollar	48.8	65.4	11.4	27.8	15.5	3.7	5.8
Korean won	27.4	42.7	21.1	11.3	7.1	1.5	1.6
Indian rupee	28.0	53.0	26.9	15.1	8.5	1.1	1.5
Latin American currencies	167.5	75.8	0.4	26.1	40.7	5.2	3.3
Mexican peso	109.6	81.0	0.3	27.5	45.7	4.3	3.2
Other EM currencies	234.0	73.7	0.1	47.5	12.3	6.2	7.7

Note: "Net/net" basis.
Data Source: BIS

According to the BIS 2013 FX survey, more than 40% of global RMB turnover was concentrated in Asian financial centers outside China (mostly Hong Kong, Singapore and, to a lesser extent, Tokyo), as shown in Table 6.4. However, trading has substantially risen since then in both Taipei (to a daily turnover of USD4 billion) and Seoul (USD0.9 billion) – easily surpassing that of Tokyo (USD0.2 billion). Outside Asia, London is the biggest RMB-trading hub globally (see Table 6.4). A recent agreement to establish a hub in Toronto may eventually spur RMB turnover in North America.

Hong Kong's dominance in the offshore RMB market and indeed globally is beyond question, as will be further discussed in Chapter 7. As of April 2013, Hong Kong's daily RMB FX turnover approached USD50 billion (on a "net/gross" basis), bigger than that in the onshore RMB FX market in Shanghai, exceeding the combined total of London and Singapore (about USD24 billion each) and equal to about one-third of the global turnover, according to the BIS FX survey (see Table 6.5).

As of end-2014, Hong Kong appears to be maintaining this lead, given that turnover in Hong Kong rose to above USD100 billion – double that of Shanghai (USD50 billion) and far exceeding Singapore

TABLE 6.5　RMB FX turnover by market (average daily turnover, April 2013)

(USD mn)	Market		
	Onshore	**Offshore**	**Global**
China	33,519		33,519
Hong Kong		49,471	49,471
London		24,279	24,279
Singapore		23,863	23,863
New York		8,620	8,620
Taipei		2,573	2,573
Paris		1,194	1,194
Others		4,051	4,051
Total	**33,519**	**114,051**	**147,570**

Note: "Net/gross" basis; total USD148 billion differs from the "net/net" estimate of USD120 billion.
Data Source: BIS

(USD70 billion) and London (USD40 billion). Based on our estimates, the offshore share of global RMB trading has risen even further. Hong Kong has been the biggest winner in this trend so far.

One key factor influencing the relative shares of onshore and offshore turnovers is the prospect of non-deliverable forwards (NDFs). These are contracts for the difference between an exchange rate agreed months before and the actual spot rate at maturity. RMB NDFs trade exclusively offshore (mostly in Hong Kong, Singapore and London) and were first developed in the mid-1990s to allow offshore investors to circumvent official restrictions on onshore deliverable forwards, known as CNY DFs. As of end-2013, NDF trading repre- sented almost 15% of global RMB turnover and two-thirds of global RMB forward trading (see Table 6.6).

With the emergence from 2011 of a fast-rising market for offshore RMB deliverable forwards, known as CNH DFs, there now exist multiple market segments: one currency (RMB), two spots (CNY for onshore spot and CNH for offshore spot) and three forwards (CNY DFs for onshore deliverable forwards, CNH DFs for offshore deliverable forwards and NDFs for non-deliverable forwards).

This segmentation has evolved in response to China's still-binding capital controls and changing underlying market demand for hedging

TABLE 6.6 RMB forwards: deliverables vs non-deliverables, 2013 (USD mn, daily turnover)

	USD mn			Share (%)		
	DFs	**NDFs**	**Total**	**DFs**	**NDFs**	**Total**
Chinese RMB						
Onshore	2,441	—	2,441	9.2	0	9.2
Offshore	7,102	17,083	24,185	26.7	64.2	90.8
Total	**9,543**	**17,083**	**26,626**	**35.8**	**64.2**	**100**
Six EM currencies						
Onshore	10,138	4,550	14,688	8.9	4	12.8
Offshore	21,543	78,170	99,713	18.8	68.3	87.2
Total	**31,681**	**82,720**	**114,401**	**27.7**	**72.3**	**100**

Notes: DFs = deliverable forwards; NDFs = non-deliverable forwards; "net/ net" basis; the six emerging-market currencies are the Brazilian real, RMB, Indian rupee, Korean won, Russian ruble and New Taiwan dollar.
Data Source: BIS

and positioning. As of April 2013, daily turnover of the three FX forward "brothers" were as follows: USD17.1 billion for NDFs; USD7.1 billion for CNH DFs; USD2.4 billion for CNY DFs. Thus, the NDFs are the "big brother."

This raises questions about the prospects for the three forwards in the run-up to 2020 (McCauley, Chang and Ma, 2014). Given a fast-expanding RMB CNH DF market, will offshore RMB NDFs continue to flourish, just hang on or eventually fade? The answer depends, *inter alia*, on such issues as restrictions, inertia and market efficiency. The experiences of the AUD in the mid-1980s and the RUB in early 2010 suggest that, even after the complete removal of FX restrictions, NDF markets can continue and even trade quite actively. On the contrary, cautious and incomplete capital opening may sustain a vibrant NDF market, allowing onshore DF and mostly offshore NDF markets to develop in parallel, as occurred with the KRW.

That said, the RMB NDF market may follow neither path. Chinese authorities are likely to maintain some restrictions on non-residents' access to the market for CNY DFs for a considerable time, as discussed in Chapter 3. Meanwhile, they are continuing to facilitate a growing RMB pool offshore, in which CNH DFs trade freely. As of 2013, CNH DF turnover was about triple the trading volume of onshore CNY DFs, but only 40% that for offshore NDFs (see Table 6.6).

But over the coming years, the much younger CNH DF market may catch up fast because of its several advantages over the more-established and bigger NDF market. The likely drivers for this include the following: a growing CNH-options market; restricted mandates regarding NDFs for some currency traders; bigger basis risks for the NDF in light of the wider daily CNY trading band; and possible liquidity support for the CNH market generally by the Hong Kong Monetary Authority (HKMA). There is anecdotal evidence of rising CNH DF turnover versus stagnating RMB NDF volume. In our view, both CNY DFs and CNH DFs may accelerate over 2013–2020, with the NDF market continuing, albeit with limited upside. We expect CNH DFs to gain ground on NDFs over this period.

CONCLUSION

In summary, the RMB's share of the global FX market has been rising rapidly. Constrained by capital controls and market underdevelopment, it punches far below its weight, but its power is increasing relatively quickly and liberalization measures will eventually lead to more equal competition. With a growing global role for China's economy, a less-managed currency and a far more open capital account, we expect RMB turnover to increase eightfold, helping make it one of the five most traded currencies by 2020. This expansion would be mostly driven by FX derivatives and offshore market trades, with DFs as the new rising stars of a more internationalized RMB. Together, these developments should result in significantly greater trading thereafter. Finally, the spreading offshore RMB markets together will knit an emerging global RMB trading network around the clock. This bodes well for the RMB becoming a global currency.

REFERENCES

BIS (2013) Triennial Central Bank Survey of Foreign Exchange and Derivatives Market Activity in 2013. Available at: www.bis.org/publ/rpfx13 .htm.

Ma, G. and McCauley, R. (2011) The evolving renminbi regime and implications for Asian currency stability. *Journal of the Japanese and International Economies* 25, 23–38.

Ma, G. and Villar, A. (2014) Internationalisation of emerging market currencies. In *The Transmission of Unconventional Monetary Policy to the Emerging Markets*, BIS Papers No. 78, pp. 71–86.

McCauley, R. and Scatigna, M. (2011) Foreign exchange trading in emerging currencies: More financial, more offshore. BIS Quarterly Review, No. 67.

McCauley, R., Chang, S. and Ma, G. (2014) Non-deliverable forwards: 2013 and beyond. BIS Quarterly Review, March, pp. 75–88.

CHAPTER 7

A SPREADING GLOBAL NETWORK FOR RMB TRADE

A trademark of a global currency is that it settles and trades against most currencies, across many markets and around the clock, so both onshore and offshore markets matter. Nevertheless, in China's case, the role of offshore markets is unique, as Beijing has been tapping offshore RMB markets to promote external use of the RMB, given its initial concerns about a more open capital account and the associated more volatile capital flows. These offshore RMB markets have served as "experimental laboratories" for freely trading RMB outside China, with Hong Kong as the premier offshore RMB center.

In just a few short years, offshore RMB centers have been established across the globe, testament to burgeoning foreign demand and a gathering momentum toward internationalization. They have been rapidly spreading, first to Hong Kong and then other Asian centers, the Middle East, Europe and the Americas, establishing a global trading network. The international use of the RMB has been rapidly advancing along the way from ground zero some ten years ago.

Eventually, these centers and a more financially open Shanghai may form a 24-hour trading network, underpinning the RMB as a potential global currency. The RMB now flows fairly freely cross-border through China's current account and has increasingly become more mobile via various managed investment schemes, which are driving holes in the Chinese wall of capital controls (see Table 3.2 earlier). In short, once it moves offshore, the RMB is, in effect, fully convertible.

THE RMB'S INTERNATIONAL POSITION

Some 10 years ago, the use of the RMB outside China was strictly banned. Then the currency was used informally in petty-cash border trade and increasingly accepted by retailers in Hong Kong, as China traded heavily with its neighbors and mainland tourists into Hong Kong exploded. In 2004, for the first time, Beijing officially permitted Hong Kong residents to convert their dollars into RMB deposits, subject to a daily limit of RMB20,000 per person. This was the first explicit official move by Beijing to experiment with offshore RMB markets while keeping the capital account regulated. In 2009, the first offshore RMB market in Hong Kong took off, following a pilot cross-border RMB trade-settlement scheme.

A decade after that first opening to Hong Kong residents, the scale of external RMB use has increased significantly and reached an impressive level. These still-nascent offshore RMB markets have so far played a central role in the rising external use of the RMB before China's capital account opens up more fully.

Some useful indicators should help put this scale in perspective. For example, RMB use in global payments surged in a few short years but still remained tiny relative to the top currencies of the USD and EUR. SWIFT (2014) data also indicate significant growth in external uses of RMB in payments over the past two years. From October 2012 to September 2014, the global gross RMB-payment flow via SWIFT nearly tripled in value, while "truly offshore" payment flows (global total, excluding China and Hong Kong) increased by 837% between November 2012 and October 2014 (SWIFT, 2014).

In addition, the RMB share of global-payment flows increased significantly in 2014. By end-2014, the RMB was the fifth most-popular currency, accounting for 2.2% of world total payment flow and doubling the amount of one year earlier (see Figure 7.1). Nevertheless, this compares with China's bigger economic weight of 13% in world GDP and remains miniscule compared with the payment flows of the USD and EUR. If the recent momentum is sustained, despite the shock of the 2015 stock-market crash, there is a distinct possibility that by 2020, the RMB can match the EUR and JPY in global payments.

The RMB is also rapidly gaining global-market share in trade finance, rising from just under 2% in January 2012 to almost 9% in October 2013, when it overtook the EUR to become the second-most used currency, albeit a long way behind the USD, which has a global

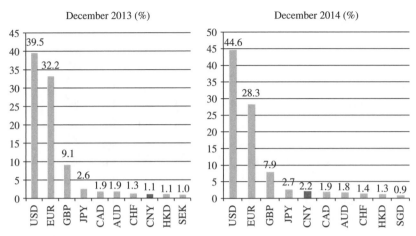

FIGURE 7.1 SWIFT global payment flow by share: top ten currencies
Data Sources: SWIFT; RMB Tracker Reports January 2014 and January 2015

share of 81% in trade financing (see Figure 7.2). China, Hong Kong, Singapore, Germany and Australia are the leading users of RMB for this purpose. Put differently, only 20% of the global RMB use in trade financing took place outside China and Hong Kong.

Not only rising RMB payment flows globally, but also the issuance of RMB-denominated bonds offshore, the so-called "dim sum bonds," is

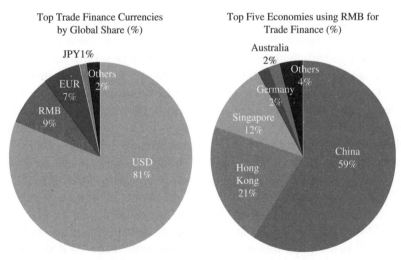

FIGURE 7.2 RMB as a trade finance currency (October 2013)
Data Sources: SWIFT; RMB Tracker Report December 2013

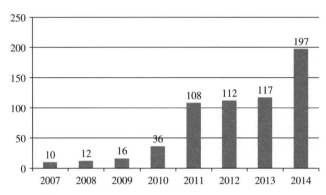

FIGURE 7.3 CNH bond issuance (2007–2014) (RMB bn)
Data Sources: Wind Information and HKMA

expanding substantially. The issuance of RMB-denominated bonds jumped from RMB10 billion in 2007 to almost RMB200 billion in 2014 (see Figure 7.3). However, the pace fluctuated noticeably over time, in response to market sentiment, currency expectations and rate differentials. Most dim sum bonds have so far been issued in Hong Kong, but a few other offshore markets have started witnessing some issuance as well. Furthermore, as will be discussed in Chapter 8, the combined offshore and onshore RMB position in the global official foreign-exchange reserves is probably rising, albeit from ground zero to still below 1% and no more than 1.5% if Chinese reserves are excluded.

The rising external use of the RMB in part reflects international market demand for RMB assets when access to the onshore RMB market remained partially hampered. It also in part indicates a market need for some issuers of dim sum bonds to hedge their long RMB positions, to fund projects in China and to take advantage of lower rates on these dim sum bonds than bank loans in China (Cheung, Ma and McCauley, 2011). In addition, it is in part policy-induced, as Beijing regularly issued RMB-denominated CGBs to build an offshore benchmark yield curve for RMB assets as well as encouraged Chinese policy and commercial banks to issue their own RMB-denominated bonds, so far mostly in Hong Kong. Other financial instruments, such as RMB deposits, have also concentrated in Hong Kong, as we will discuss later in this chapter.

The main liquidity source supporting the expanded international use of RMB is the growing cross-border RMB settlements in trade, other current account transactions, direct investment flows and even some cross-border RMB lending and portfolio flows. This will be discussed in

TABLE 7.1 RMB cross-border payments (2014) (RMB bn)

	RMB payments (A)	China total (B)	Percentage share (A/B)
Merchandise trade payments	4,384	26,240	16.7
Current account payments	6,550	33,347	19.7
Current account and direct investment payments	7,599	35,639	21.2

Data Source: PBOC and CEIC

greater detail later in this chapter. From practically zero in 2009, the cross-border RMB payments to and from China exploded (see Table 7.1). In 2014, these cross-border RMB payments amounted to 20% of China's gross currentaccount transactions and represented more than 20% of its two-way direct investment flows. Our baseline case is that the RMB settlement share in China's international trade by 2020 will rise toward 30% of total exports and imports.

HONG KONG STILL THE DOMINANT OFFSHORE RMB CENTER

The expansion of Hong Kong's RMB market was accompanied by the extension of a cross-border trade-settlement pilot scheme to 20 Chinese provinces and cities in July 2010. Hong Kong has long been a leading entrepôt and investment gateway for China, hosting a cluster of Chinese-bank affiliates and companies.

More importantly, Hong Kong's strong legal system, superior market infrastructure, robust regulatory institutions and proven crisis-management capabilities appeal to Chinese policymakers. Trust between regulators and policymakers in the mainland and Hong Kong is unmatched. However, it should not be taken for granted. Indeed, it was tested by the recent political turbulence in Hong Kong. Such trust takes decades to build but can vanish overnight.

The rapid growth of RMB deposits in Hong Kong has been due largely to net outflows from China via the cross-border trade settlement that had formed a deposit pool exceeding RMB1 trillion by end-2014 (ASIFMA, 2014; Hong Kong Monetary Authority, 2015). This deepening pool, in turn, has underpinned a nascent but rapidly expanding "dim sum" bond market in Hong Kong, as noted earlier. The resulting exposure of companies and investors to RMB currency and liquidity risk has generated demand for hedging instruments and spurred vibrant offshore RMB-FX and money markets there.

A widening range of RMB-related financial products flourish and trade freely in Hong Kong. They include the following: spots; FX and rate swaps; options and futures; CDs and wealth-management products; and even commodities-futures contracts. As of December 2014, the average daily RMB real-time gross-settlement (RTGS) turnover in Hong Kong exceeded RMB880 billion. Since some 90% of this is FX-related, the average daily FX turnover of the CNH (or offshore RMB) there could be approaching the equivalent of USD120 billion – more than twice the estimated USD50 billion daily RMB turnover in Shanghai. Hence, Hong Kong is easily the largest RMB FX market, onshore or offshore, as discussed in Chapter 6.

With its long-established trade and investment links with the mainland, first-mover advantage, a critical mass of China expertise, strong policy support and superior payment and clearing infrastructure, Hong Kong today is clearly a fully fledged and dominant offshore RMB clearing center, as can be viewed in the following five perspectives.

- RMB-trade settlements handled by banks in Hong Kong account for 80–90% of China's overall cross-border RMB trade settlements (see Figure 7.4), far exceeding Hong Kong's share of cross-border settlements (see Table 7.2). This is mainly because many of the cross-border settlements between China/Hong Kong on the one hand, and third parties on the other hand, are handled by Hong Kong-based banks. Indeed, this is even the case for some settlements among third parties.
- SWIFT Watch Data (Medana, 2014) further confirms Hong Kong's position as the premier RMB offshore center, showing that it has captured about 70% of global RMB payments (see Figure 6.7, left panel). By comparison, Singapore – which is the second-largest RMB payments hub – takes only about 8% of gross RMB payments.
- Hong Kong's RMB deposits alone may account for about half of the global offshore total, estimated at RMB2 trillion at the end of 2014. This is about three times the size of deposits in Taipei, the second-largest offshore RMB-deposit center. So far, Hong Kong probably also hosts the majority of RMB-denominated bonds issued offshore globally.

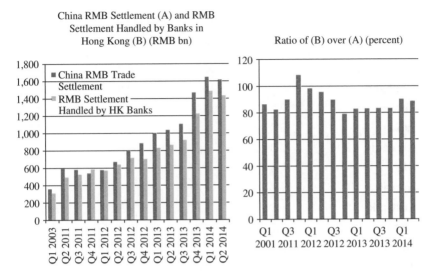

FIGURE 7.4 RMB trade settlements
Data Sources: PBOC, HKMA and BOCHK

- Hong Kong has the lion's share of the RMB270 billion total RQFII quota, dwarfing all other offshore centers combined (see Table 7.3). The Shanghai–Hong Kong Stock Connect, launched in November 2014, will ensure Hong Kong maintains its first-mover advantage in terms of China's ongoing liberalization of two-way cross-border portfolio flows. The Shenzhen–Hong Kong Stock Connect, expected to be rolled out in 2015, will further consolidate Hong Kong's lead. Hong Kong and China have agreed on cross-selling and mutual recognition of their fund management products, which gives Hong Kong-based fund managers a distinct advantage for some years.
- Hong Kong boasts the best RMB clearing and settlement infra-structure of all offshore RMB centers. Its RMB RTGS system is consistent with SWIFT and has extended servicing from 23:00 HKT to 05:00 HKT the next day – in effect, covering the business hours for most trading zones globally.

Therefore, Hong Kong's position as the dominant offshore RMB clearing center is unlikely to be seriously challenged in the foreseeable future. It continues to function as a well-integrated offshore RMB center for retail and corporate banking, as well as capital, money and FX

TABLE 7.2 Share of RMB cross-border settlements (%)

	2011	2012	2013	2014 1H
Hong Kong	61.6	55.7	57.2	53.4
Singapore	8.1	10.0	9.8	10.7
Taiwan	2.5	3.7	4.2	4.4
Japan	2.8	3.2	2.9	3.6
Germany	2.0	2.5	3.0	3.1
UK	1.4	1.7	1.9	2.7
Korea	1.2	1.1	1.7	2.3
Australia	1.5	1.7	1.3	2.1
USA	1.7	1.4	2.0	2.0
Macau	2.7	2.8	2.5	1.9
BVI	0.8	1.1	1.3	1.6
Luxembourg	1.1	1.0	. . .	1.3
Vietnam	1.6	1.5	1.5	1.3
France	1.2	1.1	1.3	1.0
Total	**90.2**	**88.7**	**90.4**	**91.5**

Note: Total is the sum of the listed regions in the table.
Data Source: PBOC

markets. In the long run, it may even develop into a parallel hub competing with a more open Shanghai.

MORE OFFSHORE CENTERS CATCH UP TO SPREAD A GLOBAL NETWORK

Beijing obviously does not want to confine the offshore RMB market largely to Hong Kong. To this end, it appears to have formulated a new global game plan, for the following three reasons.

First, for the RMB to become a global currency, it needs a much wider network of offshore trading and clearing centers. Prolonged lack of coverage in key locations could disrupt activity in major trading zones, thereby dampening economies of scale and network effects, especially in the currency market. More and widespread offshore centers may help form a market infrastructure for an aspiring global RMB.

TABLE 7.3 RMB offshore centers' clearing banks and RQFII programs (RMB bn)

Country (city)	Clearing bank	Appointment	RQFII quota	RQFII approved
		Asia-Pacific		
Hong Kong	Bank of China (Hong Kong)	Nov 2003	270	270
Macau	Bank of China (Macau)	Aug 2004		
Taiwan (Taipei)	Bank of China, Taipei branch	Dec 2012		
Singapore	ICBC, Singapore branch	Feb 2013	50	10
Korea (Seoul)	Bank of Communications (Seoul)	Jul 2014	80	3
Australia (Sydney)	Bank of China, Sydney branch	Nov 2014	50	
Malaysia (Kuala Lumpur)	Bank of China (Malaysia)	Nov 2014		
Thailand (Bangkok)	ICBC (Thai)	Dec 2014		
		Europe		
Germany (Frankfurt)	Bank of China, Frankfurt branch	Jun 2014	80	
UK (London)	China Construction Bank (London)	Jun 2014	80	11
France (Paris)	Bank of China, Paris branch	Sep 2014	80	6
Luxembourg	ICBC, Luxembourg branch	Sep 2014		
Switzerland (Zurich)	Pending	Jan 2015	50	
		EMEA		
Qatar (Doha)	ICBC, Doha branch	Nov 2014	30	
		Americas		
Canada (Toronto)	ICBC (Canada)	Nov 2014	50	
Total			**820**	**300**

Data Sources: HKMA and FGI

159

Second, competition and cooperation among offshore RMB centers will enhance innovation and market efficiency, which will directly facilitate more transactions and trading among non-residents offshore – an ultimate test of internationalization. Thus, a spreading network of offshore RMB centers facilitates the RMB's move toward global currency status.

Third, this emerging network should mutually reinforce and interact with the overseas expansion of Chinese companies, especially banks. Chinese banks had broadened their overseas presence from 29 economies in 2007 to 51 by 2013. Over the same period, the number of their overseas branches and subsidiaries grew from a mere 60 to 1,127, while the value of their combined overseas assets increased fourfold from USD0.3 trillion to USD1.2 trillion.

Beijing is actively helping the spread of this nascent global network with enabling policy measures, along with more robust overseas institutional support for market-based RMB internationalization. We highlight four key areas.

- As noted previously, the PBOC has signed 32 bilateral local-currency swaps with other central-bank peers totaling more than USD3 trillion as of June 2015 (see Chapter 8 for more details). These serve not only as liquidity facilities to promote offshore RMB market development but, according to media reports, have since been activated by some emerging-market nations as emergency funding lines to help manage external-payment pressure. Thus, these swaps may help strengthen the international financial safety net, in addition to promoting commercial use of the RMB offshore.
- Designated Chinese clearing banks initially covered only Greater China and Singapore. However, since 2014, this number has expanded to about 15 centers around the world. As well, the number of offshore RMB centers awarded RQFII quotas has grown from Hong Kong alone to more than ten, with five of them receiving official approval (see Table 7.3).
- Beijing has injected capital from its FX reserves into its two leading policy banks, CDB and China Exim Bank, strengthening their capacity to expand overseas and lend RMB. CDB's foreign-currency loans outstanding at end-2013 exceeded USD250 billion – well above the World Bank's USD152 billion of global net loans outstanding as of June 2014. CDB's total outstanding loans outside China in all currencies amounted to more than USD180 billion at end-2013 (also

exceeding the World Bank's entire loan book). Its offshore RMB-denominated loans outstanding at end-2013 amounted to RMB63 billion (or about USD10 billion). Meanwhile, the fast-growing China Exim Bank supports Chinese firms bidding for overseas infrastructure contracts.

■ Beijing has been actively using its financial strength to establish new sovereign funds and China-sponsored international financial institutions in an attempt to level the playing field globally. Beijing established the "Silk Road Infrastructure Fund," a wholly-owned USD40 billion sovereign-investment fund. China will also fund half of the USD100 billion capital for the Asia Infrastructure Investment Bank jointly with 57 sovereign members. The bank became operational in 2015. The New Development Bank is currently being set up, with USD100 billion capital and equally funded by Brazil, China, India, Russia and South Africa.

Beijing is making strong efforts to build institutions that can help spread offshore RMB centers beyond Hong Kong, first to emerging Asia, then to Europe (including the global-currency trading hub of London), the Middle East and now Toronto, the very first post in North America as well as South America. This offshore RMB network may eventually venture further into new frontiers, such as the rest of the Association of Southeast Asian Nations (ASEAN), Latin America and Africa. Beijing's game plan appears, essentially, to knit a global RMB-trading network, thus promoting its potential global-currency status.

In response to both policy and market forces, other offshore RMB centers have begun chasing Hong Kong. As mentioned earlier, by end-2014, the RMB had become one of the top five payment currencies, according to SWIFT – a leap from number 13 at the start of 2013. More than 140 countries have used the RMB for cross-border payment exchange and it has served as the tender currency in trade settlement in 220 economies (PwC, 2014; SWIFT, 2014). Currently, there are 14 fully functioning offshore RMB clearing centers besides Hong Kong.

Although Hong Kong's pre-eminence looks secure for many years, the broadening of the offshore RMB-trading network has begun encroaching on its market share. The following four recent developments illustrate this trend.

First of all, the proportion of Hong Kong's cross-border settlements handled by Hong Kong-based banks declined from 92% of the global total in 2011 to 83% in 2013, and remained below 90% in 2014 (see Figure 7.4).

TABLE 7.4 Shares of RMB deposits in major Asian offshore centers (percentage of the total of four markets)

	Hong Kong	Taipei	Singapore	Korea	Total
Jun-2013	76.8	7.8	15.2	0.2	100
Sep-2013	73.9	10.0	15.6	0.5	100
Dec-2013	67.3	14.3	15.2	3.2	100
Mar-2014	63.8	18.1	14.8	3.3	100
Jun-2014	59.9	18.9	16.4	4.8	100
Sep-2014	58.0	18.5	15.8	7.7	100

Note: Total is the sum of the four markets.
Data Sources: HKMA, CBC (Taiwan), MAS and BoK

Next, its share of RMB deposits outstanding among the four main Asian RMB centers dropped from well above 90% before 2009 to below 80% by mid-2013 and was down to less than 60% by September 2014 (see Table 7.4). We estimate that Hong Kong's RMB deposit share of the global total may have fallen to about 50% by end-2014. This trend is likely to continue.

Furthermore, Hong Kong's share of global SWIFT RMB payments has also declined noticeably, from about 80% in 2012 to 70% by end-2014 (see Figure 7.5). This trend also looks set to continue.

Finally, the number of offshore RMB centers issuing RMB-denominated bonds is likely to continue growing, which may impinge on Hong Kong's dominance of the "dim sum" bonds market, as discussed earlier.

However, Hong Kong's diminishing dominance should be viewed in the context of a rapidly expanding pie of global offshore RMB business. Hong Kong is getting a smaller share of a much bigger pie. For instance, we estimate that global daily FX turnover of the RMB probably more than doubled from USD120 billion in April 2013 to USD250 billion at end-2014, as discussed in Chapter 6. Global offshore RMB deposits probably expanded from about RMB1.2 trillion in June 2013 to RMB2 trillion at the end of 2014, and we expect them to double to reach RMB4 trillion by 2020.

Specialization has also helped the relative growth of some of the offshore hubs (see Table 7.3). For example, London may leverage its status as the top global FX center and a favorable time zone that enables it to cover Asia, Europe and the US East Coast. Meanwhile, Singapore

Global Shares in October 2014*   HK Share in Global RMB Payment

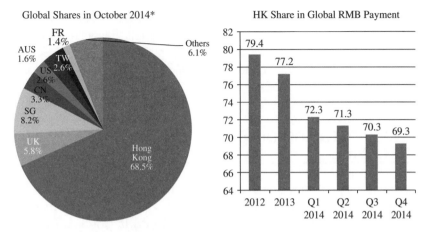

FIGURE 7.5   Global RMB SWIFT payments (2012–2014) (%)
Notes: UK = United Kingdom, SG = Singapore, TW = Taiwan, US = United
States, AUS = Australia, FR = France, CN = China.
* Simple average using monthly data.
Data Sources: SWIFT Watch and Medana (2014)

may take advantage from its position as the third-largest FX trading
center and proximity to other member countries of the ASEAN. Taipei,
Seoul and Sydney could all exploit their strong trade and investment
links to China. RMB turnover in both Taipei and Seoul has already
grown considerably since early 2014. China's energy trade with the
Middle East, Russia and Canada and its other commodities trade with
Latin America and Africa could also support offshore RMB business in
those economies.

Similarly, Luxembourg has taken a lead in offshore RMB funds
management, thanks to its reputation as a global marketing, custodian
and listing hub for the sector. Several asset managers have already
established RMB-denominated funds in Luxembourg, with total assets
under management of RMB256 billion (denominated in RMB), compared with Hong Kong's RMB61 billion in early 2014 (PwC, 2014;
Hong Kong Monetary Authority, 2015).

However, the latest agreement between China and Hong Kong for
mutual recognition and cross-selling of funds could be a game changer,
highlighting Hong Kong's determination to defend its lead in offshore
RMB business. In the foreseeable future, Hong Kong is set to maintain
its status as the global center for RMB trade settlement, financing and

asset management. It will continue to be a fully fledged leading offshore RMB center, serving both wholesale and retail financial services, including currency trading, fixed-income products, banking, equity market, insurance and wealth-management products (Hong Kong Monetary Authority, 2015).

PROSPECTS FOR OFFSHORE RMB CENTERS

As noted above, the global network of offshore RMB centers will continue to expand and may eventually interact with the onshore market.

Toronto became the first offshore RMB center in North America in 2014, offering a trading hub, as well as direct RMB/CAD quotation. SWIFT data also suggest a robust pickup in RMB payment flows with the USA, although these are miniscule compared with USD flows. From April 2013 to April 2014, the value of RMB payments increased by 327%, making the USA the third-largest offshore RMB payment center, outside China and Hong Kong (SWIFT, 2014). Nonetheless, the US share of total global RMB payments remains below 3%.

Africa, Latin America and more ASEAN countries are likely to eventually join the network of offshore RMB centers. Bilateral trade between China and Africa has doubled during the past five years, from USD210 billion to USD107 billion, underlining the huge potential for RMB trade settlements (see Table 7.5). Some African central banks have already invested part of their reserves in RMB assets. China's strong investment in Africa in recent years may help further promote international use of the RMB.

The first Latin American cross-border RMB settlement occurred in 2009 with Brazil. In 2010, CDB denominated half of a USD20 billion loan to Venezuela in RMB. In October 2013, the first RMB-denominated letter of credit in the region was issued for a Peruvian client by Citibank. Overall, ASEAN–China trade rose fivefold between 2003 and 2013 (see Table 7.5). In late 2014, two Chinese RMB-clearing banks were designated to handle transactions settlement for Kuala Lumpur and Bangkok.

However, while the network of offshore RMB centers is expanding rapidly, they remain small relative to those onshore, despite much greater media publicity. As of end-2014, total offshore RMB deposits, for example, amounted to below 2% of those onshore and even less than non-resident onshore deposits (see Chapter 5 for more details).

TABLE 7.5 Imports and exports of China to and from other regions

Value (USD bn)

	2003			2008			2013		
	Import	Export	Total	Import	Export	Total	Import	Export	Total
Asia	272.9	222.6	495.5	702.6	664.1	1,366.7	1,089.9	1,134.1	2,224.0
– ASEAN	47.4	30.9	78.3	117.0	114.1	231.1	199.4	244.1	443.5
Latin America	14.9	11.9	26.8	71.6	71.8	143.4	127.4	134.0	261.4
Africa	8.4	10.2	18.5	56.0	51.2	107.2	117.5	92.8	210.3
Europe	69.7	88.2	157.9	168.1	343.4	511.5	324.2	405.7	729.9
North America	38.3	98.1	136.4	94.1	274.3	368.3	177.7	397.8	575.5
Oceania	8.6	7.3	15.9	40.2	25.9	66.1	108.7	44.6	153.3
Total	412.7	438.2	851.0	1,132.6	1,430.7	2,563.3	1,945.3	2,209.0	4,154.3

CAGR (%)

	2003–2013			2003–2008			2008–2013		
	Import	Export	Total	Import	Export	Total	Import	Export	Total
Asia	14.9	17.7	16.2	20.8	24.4	22.5	9.2	11.3	10.2
– ASEAN	15.5	23.0	18.9	19.8	29.9	24.2	11.3	16.4	13.9
Latin America	23.9	27.4	25.6	36.8	43.3	39.9	12.2	13.3	12.8
Africa	30.2	24.7	27.5	46.3	38.2	42.0	16.0	12.6	14.4
Europe	16.6	16.5	16.5	19.2	31.3	26.5	14.0	3.4	7.4
North America	16.6	15.0	15.5	19.7	22.8	22.0	13.6	7.7	9.3
Oceania	28.9	19.9	25.4	36.2	28.8	33.0	22.0	11.5	18.3
Total	16.8	17.6	17.2	22.4	26.7	24.7	11.4	9.1	10.1

Data Sources: CEIC and FGI calculations

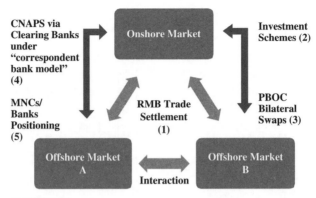

FIGURE 7.6   Channels of interactions onshore and offshore
Source: FGI

Meanwhile, global "dim sum" bonds combined probably also amount to less than 2% of the total onshore bonds and far below non-resident onshore RMB (see Chapter 4 for more details).

FX trading is an exception. The 2013 BIS survey suggests that more than three-quarters of RMB FX turnover took place offshore that year. We estimate that RMB FX turnover in Hong Kong alone at end-2014 was twice that in Shanghai (see Chapter 6 for more details).

Despite the overall discrepancies in size between onshore and offshore, we envisage a steady but rapid convergence of the two markets over time. Figure 7.6 highlights the multiple channels of interaction between onshore and offshore markets. Over time, these distinct channels can widen and reinforce each other to expand the holes in China's opening capital account.

- *Cross-border RMB trade settlements.* These allow flows both ways and are a step beyond simple convertibility under the current account.
- *Cross-border RMB flows via investment schemes.* These include the likes of stock connects, RQFII and QDFII for managing capital flows, as well as special onshore bond market-access plans, RMB cash pooling, cross-border RMB lending and borrowing, the stock-connect schemes and RMB-denominated outward direct investment (ODI) and FDI (see Chapter 3 for more details).

- *Bilateral local-currency swaps.* As discussed previously, these allow other select nations' central banks to tap official RMB liquidity lines, which can trigger both RMB outflows and inflows.
- *Clearing arrangements* (correspondent-bank model). These enable a designated Chinese "clearing" bank to directly access onshore RMB liquidity via the China National Advanced Payment System (CNAPS). These RMB clearing banks are listed in Table 7.3.
- *Foreign arbitrage and positioning.* Multinationals with a presence both onshore and offshore are able to take positions and arbitrage price differentials without engaging in actual cross-border flows.

As China's capital account opens further and the network of offshore RMB centers expands, interactions between the onshore and offshore markets will naturally increase. As discussed earlier, the RMB is "one currency with two spots and three forwards." The current literature (Leung and Fu, 2014) suggests that the causality between onshore and offshore exchange rates can run in either direction, with offshore rates even leading those onshore during market turbulence (see Figure 7.7, left panel). At least, the three forwards track each other closely.

The relationship between onshore and offshore bond yields is more complex, with the onshore yield curve so far little affected by its offshore

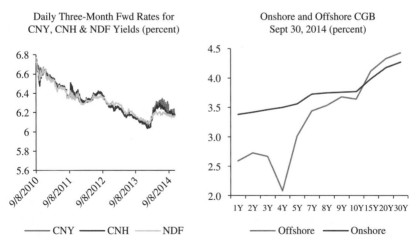

FIGURE 7.7   Daily forward rates and onshore/offshore CGB yields
Data Source: Bloomberg

counterpart. One key reason is the small size of the offshore dim sum bonds and money-market instruments relative to their onshore cousins. By contrast, offshore yields are shaped by both onshore developments and various idiosyncratic factors. As the right panel of Figure 7.7 shows: same obligor, same currency, same tenor . . . but two very distinct curves. How they converge and integrate over time remains to be seen.

To form a meaningful global RMB network, onshore and offshore centers will eventually have to link more closely. So far, market intelligence suggests that the fungibility of RMB liquidity is smooth and efficient across most offshore centers. However, multiple studies also suggest that onshore and offshore arbitrage is still far from perfect and smooth (Craig *et al.*, 2013; Cheung and Rime, 2014; Ma and McCauley, 2014). Many factors may shape their integration, but none is more important than the pace of China's capital-account liberalization (see Chapter 3 for more details).

Here, we briefly examine three technical but important issues of the RMB clearing, settlement and payment infrastructures that are relevant for a more integrated global RMB trading network.

First is the impact of the long-awaited China International Payment System (CIPS), which is reportedly due to be rolled out and tested in 2015, although it may not be fully operational for several years. It is modeled on the US Clearing House Interbank Payments System (CHIPS), and has the potential to reshape the global network of both onshore and offshore RMB clearing centers and all the cross-border RMB payment flows.

Second is the choice of bank model used for cross-border clearing. The correspondent-bank model uses the China National Advanced Payment System (CNAPS), whereas the clearing-bank model taps directly into the PBOC balance sheet. Hong Kong is the only center to use the clearing-bank model and this is due for review in 2016. Longer term, the correspondent-bank model probably makes more sense for China and the expansion of offshore RMB hubs. This is mainly because, under normal circumstances, the central bank should directly provide liquidity backstops only to domestic, not foreign, banks.

Third, the designated clearing banks for all 15 offshore hubs so far have been drawn from among only the so-called Big Five state commercial banks, with only one in each hub. This may reflect the PBOC's cautious approach to cross-border financial flows, especially via banks (Ma and McCauley, 2014). However, once the CIPS is fully functioning, foreign banks should be able to participate to a greater degree in international RMB clearing.

CONCLUSION

In sum, the offshore RMB centers are an integral part of China's three-pronged strategy to internationalize the RMB via offshore-market development, domestic financial liberalization and capital-account opening. The offshore hubs have developed well beyond the experimental stage, although the global network is still in its early days. Nonetheless, they are further evidence of China's determination to build the necessary institutions to support a potentially global RMB. It is also a testimony to the rising international market demand for RMB payments and assets. The potential for a global RMB is much higher if these widespread offshore hubs fully link up with the much bigger onshore RMB market discussed in previous chapters.

We highlight some of our 2020 outlooks for the offshore RMB markets. By 2020, global offshore RMB deposits should double to RMB4 trillion from the estimated total of RMB2 trillion at end-2014, while offshore loans will increase fourfold to RMB1.6 trillion. RMB settlements look set to expand from 20% of gross currentaccount transactions to about one-third. RMB-denominated dim sum bond issuance in Hong Kong should rise from RMB200 billion in 2014 to RMB416 billion. Outstanding "dim sum" bonds issued in Hong Kong are in line to double from RMB340 billion in 2014 to RMB680 billion. Yet no matter how impressive the outlook is for many of these offshore products, we expect a much bigger and more open onshore RMB market to dwarf the offshore one by 2020.

REFERENCES

ASIFMA (2014) RMB Roadmap.
Cheung, Y.-W. and Rime, D. (2014) The offshore renminbi exchange rate: Microstructure and links to the onshore market. Draft article.
Cheung, Y.-W., Ma, G. and McCauley, R. (2011) Renminbising China's foreign assets. *Pacific Economic Review* 16(1), 1–17.
Craig, S., Hua, C., Ng, P. and Yuen, R. (2013) Development of the RMB market in Hong Kong SAR: Assessing onshore–offshore market integration. IMF Working Paper, WP/13/268.

Hong Kong Monetary Authority (2015) Hong Kong: The premier centre for offshore renminbi business.

Leung, D. and Fu, J. (2014) Interactions between CNY and CNH money and forward markets. Hong Kong Institute for Monetary Research Working Paper, 13/2014.

Ma, G. and McCauley, R. (2014) Financial openness of China and India: Implications for capital account liberalization. In Song, L., Garnaut, R. and Fang, C. (eds), *Deepening Reform for China's Long-Term Growth and Development*. Australian National University Press: Canberra; pp. 295–314.

Medana, A. (2014) RMB Seminar AmCham (PowerPoint presentation), December 3.

PwC (2014) Where do you renminbi? A comparative study of cross-border RMB centers. Available at: www.pwc.lu/en/china/docs/pwc-where-do-you-RMB.pdf.

SWIFT (2014) SWIFT RMB Monthly Tracker Reports: various issues.

CHAPTER 8

BRIEF EXAMPLES OF BUSINESS USE OF THE INTERNATIONALIZING RMB

Theoretical analyses of the size of various potential RMB markets lead to impressive growth numbers and Chinese government policies to promote RMB internationalization may sound very thoughtful, but they count for nothing unless businesses see important opportunities to raise profits and cut costs and then act on those opportunities. Behind many of the numbers we have analyzed in previous chapters are real businesses making real business decisions.

In theory, any relaxation of a market constraint should immediately lead to more efficient flows of funds. That is the theory. In the real world, what often happens is, to take the words of a famous Robert Burns' poem of 1785, "The best-laid schemes o' mice an' men/Gang aft agley." In the case of RMB internationalization, so far the theory is actually working. To show how actual businesses are moving, we have chosen a few very brief case studies. None is clearer than the situation of Samsung, a huge, complicated and particularly successful investor in China.

SAMSUNG'S USE OF RMB TO REDUCE FOREIGN EXCHANGE CONVERSION COSTS

Samsung invests USD16.8 billion and employs 123,998 people in China. In 2013, Samsung China achieved a record of USD93.9 billion in revenue and USD43.2 billion in exports (Samsung China, 2013). In March 2013, Samsung China became the first client of the RMB settlement netting service, which benefits from the new deregulation

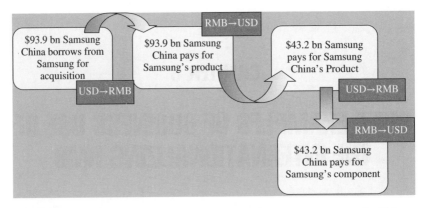

FIGURE 8.1 Samsung cash flow using USD as its treasury currency in China
Data Source: FGI analysis

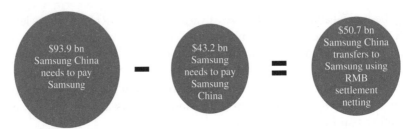

FIGURE 8.2 Samsung treasury management using RMB settlement netting service
Data Source: FGI analysis

policy in China. Prior to this policy, Samsung China needed to pay FX commission fees four times, as the trade and investment along with the inflow and outflow needed to be separate under the previous capital-control policy (Figure 8.1). When RMB could be used as its treasury currency, it saved up to 50–80% of the FX trade and money transfer commission fees (Figure 8.2). China's State Administration of Foreign Exchange (SAFE) in Beijing reports that Samsung China saved up to RMB20 million in costs in a quarter.[1]

A more complicated example is Alstom's revision of its corporate treasury system to incorporate the RMB as one of its treasury currencies.

---

[1]www.financialnews.com.cn/jj/dfjj_1/201305/t20130522_33293.html.

ALSTOM'S USE OF RMB AS CORPORATE TREASURY CURRENCY

Alstom is a leading French company in the area of power, grid and rail solutions with over 30 subsidiaries and 9,000 employees in China. About 80% of the receipts and payments by Alstom China are associated with its intergroup company members outside China.

Alstom China is an early explorer in the field of using RMB as a corporate treasury currency. With the assistance of HSBC, it issued a RMB500 million dim sum bond in Hong Kong in 2012. It was one of the pilots chosen to conduct cross-border netting in China in 2013, and its success led to the February 2014 announcement of the RMB cross-border two-way sweeping cash-pool policy in the Shanghai Free Trade Zone. (In other words, the company was allowed for the first time to treat its offshore and onshore RMB as part of one pool, rather than being required by capital controls to manage them separately.) This policy initiative has just been broadened to cover all multinational companies (MNCs) in China.[2]

Alnet is the current multi-currency payment netting service system in Alstom covering its global intergroup cash receipts and payments, including trade, service and software licenses. Initially, it was not easy to add RMB into Alnet; conversely, the addition means a dramatic change for this multinational company with a business presence in over 100 countries. The successful implementation of RMB centralized payment and netting significantly improves the efficiency of RMB transactions.

Previously, the treasury department at Alstom Beijing needed to confirm the contracts and invoices with various banks in Beijing by telephone, and the onshore RMB hedging required even more compli-cated paperwork. With the introduction of RMB as a corporate treasury currency, all the documents above are delivered by the IT system and the workload quickly declines. In this new system, all the other companies outside China follow the monthly payment schedule on a particular date each month. On the monthly netting day, Alnet will formulate a general report to the global treasury officials, which lists the value and receivers of each payment item and a net balance payment value between all the companies of Alstom in China and the rest of the global members. At this net value, after all the payments in China are first summed into a CNY general account in China, and those outside China to a CNH general account at its treasury center in Hong Kong, these two general accounts

---

[2]cn.reuters.com/article/chinaNews/idCNKBS0IQ04D20141106.

conduct the netting. Xu Liansheng, its Asia-Pacific treasury official, explains that this type of netting system is most suitable for those MNCs with a large volume of intergroup payments between onshore and offshore markets.[3]

Because the banks have checked the invoices, the treasury department just needs to list the invoice information in an Excel spreadsheet, and upload this spreadsheet into the SAFE system to comply with the requirement to report external trade income. When all the payments go through the standard procedure with a protocol of RMB receipts and payments for the global intergroup deal, there will be a reduction of the number of bank accounts in China and of the need for working capital, particularly in foreign currency in its offshore treasury centers. Also, it reduces third-party foreign currency working capital and the number of accounts payable, along with the related FX conversion fees and workloads. It saves more than RMB1 million in costs per year.

Increasingly, MNCs with production presence and sales in China are using RMB to invoice trade with China. With sales in China, the MNCs have a revenue stream in RMB. Starting on July 10, 2013, PBOC[4] allowed intragroup cross-border lending and cash pooling in RMB between onshore and offshore affiliates of the same company. This has helped unlock idle RMB cash in China, which can be used offshore by the MNCs to settle cross-border trade. This is part of a widening trend that MNCs use RMB as a treasury currency for their trade, investment and acquisitions in China. The potential for this to grow is huge, given MNCs' role in China's exports. It is estimated that MNCs contribute over half of China's exports and about 8% of its national GDP. In Shanghai, where 470 MNCs locate their regional headquarters,[5] MNCs create 21% of municipal GDP.[6]

Take the example of Ericsson, the world's leading telecom device and solution provider. About 7% of its global sales and 8% of

[3]blog.sina.com.cn/s/blog_695557320102v42y.html.

[4]The People's Bank of China issued its Circular on Simplifying the Procedures for Cross-Border RMB Business and Improving the Relevant Policies (No. 168) in July 2013. Available at: www.mizuhobank.com/service/global/cndb/express/pdf/R419-0276-XF-0105.pdf. PBOC Shanghai explains its background in *China Finance*, No. 23. Available at: www.cnfinance.cn/magzi/2013-09/25-17993.html.

[5]finance.ifeng.com/a/20141011/13175752_0.shtml.

[6]district.ce.cn/newarea/roll/201408/13/t20140813_3344796.shtml.

expenditures are settled in RMB. Another case is IKEA, which started in 2010 to make payments to selected suppliers in China using RMB from the income of its stores in China.[7] Globally, Volkswagen from Germany has more payments in RMB than in USD. General Motors and General Electric from the USA, Asia Symbol from Singapore and Lion from Japan similarly make large-scale use of RMB treasury.

CHINESE IMPORTERS' PROFIT INCENTIVES FROM USE OF RMB TRADE SETTLEMENT: CHANGHONG

Changhong Electronics is a leading electronics device producer in Sichuan, China, with over RMB58 billion in revenue. Since 2010, it has cooperated with PBOC and PBOC Hong Kong in a trade finance model using RMB letters of credit (LCs) through its subsidiary in Hong Kong (Figure 8.3).[8]

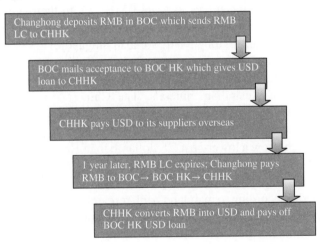

FIGURE 8.3 Changhong case: an importer's RMB LC + offshore USD loan
Data Source: FGI analysis

---

[7]www.dfdaily.com/html/113/2012/9/27/869399.shtml. Zhejiang Jiaxing Yongfa Company, a stainless steel sink manufacturer, became one of the first Chinese suppliers to IKEA in Sweden with the payment settlement entirely in RMB (jx.zjol.com.cn/05jx/system/2013/09/03/019573189.shtml).

[8]www.wccdaily.com.cn/epaper/hxdsb/html/2011-12/06/content_404498.htm.

Previously, Changhong paid its suppliers overseas by T/T; now it delays its payment for a year and guarantees the Chinese bank's issuance of an RMB LC to its subsidiary in Hong Kong, which pays its suppliers in USD without any delay. So, its suppliers would not experience any difference from RMB internationalization at this phase.

The benefit for Changhong is that its payment now yields an RMB interest income at 5.3% by purchasing a one-year financial product from the BOC. Its cost is a US dollar loan for an interest rate of 2.6% in Hong Kong. Thus, the profit margin is 2.7% with an additional gain or loss due to RMB/USD FX rate volatility. Formerly, this provided a virtually guaranteed gain from appreciation, but the RMB now moves in both directions.

There are several sources of increased profit and reduced cost for a company like Changhong using RMB trade settlement.

Interest-Rate Arbitrage

A considerable driver behind the sharp growth in trade settlement is Chinese importers' incentives to issue RMB LCs to their subsidiaries, which are used for swapping into lower-cost US dollar loans in offshore centers (predominantly Hong Kong, some in Singapore) to settle China's import payments. In a typical transaction, the Beijing-based bank of a Chinese importer issues an LC to the importer's affiliate in Hong Kong for purchase of Australian minerals. The Chinese importer deposits collateral with the RMB LC issuing bank. The collateral earns an attractive interest-rate return. The Hong Kong affiliate uses the LC as collateral to borrow a lower-cost US dollar loan in Hong Kong to pay for the commodity imports. The interest-rate arbitrage between the Beijing deposits and the US loan adds a profit margin of about 2.33% to the import trade, according to mainland bank research. Such is the additional profit incentive for Chinese buyers to settle commodities trades with global commodity importers via RMB LCs.

FX Spot- and Forward-Rate Arbitrage

As shown by the Changhong model, RMB payments could yield an automatic gain or loss from RMB appreciation, unless a CNH forward contract is purchased to hedge this "risk." Mostly in 2009–2013, the downside risk was relatively low because of strong foreign appreciation pressure on the RMB rate (left axis in Figure 7.7). Another realistic factor is that it is cheaper for a Chinese importer to buy a cross-currency swap of USD for RMB in Hong Kong than in mainland China through the banks at the Foreign Exchange Trade Center in Shanghai. In 2012–2013, the difference was around 100–200 basis points (right axis in Figure 7.7).

Regulatory Arbitrage

There is strict regulation of US dollar loan and credit business by China's SAFE. In some period of 2011 and 2013, some Chinese traders financing real business deals (as opposed to purely financial operations) often found it was difficult to get the USD LCs, as they were informed that the FX loan and credit quota of commercial banks was exhausted. Meanwhile, Rule #145 from PBOC in 2011[9] clarifies that RMB LCs are not limited by the FX debt exposure quota on a commercial bank and its branches. Rule 20 from SAFE[10] in May 2013 controls each bank branch's scale of foreign currency loans by expanding the requirement of the foreign currency loan/savings ratio below 75%. Our interviews

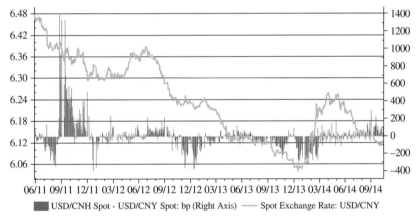

FIGURE 8.4   FX spot rate spread between onshore and offshore markets
Data Sources: Wind Information, PBOC, HKMA, FGI analysis

---

[9]The People's Bank of China issued its Circular on Clarification of Relevant Issues in Connection with Cross-Border RMB Business (No. 145) in June 2011. Available at: www.lawinfochina.com/display.aspx?lib=law&id=8848.

[10]The State Administration of Foreign Exchange issued its Circular on Strengthening the Administration of Foreign Exchange Capital Inflows (No. 20) in May 2013. Available at: www.gov.cn/zwgk/2013-05/06/content_2396347.htm.

with commercial banks in China confirm that these regulatory factors make the RMB-based transactions more attractive.

Reduced Risk

Interviews with businesses confirm that, not surprisingly, as the RMB becomes more volatile, moving in both directions (Figure 8.4), hedging the FX risk becomes much more important. This expands the use of RMB derivatives.

Use of RMB trade settlement reduces risks for the Chinese side, so Chinese buyers and sellers are often willing to give discounts in return for foreigners' acceptance of RMB settlement. US importers like Ford Motor and Victoria Classics have increasingly used RMB settlement with their trade partners from China, who often offer a price discount for the RMB payment. Companies that do not have a source of RMB would obtain RMB short-term loans from banks based in Hong Kong or swap their dollars for RMB in the FOREX market.

CONCLUSION

For the first time, China's outward direct investments are larger than its inward investments. As Chinese companies set up overseas, followed by Chinese banks, they are increasingly using RMB for procurement and investments, as they do in Hong Kong and Singapore. Industrial and Commercial Bank of China (ICBC), which has grown internationally, reported that RMB transactions account for a third of its profits overseas.

As the regulatory environment changes, and as the RMB infrastructure develops, companies are responding more and more quickly to the opportunities. Because China is a huge market, these gradual openings and marketizations, which are often too small to attract media attention, can quickly make million or multi-million dollar differences to companies operating in China or trading with China. The RMB-based modes of operation often start slowly, as China gradually changes the rules and makes institutional adjustments, banks structure new products and, as with Alstom, companies allocate significant efforts and expenditures to adopt new practices. These few examples show how this is working on the ground.

REFERENCE

Samsung China (2013) Social Responsibility Report. Available at: china.samsung .com.cn/News/downfile.

CHAPTER 9

THE RMB AS A RESERVE CURRENCY

Popular discussion about the rise of the RMB typically focuses on whether and when it might challenge the USD as the world's principal reserve currency. This is an interesting question, but we need to keep things in perspective. The RMB is quickly rising in prominence in the day-to-day functioning of the world economy, but its use as a reserve currency will be gradual – while likely impressive over an extended period of time. For many years yet, it will primarily serve purposes other than being the principal buffer against a crisis. Only if we were to experience a global catastrophe is it likely that there would be an early replacement of the USD in this regard. More likely, the RMB will become a second-tier reserve currency like the pound and the yen in the next five years and well beyond.

GLOBAL PERSPECTIVES

The structure of official reserve assets held by central banks has undergone a significant change during the past 15 years – a period in which FX reserves have swollen from USD2 trillion to USD12 trillion, according to the IMF's Currency Composition of Official Foreign Exchange Reserves (COFER) data (IMF, 2015). This growth is partly an attempt by some emerging nations to create a buffer of foreign funds that can be deployed in the event of financial stress, as occurred in the Asian financial crisis. It is also a result of more general imbalances in the

TABLE 9.1 Reserve currencies (as a share of total allocated reserves, %)

	Claims in USD	Claims in GBP	Claims in JPY	Claims in EUR	Claims in other currencies
2003	65.4	2.9	4.4	25.0	2.2
2004	65.5	3.5	4.3	24.7	2.0
2005	66.5	3.7	4.0	23.9	1.9
2006	65.1	4.5	3.5	25.0	2.0
2007	63.9	4.8	3.2	26.1	2.0
2008	63.8	4.2	3.5	26.2	2.3
2009	62.0	4.2	2.9	27.7	3.1
2010	61.8	3.9	3.7	26.0	4.6
2011	62.4	3.8	3.6	24.7	5.5
2012	61.3	4.0	4.1	24.2	6.3
2013	60.9	4.0	3.9	24.5	6.8
2014	62.9	4.9	4.0	22.2	6.9

Data Source: IMF: Currency Composition of Official Foreign Exchange Reserves

global monetary system. As a result, reserves have swollen more dramatically among emerging-market economies.

Such growth has occurred as yields in reserve-currency assets have fallen – a trend that has become more marked since the GFC. The extraordinary monetary policies adopted by the US Fed, the ECB, the BoJ and the BoE to prevent a meltdown of the financial system and real economy are among the principal causes of this yield compression. For example, during the six years from September 2008, yields on 10-year JGBs fell by 97 basis points, US treasuries by 148, British gilts by 238 and German bunds by 339.

Razor-thin or negative real returns – coupled with increasing risks associated with the fiscal strength of some developed economies – have forced reserve managers to reappraise the value of buying what were once believed to be "risk-free" assets. Central bankers have made a partial reallocation of their foreign reserves to alternative currencies and instruments. As a result, holdings of "other" currencies have more than tripled in a decade (see Table 9.1). This includes the purchase of RMB-denominated assets, despite the RMB being the only one expressly designated as not a reserve currency as it did not meet the IMF's "freely usable" criterion (IMF, 2010). (That could change by the time this book is published. See the section on SDR review below.)

SCALE OF RMB HOLDINGS

The absolute value of RMB assets held by central banks is unclear, since they do not break out these holdings when reporting COFER data to the IMF. According to the latest estimate of the PBOC (2015), central banks globally hold some RMB667 billion (USD110 billion) of their foreign reserves in RMB as of early 2015, about 1% of the world total or 1.5% of the non-Chinese reserves. This is about the same amount as the Australian dollar or the Canadian dollar as of end-2014, two of the three currencies the IMF publishes breakdowns for outside the SDR currencies (the Swiss franc is the third, and tiny). By comparison, USD-denominated assets account for more than 60% of declared official reserve holdings. Indeed, the IMF has cited this low use of the RMB, compared with the overall size of China's economy, as a circular reason for not yet including it in the basket of "reserve currencies" that make up its SDRs. Currently, these hybrid international reserve assets are based on a weighted average of the USD, EUR, JPY and GBP. The next review of the SDR composition is due in October 2015 and, as discussed earlier, may have significant ramifications for central-bank RMB holdings.

Although the absolute size of RMB investments is still small, the number of central banks holding RMB reserves has risen significantly. As of late 2014, more than 30 central banks had invested in RMB assets by some accounts. However, there is good reason to believe the figure may already be more than 60, although that is still one-third of the total 177 central banks in the world. More significantly, the increase reflects a fundamental shift in the attitude of central bankers toward the RMB over the past five years, as many more central banks become interested in onshore and offshore RMB markets. This is despite central bankers typically being slow to adapt their reserve-management policies. As such, it may represent a change in how reserve managers are interpreting their traditional investment goals of safety, liquidity and return.

The participation of a number of OECD-member central banks in the RMB markets in recent years represents a major development. Among the more prominent joining the "RMB Club" in 2014 were Banque de

France (BDF), the Reserve Bank of Australia (RBA) and the Swiss National Bank (SNB).

DRIVERS OF CHANGE

There are two key, interconnected dynamics driving RMB use by central banks. First, perceptions about the return and risk of traditional reserve currencies have changed. Yields from assets such as US treasuries, German bunds, JGBs and UK gilts have declined or become negative in real terms. At the same time, the perceived risk associated with these supposedly safe assets has risen. The so-called "Triple-A Club" – economies whose sovereign debt retains the highest credit rating – is becoming ever smaller. The USA, the UK, France, the Netherlands and Finland are among those that have been downgraded by at least one of the three major ratings agencies during the past four years. Japan has been out of the club since the 1990s.

The New Dynamics of Risk and Return

Although the logic of some of the downgrades is questionable, there is no denying the fiscal vulnerability of all the major reserve-currency nations. And this looks set to grow, given their aging populations. According to the IMF (2013), Japan's gross government debt as a percentage of GDP at the end of 2013 was 237.9%; for the USA, it was 106.5; and for the UK, it was 90.3. Increasingly, central bankers describe investments in traditional reserve-currency assets not as "risk-free returns" but as "return-free risk."

Of course, central bankers are concerned primarily with safety and liquidity, rather than returns. After all, ultimately they hold FX reserves to cover import payments, counter portfolio outflows and meet other obligations deemed vital to the smooth running of their economies during crises. Their primary goal is to be able to access the funds when they are needed. Nonetheless, returns from reserves management represent an important revenue stream that, along with seigniorage, covers the cost of many other central-bank activities.

Absent sufficient investment returns, they must raise funds elsewhere. As a worst case, that may involve seeking a government cash injection, with the risk of awkward conditions being attached. Tapping government funds can also publicly highlight the often high cost of carry related to holding central-bank reserves. For example, an emerging nation's sovereign bonds could pay a return that was, say, 50 basis points more than US treasuries. If the central bank invested USD100 billion in US treasuries, rather than domestic bonds, the cost of investing would be USD500 million a year. Indeed, the "paper cost" would be even greater if the country's currency appreciated against the USD.

Nonetheless, a number of central banks, such as the RBA, have secured cash injections when faced with weakened balance sheets and attracted little public criticism (Government of Australia, 2013). However, seeking such help can be challenging for some central banks, especially those at risk of government encroachment in other areas such as setting monetary policy.

These drivers of change have led central banks around the world to reappraise the risks versus returns of their FX holdings in recent years. Many now view alternatives to the likes of low-yielding US treasuries more favorably. Among the increasingly popular alternatives are inflation-linked debt, non-SDR-currency sovereign bonds and deposits, non-government fixed-income debt, emerging-market sovereign debt (denominated in both USD and domestic currencies), equities and even exchange-traded funds (ETFs).

The second important dynamic is the attractiveness of investing in RMB assets. This has been growing now for several years. In part, it reflects China's growing role in international trade, settlement and finance, as well as recognition of Beijing's efforts to promote RMB use in cross-border commercial and financial transactions (see Chapter 7 on offshore RMB markets).

Rise of the RMB

The RMB is now used in about 20% of China's trade. Although this is rising, it is still far lower than the Eurozone's 50–60% and Japan's 30–40%. China's trading partners, especially those that pay for imports in RMB, will need to have easy access to the currency to meet their bills during crises. As a result, holding RMB reserves appears to be sensible in terms of asset and liability management at the national level, providing the country's central bank can access the funds.

One development, albeit untested, that emboldens central banks in this regard is the PBOC's pursuit of a large number of local currency-swap agreements. Table 9.2 shows that by early 2015, the PBOC signed swaps with 32 other central banks exceeding RMB3 trillion (USD485 billion) in total.

TABLE 9.2 China's bilateral local currency swap agreements

Date	Partner central bank	Amount (RMB)	Remarks	Status
20 Jan 2009	Hong Kong Monetary Authority	200 bn	Expires in three years (Jan 2012)	Renewed Nov 22, 2011
8 Feb 2009	Bank Negara Malaysia	80 bn	Expires in three years (Feb 2012)	Expired/renewed Feb 8, 2012
11 Mar 2009	National Bank of the Republic of Belarus	20 bn	Expires in three years (Mar 2012)	Renewed to local currency settlement
23 Mar 2009	Bank of Indonesia	100 bn	Expires in three years (Mar 2012)	Renewed Oct 1, 2013
24 Mar 2010	National Bank of the Republic of Belarus	Agreement on bilateral settlement in local currencies	The first time that China has signed an agreement in local-currency settlement for transactions in general trade with a non-neighboring country	N/A
9 Jun 2010	Central Bank of Iceland	3.5 bn	To promote bilateral trade and investment and strengthen financial cooperation	Renewed Sep 11, 2013
23 Jul 2010	Monetary Authority of Singapore	150 bn	To promote bilateral trade and direct investment	Renewed Mar 7, 2013

22 Nov 2010	Central Bank of the Russian Federation	Direct trading of the Russian ruble with the RMB on the interbank FX market	On Dec 15, 2010 the Russian Moscow Interbank Currency Exchange (MICEX) formally launched RMB/ruble trading	N/A
18 Apr 2011	New Zealand Reserve Bank	25 bn	Expires in three years (Apr 2014)	Renewed Apr 25, 2014
19 Apr 2011	Central Bank of the Republic of Uzbekistan	700mm	Expires in three years (Apr 2014)	Expired
6 May 2011	Central Bank of Mongolia	5 bn	Expires in three years (May 2014)	Renewed Mar 20, 2012
13 Jun 2011	National Bank of Kazakhstan	7 bn	Expires in three years (Jun 2014)	Expired
23 Jun 2011	Central Bank of the Russian Federation	150 bn; bilateral local currency settlement agreement	Expansion of geographical coverage to general, not just border, trade; two countries can conduct settlements and payments for trade in goods and services with the currency of their choice; to deepen financial cooperation and promote bilateral trade and investment	Renewed Oct 13, 2014

(continued)

TABLE 9.2 (*Continued*)

Date	Partner central bank	Amount (RMB)	Remarks	Status
26 Oct 2011	Bank of Korea	360 bn; increased from 180 bn	Renewal; expires in three years (Oct 2014)	Renewed Oct 11, 2014
22 Nov 2011	Hong Kong Monetary Authority	400 bn; increased from 200 bn	Renewal; expires in three years (Nov 2014)	Active
22 Dec 2011	Bank of Thailand	70 bn	Expires in three years (Dec 2014)	Active
23 Dec 2011	State Bank of Pakistan	10 bn	Expires in three years (Dec 2014)	Active
17 Jan 2012	Central Bank of UAE	35 bn	Expires in three years (Jan 2015)	Active
8 Feb 2012	Bank Negara Malaysia	180 bn; increased from 80 bn	Renewal; expires in three years (Feb 2015)	Active
21 Feb 2012	Central Bank of the Republic of Turkey	10 bn	Expires in three years (Feb 2015)	Active
20 Mar 2012	Central Bank of Mongolia	10 bn; increased from 5 bn	Bilateral local currency swap supplement agreement	Revised Aug 21, 2014
22 Mar 2012	Reserve Bank of Australia	200 bn	Expires in three years (Mar 2015)	Active

(continued)

Date	Institution	Amount	Detail	Status
26 Jun 2012	National Bank of Ukraine	15 bn	Expires in three years (Jun 2015)	Active
8 Feb 2013	Monetary Authority of Singapore	Opening of the clearing house for RMB business in Singapore	Industrial and Commercial Bank of China (Singapore)	N/A
7 Mar 2013	Monetary Authority of Singapore	300 bn; increased from 150 bn	Renewal; expires in three years (Mar 2016)	Active
26 Mar 2013	Banco Central do Brazil	190 bn	Expires in three years (Mar 2016)	Active
22 Jun 2013	Bank of England	200 bn	Expires in three years (Jun 2016)	Active
9 Sep 2013	Magyar Nemzeti Bank (Hungarian National Bank)	10 bn	Expires in three years (Sep 2016)	Active
11 Sep 2013	Central Bank of Iceland	3.5 bn	Renewal; expires in three years (Sep 2016)	Active
12 Sep 2013	Bank of Albania	2 bn	Expires in three years (Sep 2016)	Active
1 Oct 2013	Bank of Indonesia	100 bn	Renewal; expires in three years (Oct 2016)	Active
8 Oct 2013	European Central Bank	350 bn	Second-largest swap; expires in three years (Oct 2016)	Active

TABLE 9.2 (*Continued*)

Date	Partner central bank	Amount (RMB)	Remarks	Status
25 Apr 2014	New Zealand Reserve Bank	25 bn	Renewal; expires in three years (Apr 2017)	Active
18 Jul 2014	Central Bank of Argentina	70 bn	Expires in three years (Jul 2017)	Active
21 Jul 2014	Swiss National Bank	150 bn	Expires in three years (Jul 2017)	Active
21 Aug 2014	Central Bank of Mongolia	15 bn; increased from 10 bn	Expires in three years (Aug 2017)	Active
16 Sep 2014	Central Bank of Sri Lanka	10 bn	Expires in three years (Sep 2017)	Active
11 Oct 2014	Bank of Korea	360 bn	Expires in three years (Oct 2017)	Active
13 Oct 2014	Central Bank of the Russian Federation	150 bn	Expires in three years (Oct 2017)	Active
3 Nov 2014	Qatar Central Bank	35 bn	Expires in three years (Nov 2017)	Active
11 Nov 2014	Bank of Canada	200 bn	Expires in three years (Nov 2017)	Active

18 Mar 2015	Central Bank of Suriname	1 bn	Expires in three years (Mar 2018)	Active
25 Mar 2015	Central Bank of Armenia	1 bn	Expires in three years (Mar 2018)	Active
10 Apr 2015	South African Reserve Bank	30 bn	Expires in three years (Apr 2015)	Active
25 May 2015	Central Bank of Chile	22 bn	Expires in three years (May 2018)	Active

Data Source: The People's Bank of China: Highlights of China's Monetary Policy. Available at: www.pbc.gov.cn/english/130727/130882/2881076/index.html

As long as these swaps can be used to back up liquidity for bilateral trade, they can support real market demand for the RMB. There appears to be some confidence that they will. As the BoE's executive director for markets, Chris Salmon, told a National Asset-Liability Conference in 2014: "If RMB activity does grow in London, and if in the future a mismatch in RMB assets and liabilities were to cause financial instability, then the swap would provide a stability-supporting backstop – just as the USD swap did after 2008." The PBOC estimates that as of end-2014, cumulatively more than RMB2 trillion worth of these bilateral swaps had been activated (PBOC, 2015).

EXCHANGING RMB IN A CRISIS

Emergency RMB liquidity facilities are now in place across the globe and are now larger in size than the USD swaps offered by the Fed to cover offshore-trade shortfalls. Meanwhile, RQFII funds have been set up in ten offshore financial centers (see Table 7.3 in Chapter 7 on offshore RMB markets). The UK has enthusiastically pursued RMB business. It has an RMB80 billion RQFII quota (license), offshore clearing via the China Construction Bank, an RMB200 billion swap line with the PBOC and direct GBP/RMB trading in Shanghai. In October 2014, it became the first developed economy to issue an offshore RMB bond, with the RMB3 billion (USD485 million) proceeds added to the BoE's reserves. Until then, the UK's reserves comprised only USD, EUR, JPY and CAD. Nonetheless, the issuance was largely symbolic, amounting to only a fraction, for example, of a GBP2 billion (USD3.1 billion) debut Islamic bond, or *sukuk*, issued a few months earlier, in June 2014.

Offshore clearing is now possible in at least 15 offshore RMB markets (see Table 7.3). The net result of these initiatives is that RMB assets now are being traded more frequently, in more markets and in larger sizes, making them increasingly attractive to reserve managers and other investors.

ONSHORE AND OFFSHORE ACCESS

Most central banks, particularly from larger economies, access RMB investments directly via onshore RMB markets. This is where most

CGBs are traded and investors often can secure better returns than offshore (see Chapter 4). The same CGB, for example, could pay well over 100 basis points more onshore, although since the end of 2014 the spread has narrowed significantly (for more details, see Chapter 6 on offshore RMB markets). Many central banks have longstanding relations with the PBOC that help them invest onshore via the QFII scheme. The BDF's deputy director of market operations, Philippe Mongars, recently described negotiating access as "not a painful, but a lengthy process," due mainly to "some legal hurdles." He advised others seeking access to adopt a new mindset. "The way of communicating can be quite different. Swift messages and emails are not necessarily the best approach." Once a license is approved, central banks then have to address being able to trade in the local time zone.

Fixed-income dealers in Shanghai estimate that 50 to 60 central banks are currently active in China's onshore market. They typically invest in sovereign or policy-bank debt (essentially instruments from institutions with zero risk, as defined by the Basel Accord) and hold to maturity. Indeed, most of their trading activity entails no more than changing the maturity profiles. The PBOC offers clearing services for central banks.

OFFSHORE ALTERNATIVES

Some central banks choose to hold deposits with commercial banks and multilateral bodies offshore or invest via financial-market instruments (see Chapter 7 for more details). This is easier than the onshore option because they do not have to apply for quotas. That said, there are credit risks and exposure limits for both parties. However, the lack of exchange controls provides comfort that the banks could draw on the offshore funds more easily during a crisis, albeit potentially with an uncomfortable "haircut" if it were a severe event. These factors can outweigh the downsides, such as the spread between the onshore and offshore markets, especially for small amounts.

While central banks have totally free access to any offshore RMB markets and the RMB investment products therein, they have also been offered special allocations of RMB-denominated CGBs issued in Hong Kong in a bid to attract longer-term investors. In 2014, RMB2 billion was allocated to seven central banks and monetary authorities. Other central banks have bought offshore government bonds and some are active in RMB futures and other derivatives.

CONSERVATIVES CHANGE COURSE

Apart from Norway, Asian and emerging-market central banks, particularly from Africa and Latin America, were the first to take up RMB investments. For some, this was a natural move, given their proximity to China or their substantial bilateral trade and investment ties with it. As well, central banks with large reserves relative to GDP are more likely to hold assets in excess of their core "liquidity tranche." These excess holdings are usually known as "investment" or "tactical" tranches, and typically they are the sources of RMB investment. This is because of lingering concerns about being able to quickly liquidate the assets, which is a prerequisite for funds held in the liquidity tranches. Yet, the risk–return profiles for assets in some non-SDR currencies may become more attractive, including a strong and higher-yielding RMB. Having said that, RMB liquidity during a crisis has yet to be tested. Since many Asian central banks have built up large FX reserves as a buffer against devaluation pressures, they have sought alternatives to SDR currencies for their investment tranches.

The central banks of more developed economies tend to hold proportionally lower reserves, as they are less concerned about being able to defend their currencies during times of stress. However, these institutions have shown the most marked change in attitude toward the RMB during the past three years. Although they are also largely concerned about being able to liquidate their assets quickly during crises, and they have invested primarily in USD and EUR assets (and to a lesser extent GBP and JPY instruments), they have become more interested in RMB assets recently.

Liquidity, Liquidity, Liquidity

Reserve managers with proportionally lower reserves are usually confident they can liquidate billions of USD treasuries at times of stress. Indeed, the depth of this market was highlighted during the worst of the GFC (see Chapter 4). There has been no such test of the liquidity of RMB assets. Major foreign banks operating in Shanghai, who estimate that central banks hold about RMB300 billion in onshore CCBs and policy-bank debt, say these portfolios are rarely adjusted, other than in terms of maturity profiles. As a result, secondary trading is light and no central bank appears to have exited its sovereign-bond positions outright.

Although untested, there are good reasons to believe that the PBOC would meet its obligations. After all, failure to deliver would have significant ramifications for its reputation. Besides which, China has nearly USD4 trillion of its own reserves to call on if necessary.

Following the Crowd

These are probably among the reasons that a growing number of the world's more conservative central banks have begun investing in RMB. As well, more developing and emerging-market central banks have overhauled their reserves-management strategic-asset allocations. The South African Reserve Bank (SARB), for example, largely followed the strategy of its developed-world peers until three years ago. However, as our case study below shows, it radically changed its approach in 2013, as South Africa's trade and investment exposure to China increased substantially in recent years.

A key reason for these mindset changes is a keener focus on the real asset- and liability-management positions of home countries. As trade with China has grown, especially that denominated in RMB, it has become increasingly important to hold RMB assets to match those liabilities. Such investments also offer the potential for higher and more diversified returns. As well, there is a political dimension. Some central banks have made small RMB investments in hopes of improving relations with the PBOC. Others are pressed to do so by governments keen to boost trade with China. These reasons justify holding RMB in small amounts and accordingly we see large numbers of countries with quite small holdings. Even countries that have promised major investments (such as Nigeria, which said in 2011 that it would invest up to 10% of its reserves in RMB) have made only modest allocations.

ROADBLOCKS AHEAD?

Despite the interest in RMB investments, liquidity and safety remain concerns. As a result, many reserve managers have sought to invest in more liquid currencies they see as RMB proxies. These include sovereign-linked assets of countries that are strong trading partners of China, notably commodities-exporters such as Australia and Canada. Among the advantages are that the necessary funds for investment in AUD and CAD sovereign assets can be allocated not only from "tactical" tranches but also from the "liquidity" tranche.

However, proxy strategies are not without risk, most obviously the danger of a correlation breakdown between an invested and a tracked asset that could cause significant distortions within a portfolio.

Politics can also play a part. Just as favorable diplomatic ties can help to secure the likes of swap lines, offshore licenses and onshore quotas, a diplomatic frost could have a negative impact on central-bank relations. This is a cause for trepidation, particularly among de jure or de facto operationally independent central banks tasked with pursuing a specific monetary policy. If diplomatic relations become strained, some central banks may even pre-emptively defer investing, as appears to have occurred with the BoJ for a while, though the PBOC and the BoJ have lately agreed to cooperate to promote RMB-denominated bond issuance in Tokyo.

Dollar Growing Faster than RMB

The scale of RMB investments must also be viewed in the context of the overall growth of global reserves, which now stand at more than USD12 trillion, compared with USD7 trillion at the onset of the GFC. Table 8.1 reveals that as of 2014, more than 63% of central-bank FX assets were still held in USD and 22% in EUR. Assuming a conservative constant 60% USD allocation, central bankers have added some USD3 trillion of FX reserves to USD assets over about the past five years to 2014. This is many times greater than the entire outstanding value of their RMB holdings. A Central Banking (2014) survey shows that 20% of the 69 reserve managers surveyed (responsible for reserves worth USD6.7 trillion – or 57% of the world's total) said they had no plans to invest in RMB assets at all.

Normalization of Rates

The return of interest rates in the developed world to pre-GFC levels may significantly affect central banks' RMB holdings. With the US Fed having tapered its latest QE program and the BoE considering raising rates, some SDR currencies could become more attractive. That said, many academics and central bankers believe that, long term, rates in developed economies may be far lower than in the past. With the threat of secular stagnation and QE in the Eurozone easing, alongside QQE in Japan, it is unlikely that rates will rise substantially in the next two to three years.

RMB INCLUSION IN SDR

Similarly, the IMF's decision in October 2015 about whether to include the RMB as one of its SDR-component currencies would impact RMB use broadly and in reserves in particular. The review will focus on whether the RMB is "freely usable," given that there is no question of China's already being a "major trading country," which is the other main prerequisite. By some measures, the RMB is already "freely usable" because of offshore trading, China's RMB3 trillion central-bank swap facilities, as well as the creation of the SFTZ and the Hong Kong–Shanghai Stock Connect (see Chapter 3 for more discussion). Some believe that the RMB today may be more convertible than the yen was when it became part of the SDR. Others argue that the inclusion of the RMB in the SDR basket would strengthen the role of the SDR in the international monetary system, whereas its continued omission might exacerbate fragmentation of Bretton Woods institutions and hasten a shift toward a more multipolar world.

The contrary argument, made notably by some US scholars and officials, is that central banks will never, and should never, accept a currency that is subject to capital controls as part of their liquidity reserves.

The RMB's inclusion in the SDR would represent an official acknowledgment of its reserve-currency status. As well, all the central banks of all IMF-member countries would automatically gain RMB exposure via their SDR holdings. It would also probably encourage more central banks to invest in or increase their RMB assets. A publication by the Official Monetary and Financial Institutions Forum (OMFIF) central bank watcher (Marsh, 2015) estimates that it would probably trigger decisions by central banks to roughly double RMB reserve holdings to the equivalent of USD200 billion. Bringing RMB holdings up to the level of the yen or pound sterling would eventually add another USD300 billion. As Marsh notes, this needs to be compared with global official sector assets of USD30 trillion.

Ultimately, therefore, the decision is largely symbolic, given that SDR use is limited. At the Fung Global Institute's June 7, 2015 conference on the RMB, Robert Aliber reminded the audience that Charles Kindleberger had said the SDR is like the universal language Esperanto – a nice idea but not of much practical use. However, the symbolism would be significant, especially in view of the failed US opposition to the AIIB. If the USA strongly opposes the RMB's entry, following its opposition to allies joining the AIIB, it will be understood in China and much of Asia as part of a US campaign to constrain China's influence. That could in turn affect the degree of future cooperation between the established US-oriented institutions (IMF, World Bank, ADB and established clearing institutions) and the newer Chinese-sponsored institutions.

In that context, the key question is whether the world is headed toward an integrated or a divided monetary/financial system. Thus, the decision is less a technical than a political one.

CASE STUDY: THE SOUTH AFRICAN RESERVE BANK

The SARB began to overhaul its reserves-management approach in early 2013, culminating in the rollout of internally and externally managed portfolios from late 2013 to mid-2014. At the heart of the new strategy were changes to the central bank's tranching methodology. SARB created a more traditional "liquidity tranche," containing reserves with an investment horizon of one year that could cover a one-standard-deviation event of capital outflows. The rest of the reserves were then placed in an "investment tranche." The two tranches in total should be able to cover a two-standard-deviation event of capital outflows.

Whereas liquidity-tranche assets must be held in liquid government bonds and cash in liquid currencies, gold and IMF SDRs, investment-tranche assets can be deployed more aggressively, with the aim of mitigating the cost of holding liquid assets on the central bank's balance sheet. Previously, US, UK and European government debt accounted for 95% of SARB's reserve assets. However, its new approach allows for investments in, among others, Chinese, South Korean and Australian debt. SARB also included collateralized-credit instruments in its strategic-asset allocation for the first time.

Investments in China's onshore bond market, as well as the Korean bond market, were completed during the first half of 2014. SARB's head of reserves management, Zafar Parker, says: "Both the Chinese and Korean bond markets are fairly sophisticated, adequately liquid and provide a meaningful risk-adjusted return to the total foreign-exchange reserves."

SARB has explained its new reserves regime at Reserves Advisory and Management Program (RAMP) workshops run by the World Bank. The RAMP scheme is offered to central banks to help them develop sound frameworks with which to manage their reserves.

To activate its onshore RMB portfolio, SARB's financial-market department had to open cash and bond accounts with the PBOC. Once they were open, it then had to fund the accounts by swapping some of its USD into RMB, which were then invested in the onshore bond market. Time-zone and language issues had to be addressed by portfolio managers in South Africa working through Asian trading hours and SARB developing new relationships with local Chinese banks.

CAPITAL-ACCOUNT REFORM

Much will depend on the speed of China's capital-account reform and how the process is managed. Capital-account liberalization will have a major impact on the domestic economy and the global financial system. On the one hand, faster capital-account opening would make the RMB more "freely tradable" and thus better suited to be a reserve currency. On the other hand, central banks and other investors regard the safety and stability of their investments as paramount and would be opposed to policies that could destabilize China's economy and hurt the international system.

As noted in Chapter 3, China has been accelerating its financial liberalization. Interest-rate liberalization, an important support for capital-account opening, is now far advanced. A deposit insurance system has been established to support the banking system, which in turn is to be put on more of a market basis. These decisions provide the foundation for more rapid capital-account opening and, as emphasized in Chapter 3,

Beijing is punching holes in the capital-account controls at an increasing pace.

CONCLUSION

The rise of the RMB as a reserve currency is likely to continue and even accelerate. But this does not mean that the RMB will dislodge the USD any time soon. Nor, indeed, is there any suggestion that this is Beijing's ultimate goal. Barring some catastrophic global event, the USD will remain the dominant reserve currency and the USA will continue to have the deepest financial markets for the foreseeable future. A return to more "normal" levels of interest rates there may even lead to an increased proportion of USD allocations. The EUR will also continue to be an important reserve currency, but if China unifies its bond markets and Europe does not, then the RMB will eventually become far more important. Overall, the global monetary system looks likely to become more multipolar, with the RMB potentially becoming one of the top-three reserve currencies in the next 10 years. In the prudent world of reserve management, the rise of the RMB has been anything but slow.

Under reasonable assumptions about the Chinese bond market development and market opening (see Chapter 4 for more details), the combined foreign holding of CGBs and CDB bonds is expected to rise tenfold between 2015 and 2020, approaching USD1 trillion or 8.5% of the 2014 global foreign reserve of USD11.6 trillion. If half of this is held by reserve managers, then CGBs and CDB bonds could reach 4–5% of the global foreign reserves, easily quadrupling the 2015 level. This would rival the yen or pound shares at the end of 2014. If we exclude the Chinese foreign reserves from the global total, the foreign holdings of CGBs and CDB bond holdings could reach 13% of the 2014 non-Chinese reserve by 2020. Again assuming half of the expected foreign CGBs and CDB bond holdings are under reserve managers, RMB reserve assets in the form of CGBs and CDB bonds can easily exceed 6% of the global non-Chinese reserve by 2020.

Where the RMB will be most important, in what we might characterize as a "reserve function," is in the expanded use of swaps. Increasingly, these are a preferred method of responding to crises. RMB swaps are now larger and more numerous than their USD counterparts (see Table 9.2). This is an important development and may even turn out to be more important than it appears today.

REFERENCES

Central Banking (2014) Central Banking's HSBC Reserve Management Trends 2014.

Government of Australia (2013) Strengthening the Reserve Bank of Australia. Statement by Hon. Joe Hockey, Treasurer, October 22. Available at: jbh. ministers.treasury.gov.au/media-release/011-2013.

IMF (2010) IMF Executive Board Completes the 2010 Review of SDR Valuation. Public Information Notice (PIN), 10/149, November 17.

IMF (2013) World Economic Outlook. Available at: www.imf.org/external/pubs/ft/weo/2013/01/weodata/index.aspx.

IMF (2015) Currency Composition of Official Foreign Exchange Reserves (COFER). Available at: data.imf.org/?sk=E6A5F467-C14B-4AA8-9F6D-5A09EC4E62A4.

Marsh, D. (2015) Chinese SDR inclusion could trigger global asset shift. OMFIF Briefing, May 26, 6 Ed 22.2. Available at: www.omfif.org.

PBOC (2015) A Report on Renminbi Internationalization, May.

CHAPTER 10

CONCLUDING REFLECTIONS

We provided an overview of our findings in Chapter 1 and we shall not duplicate that here. But, after working through the intricacies of what is required for the RMB to become a global currency, a few reflections are appropriate.

The rising use of the RMB as an international currency has been spectacular. Partly because of the low base, the rates of increase sometimes look like rocket trajectories. But it is not just the low bases. China's currency is 1% of global currency trading and its economy will soon be 18% of the global economy. Given the "winner-takes-all" nature of the currency hierarchy, we do not expect the RMB to come anywhere close to 18% of trading within the foreseeable future, but we do see a very fast rise to a much larger share. We expect the RMB to be one of the major global currencies. If the current account opening continues, and if the bond market is unified, the RMB should eventually develop a substantial advantage over the yen and the euro. We do expect to see the RMB recognized as a core reserve currency and a component of the SDR, if not in 2015, then within a few years. In some areas, such as trade settlement, the rise of the RMB is already proving transformative.

Rapidly increasing use of the RMB does not occur just because governments plan it and facilitate it. Businesses make the actual decisions, and businesses have found use of an internationalized and less-controlled RMB to be very profitable. Small changes make a huge difference to business. Every relaxation of a constraint increases the profit of some range of businesses. Every time a company can avoid exchanging its RMB for dollars and then exchanging back into RMB creates profit and enthusiasm.

This book-length review of all the changes required to make the RMB a truly global currency has probably taxed the reader. That should remind us of the extraordinarily complex and long list of things that Chinese leaders have to accomplish in order to achieve their goal. They need to move the Chinese economy into a quite new growth model, based on services, SMEs, domestic consumption and innovation rather than copycat manufacturing, SOEs, investment and exports. They need to transform the financial system to allocate resources more efficiently. In the short term, they need to deleverage their economy from serious overindebtedness. They need to transform their stock and bond markets. These tasks, summarized in a few short sentences here, are so complex that it has taken a book to delineate them and to display some of the choices that must be made properly for the process to proceed smoothly.

Behind these economic and financial imperatives are political assumptions. The political system must remain stable; it can change but must do so in a non-disruptive fashion if economic and financial maturation are to succeed. The central government must be able to lead or impose vast changes on local governments and on society. The leadership must be able to get gigantic institutions – PBOC, MOF, NDRC and others – to abandon narrow self-interest and work together to unify the bond market. It must govern with a sufficiently light touch to allow the market to drive the economy and foster innovation, but it must govern with sufficient authority to enforce conflict of interest rules, environmental regulations and much else on a very diverse and turbulent society. These necessities would be difficult in any country; they are ultimate challenges in a society that comprises one-sixth of humanity. We have not dwelt on political prerequisites, but we would be remiss not to note the assumptions.

The complexity of what China faces is daunting. The relatively optimistic tone of our analysis rests on several things. The requirements of RMB internationalization are largely the same as the requirements of reforming the economy for its next stage of growth. Chinese leaders have proven adept at implementing reforms in the face of complexity and conservative opposition. They have set a standard, probably superior to any other government in the modern world, of facing up to the economy's most serious challenges, articulating the issues publicly, designing comprehensive plans and implementing what is necessary to move forward. In the face of momentous challenges, this record is very heartening, but, as every stockbroker's prospectus says, past perform-ance is not a guarantee of future results. For the first three decades of reform, Chinese society accepted strong leadership with a modicum of unity because everyone feared collapse. With the achievement of confidence comes a more complex leadership challenge.

China will pay a substantial price for success at RMB internationalization. To the extent that the RMB is widely accepted as an international currency, there will be more demand for it and it will appreciate. That in turn will create more headwinds for China's manufacturing exports. For this reason Germany, and for long periods Japan, did not want to be home to an international currency. If China's move to a new growth model is going smoothly, such headwinds may be welcome as accelerators of needed change. If the going is rough, if jobs are scarce and workers are protesting, China's leaders could find themselves reconsidering the drive to RMB internationalization.

Likewise, if China exits promptly and thoroughly from its current financial squeeze, and if its new international financial disbursements are allocated efficiently, then all the financial commitments China is making to new international financial institutions and to its "One Belt, One Road" development program will accelerate its success. But even with China's huge financial resources it is possible to get overstretched. The USD4 trillion of reserves are very impressive, but each dollar of reserves was acquired by the government by issuing a bond for a little over RMB6. Those bonds must be serviced; the reserves are not discretionary spending money.

The rise of the RMB is not just a currency development, not just businesses enthusiastically reducing costs and raising profits. It is also part of a global system change. The existing system is based on US leadership, supportive leadership roles for Europe and Japan, USD predominance and the Bretton Woods institutions (World Bank, IMF, plus the ADB). How these interact with the rise of new economies (China, India, Brazil, Mexico, etc.), new institutions (AIIB, NDB, Silk Road Fund, CDB) and newly important currencies (mainly the RMB) is both uncertain and important. Will we gradually evolve the existing system into a new, highly integrated but more balanced system or will the financial world head toward a competing, schismatic system with a US-led part and a Chinese-led part?

Seen from Washington the current situation looks one way; seen from much of Asia it looks a different way.

Seen from much of Asia, a system that worked pretty well from 1944 to almost the end of the 20th century isn't working well anymore. In the Asian crisis of 1997–1998, IMF-imposed austerity plunged Thailand into a deep recession and forced closure of some Indonesian banks in a way that led to collapse of the Indonesian banking system. The USA did not rescue Thailand the way it had rescued Mexico in 1994 (because of congressionally imposed restrictions), and the USA opposed a Japanese effort to set up a supplementary fund that could have helped the countries in crisis because it did not want Japan second-guessing the IMF. The harsh treatment of Indonesia and Thailand was the exact opposite of how the USA and core Europe subsequently reacted to Western crises in 2008, and the IMF's post-GFC decision that capital controls are sometimes appropriate contrasted with blistering Western criticism of Asian capital controls and interventions during the Asian crisis.

In 2008, the GFC, triggered by US and European financial malpractice and weak regulation, proved extremely destructive for Asian economies. It cost many millions of jobs and created a crisis of trade finance that was terrifying to societies dependent on trade for their livelihood. In 2009, the US Congress refused to modernize the governance and capitalization of the Bretton Woods institutions to make them effective in a world where the power relationships of 1944 – when those institutions were structured – are utterly anachronistic. The subsequent, extremely stimulative, monetary policies of the rich countries created a tide of money that caused housing bubbles, staple food inflation and other problems across the emerging markets and subsequently threatened to recede and cause financial crises. The aftermath of the GFC left even Europeans, Japanese and Americans anxious about their currencies; hence the emergence of Bitcoin and other attempts to circumvent the perceived risks of established currencies.

To many Asian observers, not just Chinese, and also to others like the Russians (distinct from geopolitical quarrels), this seems like a global monetary system that is shaky and no longer serves their interests. To much of the world, the US refusal to accept modernization of the Bretton Woods institutions, and its opposition to the formation of desperately needed new institutions to supplement them, are contradictory and insupportable. All these problems add up, in such a view, to systematic malfunction of the post-World War II, US-dominated system.

Seen from Washington the system is working, albeit with some glitches. In this view, the IMF's bad decisions in Thailand and Indonesia were unfortunate, but they weren't US government decisions. That the US Congress had blocked the Treasury from supporting a country like Thailand was regrettable, but a temporary legislative foolishness that should be discounted. If the US Congress blocks modernization of the

Bretton Woods institutions, the world should understand that US presidents of both parties have the right attitude and should regard that as more important. The GFC, in this view, was unexpected and unpredictable, not evidence of a profound systemic flaw. Super-low interest rates for a sustained period were prerequisite to the US recovery and therefore good for the world in the long run; suggestions that the Fed, which is de facto the central bank of the world, should take into consideration what it is doing to the prices of housing in Hong Kong, bread in Tunisia and onions in India are out of line.

Asians increasingly argue that the role of the US Congress in blocking IMF and World Bank reform, weakening bank regulation before the GFC, blocking the Fed from considering the international implications of its decisions and blocking what had come to be expected crisis interventions are now core aspects of how the system works. The IMF's bad decisions don't come across in Asia as separate from US decision-making, but rather as malfunctions of a general system with the USA as the leader; a leader very jealous of threats to diversify the institutions or institutional leadership to take greater account of Asian concerns. In this context it is fair to ask whether, if the US Congress had allowed a more appropriate scale of fiscal stimulus, the Fed might have helped revive the US economy without so much collateral damage to emerging markets.

Influential Americans question whether diversification of the world's leading currencies and other changes will ameliorate the main problems. Certainly, the AIIB and its sister institutions will fill some of the vacuum of infrastructure finance. Will the huge build-up of Asian reserves and the network of swaps modulate the next big crisis? Will diversification of reserve currencies away from the USD reduce losses in coming waves of volatility? While Chinese motives in wanting to amend the system are understandable, the question of whether their proposals will actually reduce the system's risks has not yet been adequately answered.

In dealing with these issues, the US position is awkward at best. Because the US Congress opposes modernization of the Bretton Woods institutions (IMF, World Bank, the later Asian Development Bank), those institutions are increasingly crippled, both for lack of capital and for anachronistic governance. That means, inexorably, that new institutions must arise to fill the vacuum. Those new institutions – AIIB, NDB, Silk Road Fund, the international operations of China Development Bank – are going to have superior resources to the old ones. US refusal to participate in those institutions ensures that they will be dominated by China.

Thus, US policy undermines US influence and maximizes Chinese influence. This does not mean that Chinese leadership will be replacing US leadership and the dominant position of the USD anytime soon. It does make the global monetary system less resilient and more conflictful. In the event of some great financial or geopolitical crisis, change could come much more quickly than would otherwise be likely.

What has happened to date remains perfectly consistent with a future scenario in which the rise of a new currency and new institutions like the AIIB supplement, and modify in constructive ways, an integrated global financial system that enhances global prosperity as much as the post-World War II system did. It is worth remembering that that system facilitated China's success and US policy welcomed that success.

Equally, everything that has happened is perfectly consistent with a future scenario in which US and European jealousy of challenges to their established power leads them to defend a system whose governance is incompatible with the global economic structure of the 21st century, and whose domestic legislative foibles impose ever-greater costs on other countries. Combined with rising Asian nationalism, in India and Indonesia as well as China, which sometimes sees threats where there are none and sometimes asserts itself without adequately reflecting on the consequences, this could lead to a hostile competition that serves nobody well.

The outcome for the international monetary system depends on leadership, not on inexorable laws of politics or economics.

APPENDIX A

CHINA RMB FINANCIAL STATISTICS AND FORECASTS BY OTHER INSTITUTIONS

B ecause much of the material in this book is based on assumptions about the Chinese economy, and because forecasts and scenarios can be controversial, we provide here in Table A.1, for comparison with our own, some current forecasts by the most reputable institutions.

TABLE A.1 Forecast China RMB financial statistics and forecasts by other institutions (for reference)

	RMB current status	Yen current status	HSBC forecast[*]	Standard Chartered forecast[**]	Deutsche Bank forecast
China trade RMB settlement	RMB4.6 trn, 18% of China's trade, 1Q 2014 14% of China's trade, 2Q 2013 An annualized total of USD700 bn (SC)	30–40% of Japan's trade was settled in yen, 2014 (HSBC)	30% of China's trade, 2015; 50% of China-EM trade in RMB, 2015	USD1.167 trn by 2015; 3,043 trn by 2020 28% of China's international trade in RMB, 2020	20%, 25% and 30% of China's trade in 2014, 2015 and 2016
RMB global trade settlement	1.6% of global trade, March 2014 (SC)	2.6% of global trade was settled in yen, October 2013 (SC)	USD2 trn annual trade flows, 2013–2015	3% of global trade, 2020	
FX RMB, daily transaction	USD120 bn, 2013 2.2% of total global FX turnover; 1.3% of GDP and 2.8% of merchandise trade USD34 bn spot + 28 bn outright forwards + 40 bn FX swaps + 17 bn FX options = 119 bn (SC quote BIS data)	Around USD1200 bn, 23.9% of GDP and 83.6% of merchandised trade, 2013 (SC)		Baseline estimate USD500 bn, 2020 USD1 trn, 2020 assuming RMB as fully deliverable currency	

(continued)

Government bonds	SC quotes BIS, mainland accounts for 44 bn, but SC estimates 70% of spot trading is onshore, HK 20%	LCY government bond market 64.9% June 2014 (ADB)	LCY government bond market 92.3%, June 2014 (ADB)
Corporate bonds (including corporate, enterprise, MTN and commercial papers)		25% of total bonds, 12.5% of GDP, 2Q 2013 (HSBC) LCY corporate bond market 35.1%, June 2014 (ADB)	29% of total bonds, around 15% of GDP, 2Q 2013 (HSBC) LCY corporate bond market 7.7%, June 2014 (ADB)
Offshore RMB bonds		Offshore RMB bonds RMB80 bn; CDs 114 bn, 1Q 2014 Dim sum bonds CNY312 bn; CDs CNY222 bn, October 2013 (SC)	Samurai bond market USD94.5 bn, end-2014 (SC)	Offshore RMB bond market will reach CNY700 bn by end of 2014; CNY2 trn by end of 2018; and CNY3 trn by end of 2020. CNY1.8 trn by 2020 as a conservative scenario

TABLE A.1 (*Continued*)

	RMB current status	Yen current status	HSBC forecast[*]	Standard Chartered forecast[**]	Deutsche Bank forecast
Direct financing/total social financing	12.6% of total financing, 2013 (HSBC)		15% of total financing 2015		
HK RMB deposits	RMB950 bn, 1Q 2014 (SC)				CNH2.25 trn, 2014; 4 trn, 2015
HK RMB loans	Around CNY110 bn, 2Q 2013 RMB loan-to-deposit ratio 16%, 2Q 2013; 72% for all currencies in HK (SC)			HKD2.3 trn (20% of HK bank loans), end-2020; should higher exposure shift to RMB (HKD pegged to CNY), it will reach HKD3.8 trn (33% of total bank loans), 2020	RMB bonds and loans CNH870 bn, 2014
Total offshore RMB deposits	RMB1, 411 bn, January 2014 Four major centers Deposits, CDs, bonds and loans reach RMB1.88 trn, end-2013 (SC) Offshore RMB bonds and CDs RMB634 bn, February 2014 (SC)			RMB1.8 trn, end-2014	

Onshore foreign bank total deposits	RMB1, 455 bn, 1.6% of total, 2013 (PBOC)	1.5% of total August 2014 (BoJ, KPMG, FGI)
Onshore foreign bank total loans	RMB2, 075 bn, 1.9% of total, 2013 (PBOC)	1.3% of total August 2014 (BoJ, KPMG, FGI)
Onshore foreign bank total assets	RMB2, 581 bn, 1.82% of total bank assets, 2013 (PBOC)	Yen44,555 bn, 4.79% of total bank assets, 2014 (BoJ, KPMG, FGI)

*HSBC expects RMB fully convertible within two to three years (2016–2017).

**SC projects that China's capital account will be open by 2020.

SC projects China's GDP will reach USD21.8 trm by 2020 on a conservative estimate at 4.6% annual GDP growth.

SC expects the RMB exchange rate to be basically free-floating by 2020.

SC expects RMB CIPS to be fully operational by 2015.

SC looks for the offshore RMB debt market to grow 30% a year, to be worth CNY3 trm by 2020.

Data Sources: FGI analysis, PBOC official website, Bank of Japan official website, Asia Development Bank official website, September 2014. ASIFMA, Standard Chartered Bank and Thomson Reuters, 2014. RMB Roadmap, May 2014. Standard Chartered Bank, 2013. The Renminbi's 2020 Odyssey, November 4, 2013. Qu Hongbin, Sun Junwei, Paul Mackel and Ju Wang, The Rise of the Redback III – The World's Next Reserve Currency, HSBC Global Research, March 2014. Deutsche Bank, 2014. At the Center of RMB Internationalization – A Brief Guide to Offshore RMB, March 2014. KPMG, 2014. Foreign Bank in Japan Survey, March 2014

GLOSSARY

AIIB	Asian Infrastructure Investment Bank
ASEAN	Association of Southeast Asian Nations
BDF	Banque de France
BIS	Bank for International Settlements
BOCHK	Bank of China (Hong Kong)
BoE	Bank of England
BoJ	Bank of Japan
BoK	Bank of Korea
CAGR	compound annual growth rate
CBC (Taiwan)	Central Bank of China (Taiwan)
CBRC	China Banking Regulatory Commission
CDB	China Development Bank
CGB	Chinese government bond
CIFR	Centre for International Finance and Regulation
CLS	Continuous Linked Settlement
CNH	deliverable RMB exchange rate offshore
CNY	RMB exchange rate in onshore market
COFER	Composition of Official Foreign Exchanges Reserves (IMF compilation)
CSRC	China Securities Regulatory Commission
ECB	European Central Bank
ESM	European Stability Mechanism
ETF	exchange-traded fund
FDI	foreign direct investment
FGI	Fung Global Institute
GFC	global financial crisis
HKEx	Hong Kong Exchange and Clearing Limited
HKMA	Hong Kong Monetary Authority
ICC	International Chamber of Commerce

IMF	International Monetary Fund
IPO	initial public offering
JGBs	Japanese government bonds
LC	letter of credit
LGFV	local government financing vehicle
LME	London Metals Exchange
MAS	Monetary Authority of Singapore
MNC	multinational corporations
MoF	Ministry of Finance
NBS	National Bureau of Statistics
NDF	non-deliverable forward
OTC	over-the-counter
PBOC	People's Bank of China
QDII	qualified domestic institutional investor
QE	quantitative easing
QFII	qualified foreign institutional investor
RAMP	Reserves Advisory Management Program (World Bank)
REER	real effective exchange rate
RMB	renminbi: the Chinese currency, one unit of which is a yuan
RQDII	renminbi qualified domestic institutional investor
RQFII	renminbi qualified foreign institutional investor
RTGS	real-time gross settlement
SAFE	State Administration of Foreign Exchange
SDDS	Special Data Dissemination Standard (IMF)
SDR	special drawing rights
SHFTZ	Shanghai Free-Trade Zone
SIFMA	Securities Industry and Financial Markets Association
SOE	state-owned enterprise
SWIFT	Society for Worldwide Interbank Financial Telecommunications
T/T	telegraphic transfer
UK DMO	UK Debt Management Office
US MBS	US Mortgage Backed Securities
YoY	year on year

INDEX